THE
HUNGRY
SOUL

THE
HUNGRY
SOUL

*Eating and the Perfecting of
Our Nature*

LEON R. KASS, M.D.

WITH A NEW FOREWORD

THE UNIVERSITY OF CHICAGO PRESS

Chicago and London

The University of Chicago Press, Chicago 60637
The University of Chicago Press, Ltd., London
Published 1994 by The Free Press, a division of Macmillan, Inc.
University of Chicago Press edition 1999
© 1994, 1999 by Leon R. Kass, M.D.
All rights reserved.

18 17 16 15 14 13 12   6 7 8 9
ISBN-13: 978-0-226-42568-9
ISBN-10: 0-226-42568-1

Selections from "Babette's Feast" (used in Chapter 5) are taken from *Babette's Feast
and Other Ancedotes of Destiny* by Isak Dinesen, Copyright © 1953, 1958 and renewed 1981,
1986 by Isak Dinesen. Reprinted by permission of Random House, Inc.

Library of Congress Cataloging-in-Publication Data
Kass, Leon,
    The hungry soul : eating and the perfecting of our nature / Leon
R. Kass.
        p.   cm.
    Originally published: New York : Free Press : Toronto : Maxwell
Macmillan Canada : New York : Maxwell Macmillan International,
© 1994. With new foreword.
    Includes bibliographical references and index.
    ISBN 0-226-42568-1 (pbk. : alk. paper)
    1. Eating (Philosophy)   I. Title.
[BD450.K345   1999
641'.01—dc21   98-32259
                                                                      CIP

♾ The paper used in this publication meets the
minimum requirements of the American National Standard
for Information Sciences—Permanence of Paper for
Printed Library Materials, ANSI Z39.48-1992.

To Amy

Contents

List of Illustrations   *ix*
Credits   *x*
Foreword to the Paperback Edition   *xi*
Preface   *xix*

Introduction:
"Good for Food . . . to Make One Wise"   1

1. Food and Nourishing:
   The Primacy of Form   17

2. The Human Form: 57
   Omnivorosus Erectus

3. Host and Cannibal: 95
   From *Fressen* to *Essen*

4. Enhancing Uprightness: 129
   Civilized Eating

5. Freedom, Friendship, and Philosophy: 161
   From Eating to Dining

6. Sanctified Eating: 193
   A Memorial of Creation

   Conclusion: 227
   The Hungry Soul and the Perfecting of
   Our Nature

   Notes   *233*
   Index   *239*

List of Illustrations

Lucas Cranach the Elder, *Adam and Eve and the Animals*   Frontispiece

Albrecht Dürer, *Animals Fighting*   18

Andreas Vesalius, *The Structure of the Human Body* (contrasted with pig from Pieter Bruegel the Elder's *The Fair at Hoboken*)   58

Rembrandt Harmensz. van Rijn, *Abraham Entertaining the Angels*   96

Jan Steen, *The Fat Kitchen*   130

Paul Emile Chabas, *End of the Table*   162

Claus Jansz. Visscher (after Pieter Feddes), *Grace Before the Meal*   194

Hartmann Schedel, *The Work of the First Day*   195

Hartmann Schedel, *The Sanctification of the Seventh Day*   225

Credits

Grateful acknowledgment is made to the following institutions for providing the photographs of works of art and for the permissions to use them:

Art Resource, New York: Rembrandt Harmensz. van Rijn, *Abraham Entertaining the Angels*, etching.

Cheltenham Museum of Art: Jan Steen, *The Fat Kitchen*.

Courtauld Institute Galleries: Lucas Cranach the Elder, *Adam and Eve and the Animals*.

Giraudon/Art Resource, New York: Paul Emile Chabas, *End of the Table (Coin de Table)*, 1904. Musée des Beaux-Arts, Tourcoing, France.

Rijksprentenkabinet, Amsterdam: Claes Jansz. Visscher (after Pieter Feddes), *Grace Before the Meal*.

The University of Chicago Library, Department of Special Collections: Hartmann Schedel, *The Work of the First Day* and *The Sanctification of the Seventh Day*, woodcuts from the *Liber Chronicarum (The Nuremberg Chronicle)*, 1493.

Foreword
to the Paperback Edition

When the first edition of this book was published, friends of mine who looked for it in bookstores were astonished to find it among the cookbooks, sandwiched in between thin books on French pastries and thick books on fat-free diets. My former publisher, encouraged by his marketing advisors, believed it best to categorize this hard-to-classify book as a "food book," for the simple reason that many more people buy books on food than buy philosophical essays. That the Caravaggio painting on the cover, which I had selected to invite reflection on the hungers of the soul, offered mouth-watering fruit, and that the author happened also to be a medical doctor, would surely strengthen, it was argued, the book's immediate (if only superficial) appeal to the gourmandizing or health-minded food-book shopper.

The strategy proved only a partial success, at best. The book did get reviewed by some distinguished food editors. But they had little interest in, and less understanding of, what the book is actually about. For example, one reviewer was hoping to find socioeconomic explanations for certain contemporary American gastronomic phenomena, especially our current confusions about what to eat. But my purpose is instead philosophical: a wisdom-seeking inquiry into human nature and its perfection. I treat certain common phenomena of eating, however interesting in their own terms, primarily as evidence in my search for what is universally, permanently, and profoundly true about the human animal and its deepest hungerings.

This is not to say that such a philosophical inquiry into the higher meanings of eating should close its eyes to the contemporary scene, in which public attention to food, cooking, and eating is steadily growing. No longer innocently content or simply grateful to have food on the table, many Americans are increasingly preoccupied with what and where they eat, some to the point of making a fetish of their food and its preparation. A concern for health and the fear of death determine many a diet, sometimes sensibly sometimes not, as people struggle to adjust to the ever changing and often conflicting medical pronouncements about the harms (or is it benefits?) of salt, fats, and dairy products or the benefits (or is it harms?) of fiber, fruit, and a glass of red (or white?) wine with dinner. Organic and health food stores do a booming business, often supplementing their produce with quasi-religious publications proclaiming the salvific power of "pure foods." Food books do in fact abound in the publishing world: in 1997 alone there were over 1,600 new cookbooks and nearly 400 new diet and weight-loss books published in English, not to mention the scores of other books on anorexia, bulimia, cholesterol, dyspepsia, eructations, flatulence, and the rest of the gastrointestinal alphabet.

But, as the plethora of cookbooks indicates, our fascination with food is prompted as much by love of pleasure as by concern for health. Catering to epicurean cravings, most major newspapers feature elaborate food sections and regular restaurant guides, reviews, and ratings. On radio and television, cooking shows are ubiquitous, with cable television sporting The Food Channel, entirely devoted to food and especially to gourmet cooking. Dining clubs offer members large discounts at thousands of participating fine restaurants nationwide. Yes, the nightly family meal may be in decline, and hosts and hostesses of dinner parties may be burdened as never before by the need to accommodate the numerous dietary idiosyncrasies of their many guests. But cosmopolitan dining on the town is more in vogue than ever, and not only among the well-to-do. As I write this foreword, more than four million people (a record-breaking number) are attending the "Taste of Chicago" festival in Grant Park, sampling the ethnically diverse cuisine brought forth by dozens of Chicago's famous restaurants.

Finally, food has also made it big time in the movies. First there was *Babette's Feast*, a beautiful movie based on Isak Dinesen's short story (which I discuss at length in Chapter 5). Then the foreign art films, *Tampopo, Like Water for Chocolate*, and *Eat, Drink, Man, Woman*, explored the relation between hunger and eros, between food and love. Recently popular has been *Big Night*, a movie about two brothers—one a cooking genius—struggling to maintain an Italian restaurant without compromising culinary excellence. In some circles, the movie has become something of a cult film, combined of course with dinner: in what is known as a "*Big Night* Event," people gather to see the movie and then dine at an Italian restaurant that prepares for them the spectacular meal served in the film.

Something is going on here—probably many things. The cynical explanation is consumerism: affluent people with disposable income are engaged, quite literally, in conspicuous consumption, seeking to sample the strange, to buy the best, to be first among their friends to try this or taste that. Chasing around in search of new pleasures and sensations has long been the preferred distraction of those who could afford them, especially in times in which deeper sources of satisfaction and meaning are thought to be lacking; some people maintain that our growing gastronomania is in fact evidence that we live in such spiritually troubled times. More optimistically, the new preoccupations with finer eating may represent, at least for some, a genuine delight in taste and refinement, a cultivation of the aesthetic dimension of life to which (as I argue) eating provides a regular opening.

I leave it to others more sociologically astute to try to decipher the meaning of these new hungerings. But to make sense of our present appetites requires seeing them against the background of the native and more fundamental hungers of the human soul. *The Hungry Soul* is about these deeper desires, appetites, and longings as they reveal themselves in human eating.

This inquiry belongs, therefore, to the now sadly obsolescent science of "anthropology," in its original meaning: the knowledge of the human being. As Immanuel Kant first developed the notion, such knowledge has two aspects: the physical or physiological, what nature has made of man, and the practical or pragmatic, what man has made of himself. Focusing on the most basic of human functions, eating, *The Hungry Soul* seeks to supply part of such an anthropology, examining and uniting both the physiological and practical aspects. The first two chapters treat the general bodily and psychic aspects of feeding, animal and human; the other four chapters deal with how human beings transform feeding into eating and dining, governed always by moral notions of the legal or just, the beautiful or noble, the sacred or holy. The two parts of the book are connected, the first serving as the ground for the second. Most provocatively, and against the stream of current orthodoxy, the book explores the possibility that an appreciation of what is given to us by nature could point us toward humanly instituted practices and beliefs that perfect our given nature. If true, this would imply that some practices really are just, noble, and holy, and that we can discern or discover what they are.

Anthropology as practiced today usually has little use for such a universalizing approach to human nature and its cultural and moral adornments. On the contrary, concerned primarily with the differences between one culture and the next, most academic anthropologists are inclined to treat all moral notions and practices as socially constructed and culturally relative. Common human nature they either deny or regard as trivial compared to the weighty significance of the diverse and diversifying cultures. Indeed, the most common complaint against this book is that it does not make sufficient use of non-Western sources and does not pay sufficient attention to the wide sweep of the world's peoples. But such criticism misses the point, and, I venture to say, predictably. For if one is preoccupied with the divergent variations, one may have forgotten about the common theme; and, having forgotten the theme, one may never see that it might be readily discernible even without collecting every last variation. Yes, some people bury their ancestors, others cremate them, while still others may eat them; but, more important, we human beings everywhere and always do something to honor the mortal remains of our forebears. Yes, some people eat with forks, others with chopsticks, some at elevated tables, others on carpets; but, more important, we human beings everywhere and always ritualize our eating, showing thereby our self-conscious recognition that we differ from the animals. In addition, insofar as current anthropology—unaccountably—denies or disparages human nature, it will necessarily also be blind to a search for how our nature may be perfected.

If one is trying to show how customs and practices of eating *can* perfect our given human nature, it is not necessary to scrutinize all customs; any such customs may serve as illustrative. But to consider the perfecting of our nature means looking first not to custom but to nature, to the meaning of what is naturally given to us as human beings, here and everywhere, now and always: our need for food, our native omnivorousness, our special upright standing in the animal world, and our uniquely human self-consciousness of all these matters. If properly considered, these and other such simple natural facts, accessible to us through the testimony of our own lived experience, can provide a royal road to appreciating what we are and discovering what we might become.

At the center of any philosophical anthropology will be an account of the human difference, of what is peculiarly human about human nature and the human animal. The second chapter, "The Human Form," provides (in part) such an account of the naturally and universally human; all subsequent explorations of the perfecting of our nature, through customs just, noble, and holy (described in Chapters 3–6) take their bearings from and look back to this presentation of our natural humanity. But to know the human, if only by contrast and relation, we need to know also the nonhuman, especially the animal. For though we may be, as claimed in many traditions, the most godlike of the animals, we live always an animated and necessitous existence just like our fellow animals. Yet because modern biology with its materialistic and mechanistic biases fails to do justice to the evident vitality of animal life, it will fail also to do justice to our humanized animality. Thus, partly to locate the human within the animal world, partly to show how we might acquire a richer and truer science of all living things, I begin with a chapter on animal feeding—on food, nourishing, and animal form. It is here that the reader may benefit from some advance warning and advice. The latter parts of Chapter 1—the sections entitled "Form and Material," "The Primacy of Form," and "The Three Great Powers of Organic Form"—are the most difficult and abstract parts of the book, precisely because they move away from common experiences to speak about their causes. I hope readers who find this material slow going will persevere, for after Chapter 1 they will find themselves back in familiar territory, able to judge everything I say in the light of what they already know or can easily come to see. The last two pages of Chapter 1 provide a summary of the argument, useful I hope to all, but especially helpful to readers who wish to skip the more demanding parts of the chapter or who are eager to get to the specifically human phenomena.

If the near boundary of the human is the animal, the far boundary is the divine. Recognition of this boundary also finds its way into human eating, whether in expressions of gratitude for the bounty of food or in commemorative meals celebrating religious holy-days. This book ends with a look at sanctified eating, in which I treat *as illustrative* the dietary laws of Leviticus, part of the so-called holiness code of Ancient Israel and still observed by traditional Jews today. I fear that nothing I can say will prevent some readers from mistakenly attributing this choice to ethnocentric prejudice or to my wish to promote a parochially Jewish understanding of the sacred and divine. In this regard, some readers will wonder, with reason, why I did not conclude with the Eucharist, the ingestion—some think symbolic, others literal—of the body and blood of Christ. There are at least three reasons for this choice and this omission, one personal, two substantive. First, given what appeared to this outside observer to be the hard-to-adjudicate controversies about the meaning of the Eucharist, I thought it wiser to leave it for someone steeped in the Christian tradition who could come at the subject "from the inside." Second, I was looking for a religious ritual that informs everyday eating in the home, rather than a practice performed away from the table in church or synagogue. Third, and most important, I wanted a ritual practice whose content recalled and celebrated the fundamental yet precarious principle of *form* that, as I argue near the beginning of the book, lies at the heart of our multiform and articulated natural world. As clarified in Chapter 6, the dietary laws of Leviticus fit these requirements perfectly; the Eucharist does not. I freely acknowledge that the Eucharist may, on other grounds, be a superior example of sanctified eating, and I would be pleased if someone else were moved to write the "missing" seventh chapter to this book.

Mentioning matters theological and metaphysical prompts me, finally, to call the reader's attention to the key word in my title: Soul. When the need for it arises in my argument, I will clarify what I mean by "soul"—it is for me primarily not a theological but a biological notion! You should know at the outset, however, that I use the term advisedly and without apology, even though I know that it will cause most scientists to snicker and many others knowingly to smile. These skeptics need to learn that it is only because they in fact have soul that they are able to find such (or any) speech intelligible, amusing, or absurd. Indeed, only the ensouled—the animate, the animal—can even experience hunger, can know appetite, desire, longing. Not the least purpose of this book is to try to make the notion of soul again respectable in the pursuit of knowledge about all of life, and especially our own.

    Bon appétit!

Preface

Be forewarned: You have picked up a strange book. It is at once a book about eating, a book about animal nature, a book about human nature, a book about human good, a book about custom and culture and their relation to human nature and human good, a book about human uprightness and human dignity, a book about where we human beings stand—and how we ought to stand—in relation to the larger cosmic whole of which we are such an unusual part.

This strange book was written by a strange author. Trained first as a physician and then as a biochemist, he now practices neither. Untrained in philosophy and literature, he teaches both without a license, studying some of their greatest works with serious students at one of the world's best universities. Yet he does not identify himself as an academic or even as an intellectual, but as a thoughtful human being—a husband and father, a Chicagoan, a first-generation American, a teacher, a Jew—who was reared on moral passion and who sustains an interest in unfashionable ideas like the true, the good, the beautiful, and the holy. Because he cooks little, has unsophisticated tastes, and rarely dines in the top-ranked restaurants, he is himself astonished that he should have written a book about eating.

So why this book? What moved the author to write it?

When I began nine years ago, I viewed it mainly as a sequel to my *Toward a More Natural Science*, in which I had called for a richer biology, psychology, and anthropology that would be truer to life as lived and that might therefore be less at odds with cultural and ethical notions about how it *should* be lived. In the subject of eating—as I will explain in the Introduction—I saw a perfect vehicle for attempting such a more natural science and for building bridges between the scientific and humanistic ways of looking at the world. But even at its inception this project was more than a philosophical enterprise. It was inspired by a strong desire to address our modern moral predicament as I then understood it: the absence of any account of human life that could ground and sustain the moral outlooks and norms necessary for living in a world massively transformed by science and technology.

Over the course of nine years anyone who has his eyes open, and especially anyone who teaches good books to good students, is likely to learn a lot. And so I have, and not only about my subject and about some superb books that illuminate it. I have become more aware of the depth of our modern predicament and more passionately eager to address it.

As the curtain begins to descend on the twentieth century, we who find ourselves still on the stage are, truth to tell, more than a little befuddled about how to act and what to think. To be sure, we seem to speak our lines and play our parts no less than did our ancestors. But we barely remember the name of the drama, much less its meaning or its purpose. The playwright is apparently dead and cannot be consulted as to his original intention. Cultural memory still holds gingerly a tattered script, but many of its pages are missing and the guidance it provides us is barely audible and, even then, delivered in what appears to us to be a foreign tongue. Armed with new-fangled, electronically delivered images and phrases, we are never at a loss for words. But we are at a loss for meaning.

The problem is, paradoxically, worse for those of us who star in the performance. We fortunate few—we children of privilege, highly educated in the land of liberty, well fed and well traveled, sophisticated in the arts and sciences, emancipated from prejudice and superstition, superstimulated and supersatiated—we feel especially poignantly the incoherence of modern life. For we are better able than our less fortunate contemporaries to appreciate that the fault lies not in our stars but in our souls that we are underlings in the quest for happiness. Our troubles are not economic or political, they are intellectual, moral, and spiritual. Our souls still crave the drama of what Tolstoy called "real life": immediately meaningful work, gen-

uine love and intimacy, true ties to place and persons, kinship with
nature, family, and community, dignity, understanding, and an openness to the divine. But real life has become nearly impossible as we
have ceased to know and honor its forms. We are, of course, too sophisticated to allow ourselves to be self-deceived, to embrace any
grand illusions. We would sooner quit the scene than live a noble lie,
and so we continue (nervously) to applaud the intellectual demysti-
fiers and debunkers of our traditions and mores. We fuss over our
decadent art, our atonal music, and our haute cuisine. But when the
lights grow dimmer and we look into the mirror, we do not like what
we see: We look even to ourselves like hungry men who have been
offered nothing but sawdust and tinsel.

The causes of our spiritual distress and alienation are many and
largely well known; one of them—the scientific view of the world—I
will soon single out for special attention. Though they are mostly of
our own making, they will not easily be reversed, and certainly not
by the work of intellectuals. Yet, I submit, the root of the difficulty is
in fact philosophical: our failure to understand or even deeply to
ponder the truth about our human situation. Who and what are we?
How are we related to the rest of nature and to the cosmic whole?
What would it mean to live a dignified and truly human life, a flourishing life, a life not alienated from ourselves or our true place in the
world? How does one truly nourish the hungry human soul?

These are, to be sure, very big questions, questions that can never
be disposed of once and for all. Nevertheless, lacking some sort of
tentative answers to them, we can but strut and fret our hour upon
the stage, painfully aware that, for all our jabbering, the stories of
our lives signify nothing. Given that our inherited answers no longer
satisfy us, we have no choice but to inquire for ourselves, even
should we fail. The stakes are enormously high.

As will become clear, I am not a pessimist, nor do I share the ni-
hilistic outlook that clouds so much of our current intellectual and
moral scene. On the contrary, I remain an optimist, if not about the
state of our culture, then certainly about the goodness of human life
and the goodness of the given world. And about my own life, I remain profoundly cheerful, feeling even blessed. For I have known
and benefited from remarkable—and often remarkable because or-

dinary and typical—human generosity, thoughtfulness, and goodness throughout my life and, more pertinently, in connection with
the writing of this book these past nine years. Some of these bene-
factions I wish here to acknowledge.

The study was begun during a wonderful fellowship year
(1984–85) at the National Humanities Center in North Carolina
(with funding provided by the National Endowment for the Humanities) and virtually concluded during a second, even better fellowship year (1991–92) at the American Enterprise Institute in
Washington, D.C., where I was the William H. Brady, Jr., Distinguished Fellow in Social Thought. Many thanks are owed to Charles
Blitzer (then head of the center), Chris DeMuth (president of AEI),
and Elizabeth Lurie (president of the Brady Foundation) for their
vigorous support and encouragement. My good friends Gertrude
Himmelfarb and Irving Kristol have from beginning to end boosted
my project, my prospects, and my morale.

Earlier versions of several of these chapters were presented as the
Arnold Ravin Memorial Lectures at the University of Chicago
(1986); a version of Chapter 1 was delivered at Catholic University
in a lecture series on teleology (1992); and earlier versions of Chapter 6 were presented at the Hillel Foundations of the University of
Chicago (1983) and the University of Virginia (1992). In the spring
of 1993 a penultimate draft of the entire book was circulated among
faculty and graduate students in the Institute of Philosophic Studies
at the University of Dallas and formed the basis of five lecture-and-
seminar sessions I gave there as the Eugene McDermott Lecturer.
The discussions on these occasions, and especially at Dallas, were
enormously rich and stimulating; they led to numerous changes in
the final version. I am grateful to Dean Glen Thurow, John Alvis,
David Davies, William Frank, Tim Herman, Jack Painter, Eric Perl,
Michael Platt, Janet Smith, Sarah Thurow, Steve Vanderslice, Grace
West, and Thomas West (all members of the Dallas seminar); to
Richard Kennington, Jude Dougherty, Richard Hassing, and Father
William Wallace (Catholic University); and to Joseph Cropsey (Uni-
versity of Chicago) for their searching questions, tough arguments,
and thoughtful comments.

Four people read the entire manuscript in draft: Paula Duggan at
AEI, my designated "general reader," gave wonderful advice about

tone and the order of presentation, unerringly located the most opaque sections that demanded clarification, and encouraged me to believe that the material and the argument were not too abstract or abstruse for the unspecialized reader. Harvey Flaumenhaft of St. John's College, my dearest friend for close to forty years, gave much general encouragement and many particular suggestions for improvement, both of content and style; he thoroughly understood and sympathized with the entire argument from its inception. Buzzy Fishbane, professor of Judaica and my new colleague and friend at the University of Chicago, read the near-final version and made important substantive suggestions that I have tried to incorporate, especially in the Introduction, the Conclusion, and Chapter 6; being fairly new to my way of thinking, he enabled me to see with fresh eyes what I was in fact attempting and encouraged me to be more explicit, and so I have been, about what is morally and culturally at stake for me in this enterprise. My wife, Amy, has read many versions of each chapter and has shared speeches and thoughts about their content these many years, often over dinner. As frequently happens in such protracted conversations, it becomes difficult to separate one's own thinking from that of one's partner. But I do know that my discussions of hospitality, Homer, Herodotus, and much else besides depend decisively on her own literary studies. She also read again the final version, saving me from numerous errors and approving most of my suggested revisions. When I write I write first of all for her.

Curtis Black and Marie Rice at Chicago and Gretchen Chellson at AEI gave excellent assistance in preparing the manuscript. It benefited also from Ms. Chellson's great knowledge of cookery and her interest in manners and mores; the author was often kept in good spirits by her generous supply of fine cartoons and witty anecdotes on the subject of eating. Sue Llewellyn effected numerous improvements through her able and sympathetic copy editing. Anselmo Carini (The Art Institute of Chicago), Gerhard Gruitrooy (Art Resource), Tina Yarborough (The University of Chicago Art Library), and Robyn Krauthammer provided generous and knowledgeable help in locating suitable graphic images. At The Free Press, Nancy Etheredge gave wonderful advice regarding the artwork and handsomely prepared the images for publication; her enthusiasm for the project is much appreciated. Marion Maneker shepherded the book through all stages of production, solving all problems skillfully, promptly, and graciously. Francis DuVinage (doctoral candidate in the Committee on Social Thought) did yeoman service in helping me proofread.

My friend and publisher Erwin Glikes contributed his usual—but indeed most *un*usual—good judgment about the manuscript as a whole. One cannot exaggerate the benefits of working with a high-minded and perceptive publisher whose advice unfailingly shows that he understands entirely what one is trying to say and do.

Much of this book actually grew out of my teaching at the University of Chicago, where the students I get are too smart and too serious to be taken in by the prevailing nihilism. As all my classes are seminars, which proceed by interpretation and discussion of great texts, I always learn an enormous amount both from and because of my students. To those who have accompanied me in my studies of Genesis; Aristotle's *Nicomachean Ethics*, *Physics*, and *De Anima*; Descartes's *Discourse on Method*; Rousseau's *First and Second Discourses*; and Tolstoy's *War and Peace* (taught with my wife); and especially to the students who took Mrs. Kass's and my course on "Civility" I owe my profound gratitude.

My deepest debt, inexpressible, is to Amy.

Introduction

"Good for Food . . . to Make One Wise"

According to a very old story, well known to most readers, a woman and a man once took a fancy to a most unusual fruit. It grew on no ordinary tree, and their eating of it had no ordinary consequences: Indeed, it opened their eyes and made permanent the whole human difference. They had sought this tree not only because they thought its fruit would be good for food but also because they imagined it would make them wise. Though the consequences of their eating were both less and more than they had bargained for, though it gave them psychic indigestion, and though true wisdom eluded them, we have it on the highest authority that they in some sense succeeded: "Now the man is become like one of us, knowing good and bad." God Almighty knew that the world was arranged so as to contain deep connections among human eating, human freedom, and human moral self-consciousness. It is these connections that we here seek to discover. We, too, seek wisdom through eating; eating is the manifest theme of this inquiry.

1

Eating

Compared to wisdom eating may be a humble subject, but it is no trivial matter. It is the first and most urgent activity of all animal and human life: We are only because we eat. Much of human life is, in practice, organized around this necessity. Enormous time and energies are poured into growing, harvesting, rearing, butchering, preserving, packaging, storing, transporting, stocking, selling, buying, preparing, cooking, and consuming food. The manufacture of tables, chairs, stoves, refrigerators, dishes, glassware, utensils, and kitchen gadgets; the provision of homes with fuel for cooking, with water for drinking and cleaning, and with electricity for refrigeration; the operation of groceries, bakeries, supermarkets, restaurants, and services for garbage collection and sanitation; the scientific development of new fertilizers and animal feed, of pest-resistant crops, and of genetically engineered high-yielding livestock—all these and more follow from the increasingly complex ways in which we arrange to meet our most basic need. Indeed, at least indirectly, the need to eat makes the world go around: Most of society's work gets done largely because we workers need to make a living—that is, to earn enough to feed ourselves and our families. If we lived in a bountiful Garden of Eden, who would work? Who would do much of anything?

But these massively important socioeconomic aspects of eating are not my present concern. Neither will the reader find here gourmet recipes, suggestions for losing weight, or advice regarding the treatment of eating disorders. The spirit of this essay is philosophical rather than practical. Its first purpose is to invite reflection on the *meaning* of eating.

How little we think about what eating is, compared with how much we think about making it possible! In a way this is not surprising. The hardships and cares of life often leave little leisure for reflection. Yet even for those of us blessed with freedom from mind-numbing toil, the marvels of everyday life become indifferent by dint of becoming familiar. We must be prodded into philosophizing in order to observe once what we see every day. What, for example, makes something food? What is food for? What is the connection between the tasty and the nourishing, between what we like to eat and what is good for us?

Have you ever thought about the mouth and the meaning of its having multiple and competing functions: chewing, tasting, speaking, kissing? What about teeth? What does it mean that we human beings have multicompetent and "balanced" dentition—with a complete set of the variously specialized incisors, canines, premolars, and molars? And what about our broad and open appetites: Is there any connection between human intelligence and human omnivorousness or between human omnivorousness and the need for morality? How do nature and custom cooperate in shaping what, when, where, with whom, and how we eat? What is the point of the myriad customs regulating eating: Why cook or set the table, why have utensils or table manners, why dine or feast with company? What meanings, regarding ourselves and our relations to the world, are silently encoded in the everyday meal?

These and other related questions will become thematic in this book. We will reflect on various aspects of what it means to eat, beginning with the natural phenomena of ingestion, digestion, and metabolism and progressing to the ethical norms governing what we eat and how. Yet, although eating is my explicit theme, I am, as I confessed in the preface, tracking bigger game. In fact it is precisely this matter of nature and ethics, and their possible connection, that is my deeper concern.

Nature, Ethics, and Modern Science

What is the relation between nature and ethics? Can knowledge of nature, or even knowledge only of human nature, provide any guidance for how we are to live? Philosophers once hoped that knowledge of the cosmic whole would reveal at least our human place and at best our meaning, and would do so in ways that could inform our beliefs about how we ought to live. Though agreement was never reached, a number of grand ethical teachings emerged—in the East as well as in the West—that showed how we might live "in accordance with nature." For example, we have the Aristotelian view of human flourishing as the perfection of our distinctive nature, the Epicurean teaching of the natural primacy of pleasure, the Stoic and Thomistic versions of natural law, the early modern doctrine, begun by Hobbes and Locke, of natural rights (central to the American

Founding), and the classical Buddhist teaching of nirvana. Even today we occasionally hear moral appeals to natural law and to natural rights (more commonly, to *human* rights), and certain deeds (like matricide, infanticide, or acts of bestiality) are still sometimes condemned as "unnatural." The environmentalist movement tells us that we must learn to think of ourselves as a part of nature and to act accordingly, and it sometimes even speaks of nature in reverent, almost deified, terms ("Mother Earth," Gaia). Yet we are much more disinclined than our philosophical forebears to look to nature with any hope of gaining self-understanding or ethical help. Indeed it seems to be a basic, if only tacit, premise of the dominant contemporary modes of thought that any such hope is a delusion. The reason for this opinion is, quite simply, that we have largely adopted the view of nature associated with modern natural science. The nature we think we know through modern science is not the nature we know through ordinary experience—or at least not through experience that was ordinary before it was overwhelmed by the technological transformation of the world.

Because of a radically new idea of nature, first promulgated by Galileo, Descartes, and Bacon in the early seventeenth century, modern thought has come to teach the uselessness of natural knowledge for ethics. Science deliberately broke with ordinary human experience and gained knowledge through the mathematization of nature. It rejected natural teleology, the belief that living things are purposive and goal-directed beings, who pursue naturally given ends, fulfillments, or purposes; it denied not only that animals have purposes relative to some larger scheme of things but also that they naturally seek ends for themselves. Science adopted an analytic and reductive mode of understanding wholes in terms of parts, living things in terms of dead matter and motion. Modern philosophy, following the lead of modern science, insisted on the absolute distinction between facts and values, a distinction rooted in the view that nature itself is "objective" and indifferent to all human concerns with better and worse or with the good, the just, and the beautiful. This doctrine of objectivity necessarily removed the knower from among the things known, thus isolating the passionate and morally concerned human being ever more from nature as studied by his science. Eventually even the possibility of truth came under challenge, with various skepticisms asserting the ultimate unknow-ability of both the true being of nature and the true causes of natural phenomena.*

In all these ways nature as approached and understood by modern natural science is not the sort of "thing" that has anything helpful to say regarding human longings or anything solid to offer for grounding norms for human conduct. Moreover, certain substantive teachings of science—most notoriously Darwinism, but also corporealism and mechanism—are, *in their cultural effect*, ethically subversive. As broadcast popularly through the society, these doctrines embarrass the ethical claims of our traditional philosophical or religious teachings by seeming to contradict what they say about nature, man, and the whole. It does not matter that one can show, on careful study, that the theory of evolution is not in fact incompatible with the picture of the world presented in the first chapter of Genesis.[1] Enough damage is done by the fairly common opinion, especially prominent in enlightened circles, that science has now made "unbelievable" the biblical view of the special place of human beings in the world.

The gap between the ethically sterile nature studied by science and the morally freighted life lived by human beings has become tremendously important in the present day, largely because our new technology, based on that science, readies itself to make direct and far-reaching alterations in the human body and mind. Thanks to growing knowledge of our genes and brains, thanks to present and projected techniques for replacing body parts and for laboratory-assisted reproduction, our human nature becomes increasingly subject to our deliberate manipulations. But if nature itself cannot teach us which interventions are to be preferred, and if our traditional notions of human fulfillment and flourishing cannot be culturally sustained, how will we proceed ethically?

How, for example, will we be able to judge whether increasing the human life span, say, to 150 years, will be humanizing or dehumanizing; whether an alterable genetic predisposition toward homosexual-

---

*There remain today large controversies in the philosophy of science, and the hegemony of determinism has been disrupted by such developments as quantum mechanics and chaos theory. But these are family quarrels within broad agreements about the propositions stated in this paragraph, especially about teleology, "objectivity," and mathematization.

ity, should it be diagnosable *in utero*, ought to be regarded as a treatable condition; whether we will be better or worse off with a perfected pharmacology of pleasure? In short, how, in a world morally neutered by the effects of objectified science, will we know which genetic or functional or behavioral alterations of human nature we should welcome as improvements?

But these practical difficulties are not yet the worst of it; much worse are the consequences for belief, for self-understanding, for our sense of our place in the world. We can, perhaps, adjust to our biomedical technologies; we may even be able to muddle through without clear and well-grounded moral notions of better and worse. But we will continue to face, in mind and in spirit, the disquieting disjunction between the vibrant living world we live in and enjoy as human beings and the limited, artificial, lifeless, objectified, representation of that world we learn about from modern biology.

The disjunction between the world-as-experienced and the world-as-known-by-modern-science is, of course, an old story. For example, according to obvious experience your dining room table is hard and solid, but according to atomic physics it is mainly empty space. Most of us say, "So what?" About tables and the like this discrepancy is rarely bothersome. But when it reaches to life and to our *human* lives, it is—and will be—increasingly disorienting, troubling, and self-alienating. True, from the inside we still experience life as passionate and purposive; but the truth, according to our science, which looks from the outside, is that it is neither. Yes, we still quite naturally wonder what it means to be a human being, but our science is not interested in either being or meaning. Many of us still argue about whether something is good or beautiful; but the sophisticated ones, following the direction taken by science, know that such arguments are pointless because these "values," being of purely human construction, have only subjective and relative meaning.

Science should perhaps not be blamed for its failure to address, much less to answer, these large human questions, which, one might say, belong more to the humanities—especially philosophy and literature—and to religion. But over the last century, and alarmingly so in the last two decades, most humanists and many teachers of religion have been declaring bankruptcy regarding truth: Even leaving aside the recent malignant politicization of humanistic disciplines, with its denial of the independence of mind and its insistence that everything can be reduced to power, the humanities have long been in retreat from the pursuit of wisdom. Analytical clarity, logical consistency, demystification, and refutation; source criticism, philology, and the explication of thinkers solely in terms of their historical and cultural contexts; and the devotion to theoretical dogmas—formerly romanticism and historicism, nowadays Marxism, deconstructionism, multiculturalism, feminism, and many other "isms"—all these preoccupations keep humanists busy with everything but the pursuit of wisdom about our own humanity. Humanists may claim, in self-defense, that they have been frightened off the pursuit of truth by the scientists, whom they regard with a mixture of envy and contempt: It is the scientists, they complain, who have chilled the heart with their icy doctrines of an infinite and indifferent universe, lifeless matter, and soulless life. (The scientists can reply, fairly, that for all their possible failings they at least still believe in truth.) Our purpose, however, is not to blame but to understand, and we understand how virtually all of modern intellectual life has nothing good to say to the deepest human questions or to the most important human aspirations.

I worry that at this point many of my readers—not knowingly captives of scientism or any other intellectual school—will not recognize themselves or their stake in this controversy. Not being scientists, they will not see that their own views are to be placed on trial. But virtually all of us in the present age are at least cryptoscientists and fellow travelers. We are rationalists, and we are, at the very least, influenced by corporealism. We not only do not believe in miracles, we cannot even imagine an occurrence or phenomenon that could ever shake our faith in their impossibility. We smile knowingly when we hear the word *soul,* and we do not stand respectfully before our living bodies. We readily accept biochemical "explanations" of human emotions and eagerly embrace deterministic accounts of human (especially criminal) behavior. We even coolly "objectify" our moral norms and cultural practices to see not their wisdom (or folly) but only their origins—in the accidents of history or the arbitrary wills of dead ancestors. We may not see with a scientific eye, but we think—often unwittingly—with scientific concepts and explanations. For us mystery is but a name for that which science has not yet explained.

At the very least we are confused: on the one hand, we necessarily trust (because daily life demands that we do) our own experience and the surface appearance of things; on the other, we at least tacitly believe in the deeper truth of the abstracted scientific view. We latch on to a system of thought that provides confidence through its ability to predict and control, but we do not notice that it does not help us truly to see nature or ourselves or to understand any phenomenon right before our eyes. We have lost our way in the world partly because we no longer believe that our ordinary experience of life in the world may be the privileged road to the deepest truth.

We are today, before the large human questions, like men lost at sea without a compass. We adhere to a science that provides us with enormous power to travel but that denies the existence of knowledge about who we are and where we should go. Seduced by a siren song of progress, we are deaf to the voices of common sense, as we recklessly throw overboard our accumulated moral and cultural wisdom. The mighty ship of modern life drifts under the command of blind chance. The urgency of our moral situation recommends that we reopen the question of the nature of nature and its possible bearing on human affairs.

Against the Stream: Beginning with the Phenomena

This investigation of eating is, in fact, informed by a long-standing suspicion about the inadequacy of our contemporary notions about living nature and man.[2] Let me come clean about where I begin. Though I greatly esteem the discoveries of modern science and the insights it provides regarding *how* things work or happen, I share neither its apparent indifference to questions of *what* and *why* things are nor the explicit or tacit claims scientists sometimes make—when they choose not to be indifferent—about the *being* of living nature and man. In particular I doubt that living things are adequately understood on the corporealist premise that only lifeless *body* truly *is* or that the experientially evident wholeness, form, "inwardness," and purposive activities of living beings can be properly and fully understood, by analysis, in terms ultimately of homogeneous matter and its purposeless motions. Regarding man I am suspicious of the tendency to treat him as only an animal like any other, merely "more complex" and in all decisive respects the same. But I am at least equally doubtful of the opposite modern views, born in reaction against this "naturalistic" treatment of the human, which isolate mind and consciousness and which see man, as the "existential" or "historical" being, as simply discontinuous with the rest of nature. The "culprit" in both of these opposed and, to my mind, erroneous views of our humanity is the same objectified view of nature. Those who corporealistically assimilate man to the rest of the animals as well as those who idealistically set him in explicit opposition to nature share the scientific view of nature as blind, mechanical, mindless, and aimless.

The present inquiry, then, attempts to reconsider the now-dominant scientific view in search of a more natural and richer biology and anthropology, one that does justice to our lived experience of ourselves as psychophysical unities—enlivened, purposive, and open to and in converse with the larger world.* Substantively it is part of a quest for the place of man within the natural order, as one—but also as a special one—of the living beings, in relation to other living beings and in relation to other human beings. I hope to provide evidence that the modern corporealists—those who deprecate or deny the soul—and their modern rationalist or humanist opponents—those who deprecate or deny the body—are both mistaken, both about living nature and about man. I seek such evidence in an examination of eating.

Where to start? Let us examine the phenomenon of human eating by looking at the scientist and his views of the subject. When the scientist looks at eating, what does he see? An objective fellow, he sees coolly from the outside. Generally speaking he sees animal movements to gain food, the movement of the edible material from the outside in and down, the physical and chemical breakdown of food, the energetics of the process, and the maintenance of a steady internal environment of sugar, nitrogen, salts, and the like. More specifically the anatomist may show how the powerful masseter muscles at the angles of the mouth cause the lower jaw to move, enabling the teeth to grind the ingested food, or how the tongue and pharyngeal

---

*The present volume can therefore be regarded as a sequel to my first book (see note 2 of this chapter), for it attempts a positive contribution to "a more natural science."

muscles are coordinated with each other and with the closure of the epiglottis to ensure the successful act of swallowing without aspiration into the lungs. The physiologist can show how the sight of food stimulates the psychic phase of gastric secretion through the vagus nerve or how a rise in blood glucose after a meal releases insulin from the pancreas to facilitate the transport of sugar into the cells. The biochemist studies how the sugar is oxidized and its energy trapped by the process of oxidative phosphorylation or how stores of glycogen in the liver are released during a period of fasting. The molecular biologist can demonstrate how a certain genetic mutation produces the inborn metabolic disease phenylketonuria (PKU) or how the supply of messenger-RNA is regulated to increase the desired protein synthesis. The psychologist will show how certain stimuli ordinarily presented with food can come on their own to induce salivation or how certain childhood traumas give rise to special food aversions or to eating disorders. And the anthropologist will study how different cultures eat different foods, in different manners, and with different rituals.

But when these scientists get together for lunch, how do they look on eating? They forget their anatomy, physiology, biochemistry, molecular biology, psychology, and anthropology—and a good thing, too. For not only might their science interfere with their enjoyment of the meal, it also has nothing to do with their own tacit understanding of themselves as eaters. They choose when and what to eat, and they do so quite purposively; hunger or appetite prompts them; gustatory preferences guide their choices. They eat sitting down, at a table, where they notice temperatures and textures, enjoy seasonings and spices, and take pleasure both in the abatement of their hunger and in the sequences of courses and tastes. Some will be *Feinschmecker* and connoisseurs; others will eat with relative indifference—even though they all are supposedly doing their identical anatomical and physiological things. They converse while eating, taking as much pleasure in the company and the conversation as in their food. But one suffers loss of appetite because of grief or worry; the second finds the meat overcooked and tough to chew (for him, not for the masseter muscles); a third finds the sight of red meat repulsive; a fourth, tasting the apple pie, remembers that his mother made it better; a fifth remarks how much better the trout would taste if it had been grilled (and best of all if he had caught it himself); and the sixth is momentarily embarrassed because he has a mouth full of food when his neighbor asks him a question. None of them ever even imagines that his colleagues may be tasty or nutritious—despite the fact that their protein and carbohydrate content does not differ from that of their food. The eating of the scientists—and even the eating of the scientists' pet dogs and cats—is not eating according to their science. Their eating, like all other activities in which human beings and animals engage, is an activity of whole, unified, formed, living, active, sensitive, and desiring beings, to whom and for whom such activities matter. They live concretely and feelingly in and through their enlivened and inwardly experienced bodies, in ways that cannot even be accurately described in terms of the "dead," abstracted, objectified "body" of their—our—science.

The gap between the eating actually engaged in by our scientists and the so-called eating analyzed by our science is generalizable; it exists and, because of the premises of modern science, must exist between all activities of life as lived and those activities as understood scientifically. As we shall see, it is a gap much wider and deeper than the notorious "mind-body problem," which is primarily a problem only for those who begin with a soulless body and who then wonder how consciousness can arise from and be fused with it. The gap, unbridgeable unless we shift the basic notions of our science, exists not only regarding thinking, feeling, and imagining, but also regarding sensing, desiring, moving, and—as I will argue—nourishing. And it exists not only regarding these activities of human beings but also for the activities of the other animals.

Thus eating, albeit a fascinating topic in its own right, turns out to be a perfect subject for reopening the question about nature, human nature, and ethics. First, all living things take nutriment, and their need to do so characterizes life universally. Every animal eats. If one can find a richer and more natural account of animals and man in the phenomena of metabolism and nourishing, one can find one for *any* vital activity. Thus in thinking about eating we hope to gain a deeper understanding of both animal and human nature.

Second, since animals mostly eat other living things or their products, eating necessarily implies and illuminates the relation of one animal to other living beings. Inwardly experienced need drives animals outward into the world, and their place and way of life in relation to that world is largely defined by what and how they eat. Thus in thinking about eating we can explore the relation between an animal's nature, or between our nature, and the larger world—that is, nature as a whole.

Third, understanding human eating throws light on the relation between the nonrational and the rational in man, and between the strictly natural and the cultural or ethical. For eating is that indispensable vital activity closest to the mindlessly natural, yet it is also influenced by the emergence of mind and culture. Thus in thinking about eating we can examine the relation between our nature and our customs. We can ask whether and to what extent our customs about eating are informed by insights into our nature. We can even ask whether and to what extent our customs about eating contribute to the perfection of our nature. If we are successful, perhaps we can even show that nature is not altogether silent about, or irrelevant for thinking about, how we should live. By this I do not mean that I hope here to discover rules of conduct written, so to speak, on the cosmic stones. Rather, nature rightly understood might turn out to be a *suggestive* teacher. Nature might yield a pointing-toward, a hinting-at, a promising-forth of a wholesome direction, a propitious attitude, a dignified and fulfilling posture for our lives. Nature, and even natural necessity, might yet point the way to virtue.

A Foretaste of the Argument

This project and these aspirations appear, even to me, to be grandiose. Moreover, the topic of eating is enormous and fills vast literatures—from biochemistry to social anthropology and from cookery to theology—more than any one human being can read. My own approach is nondisciplinary and eclectic, for instead of a methodical or comprehensive treatise, I have sought to produce a thoughtful exploration that seeks to stimulate exploratory thoughtfulness in my readers. I have sought evidence and assistance in the only places one can: in the appearances—the phenomena of nature—and my own and others' experience of them, and in the opinions and writings of those who came before. I have made particular use of some of the great works of our tradition, which I consult not because they are old or traditional but because they have a depth of vision about profound human matters that we neglect at our peril. Though we attempt a reconsideration, we need not simply start afresh; precisely because we are so disoriented, we may need to be prodded by voices long dead in order to come alive to what is right before us. Moreover, because this inquiry is not about constructing just one more way of looking at things but about discovering answers to the deepest questions of who we are and how we should live, I have eagerly taken help wherever I could find it, from biologists to gastronomists, from Homer and the Bible to Miss Manners. But my gleanings from the fields of food and eating have been governed by an intellectual and moral appetite and by a philosophical menu devised to satisfy it. The topics I have chosen to treat and the sources I have selected have been guided throughout by the singular argument I am advancing regarding the moral pointings of human nature.

That argument is in six stages. In the first I examine the nature of food, feeding, and the beings that feed, arguing against modern science's corporealist hypothesis and seeking to establish the independence and supremacy of the living form in relation to its own material. In the process I expose the great paradox of eating, namely that to preserve their life and form living forms necessarily destroy life and form. This chapter's account of living animal form reveals the three great powers of soul—awareness, action, and especially appetite—that prefigure important dimensions of human life. Turning in Chapter 2 from animal nature in general to human nature in particular, I explore the special openness and social promise of the human form, implicit in our upright posture, as well as the problematic indeterminacy reflected in man's extreme omnivorousness—that strictly natural, unpremeditated bodily mark of man's dominant and mastering posture in the world and, hence, of his moral ambiguity. These protean and indefinite appetites of the "best and worst among the animals" need and receive delimitation and consequent modification by culture, the themes of the remaining four stages of this inquiry. Chapter 3 deals with those foundational conventions, more or less universal, that set outer limits to human omnivorousness, in the first place by excluding other human beings and human flesh from the realm of the edible. Chapter 4 deals with basic table manners and other regulations of eating that transform animal feeding into human eating, whereas Chapter 5 continues the movement toward freedom, friendship, and refinement by considering how eating is sometimes elevated into dining and even feasting. This ennobling of human eating—a major aspect of the general refinement and civility brought about by culture—would be further perfected if the rituals of dinner themselves reflect in their content a more or less true understanding of the nature of nature and of the place of man within it. The final chapter argues that the dietary laws of Leviticus embody one such understanding—one that pays homage to the supremacy of form over material in the living world; one that acknowledges both the problematic character of eating and the promise and peril of the hungry soul; but one that at the same time celebrates in gratitude the mysterious source of the formed and multiform world and its generous hospitality in providing food, both for life and for thought.

The argument is thus an ascent—from nature to human nature to human nature culturally clothed by the just, then the noble, then the holy—but an ascent that remains in touch with its beginnings. Like a rising spiral staircase the path revisits earlier vistas that, now enlarged, can be contemplated with greater depth of understanding, yielding insight into both the viewer and the viewed. The central thread that guides the argument in its ascent is the idea of *form*, with its multiple yet always interconnected meanings. An animal's form or organization is distinguishable (yet also inseparable) from its own materials; thanks to its form an animal is distinguishable from other kinds of animals; thanks to the psychic powers that emerge with its special form or organized embodiment, many an animal—and especially the animal that bears the peculiarly upright form—can respond to and have commerce with the myriad forms of the surrounding world. These silent forms impress themselves on the imagination and receive articulate recognition in the speech of the human animal, whose rational openness to the multiform world is, paradoxically, what makes him also its great trans*form*er. Yet the cultural forms that clothe his naked nature can also form him (or re-form or transform or de-form him), in the best case to conform him to the best and the highest possibilities implicit in his own unique form and embodiment. The cultural forms of human eating, dependent in turn on the forms of the human imagination and mind, range from the silent form of the table itself, to the gestural forms of table manners, to the aesthetic forms of refined dining and the culinary arts, to the articulate forms of dinner conversation. Finally, from the top of the spiral, gazing on the totality of the world as well as on his own peculiar ascent, the upright animal embraces forms that sanctify his eating, embodying his self-conscious awareness that he stands face-to-face with the awesome mystery of form and form's wondrous openness to mystery.

1

Food and Nourishing

The Primacy of Form

For of the soul the body form doth take;
for soul is form, and doth the body make.

—*Edmund Spenser*
"A Hymn in Honour of Beauty," line 90

The whole of nature, as has been said, is a conjugation of the
verb to eat, in the active and passive.

—*William Ralph Inge*
"Confessio Fidei," *Outspoken Essays*

Who says the earth is not the center of the universe? No, not its geometrical or material center; the earth is not even the center of its own solar system, which in turn is nothing like the center of our allegedly boundless universe, by definition incapable of having a spatial center. But, *pace* Copernicus, the earth may still be the vital, and also the intelligent, center of the universe; for it is, as far as we know, the only place in the vast cosmic sea of inorganic stuff and motion that has proved hospitable to life. Only here has the lifeless mud acquired the breath of life; only here has the cosmos through life finally become conscious of itself.

These are not just anthropocentric prejudices; they seem to be cosmic truths. In the waters, on the land, and high aloft before the heavens, the earth teems with living beings, plants and animals, large and small, manifesting and reproducing themselves according to their myriad and distinctive kinds. And we are not the least among them, not least because we *know* that we and all our other terrestrial relations are alive. We, the curious and reflective animals, give names to all our kin—to date to more than 1.4 million species of organisms.

Though plants offer splendid displays for the appreciative eye of the beholder, most people find animals more fascinating. For the animals are the truly animate, because obviously lively, ones. They move around and about and often collide with one another. They hunt and fish and sport and mate and die—as do we. Most of them operate beneath our notice, too small or too hidden to be detected except by the searching zoologist. But the larger ones especially attract a crowd. For notwithstanding their abundant variety and their manifest strangeness, we sense in their movements and expressions that their life is somehow related to our own and that they too experience an inwardness filled with some similar pleasures and pains, desires and fears. About this we are surely not mistaken, at least with respect to the business of staying alive. For every living animal is alike at least in this: It needs, seeks, and takes in food—and so do we. Moreover, being self-conscious eaters, we can sympathize with all that hungers and feeds. Not surprisingly feeding time at the zoo ranks first in popularity with occupants and spectators alike.

Taking food is not a matter of choice. It is a desired necessity, indispensable for all vital activity and sought after by all living animals. Food is needed for growth and development, for maintenance and repair, for every motion and activity. Show us an animal that is not turning over foodstuff and we shall pronounce him dead. To live is to metabolize; at least for all terrestrial beings, there is no other way. One is only if and because one eats.

Animals seek and find food in their environments. Originally outside and other, food must be brought inside and transformed into same. But what does this really mean, and what is responsible for it? What *is* the sameness that persists despite—indeed, because of—the ceaseless transformations of metabolism, transformations now occurring in every cell of your body even as you sit quietly and read? How do we understand what is responsible both for the transformations and for any persisting sameness? What kind of "world relationships" are entailed by the necessity of finding food? What enables an animal to recognize that which is nourishing? What drives it forward and outward to appropriate its food? What, finally, is the relationship between what one is and what one eats? These are the questions with which we begin our inquiry into eating. Animals, and not especially human beings, are our focus. At stake in the inquiry is the adequacy or sufficiency of a materialistic explanation of metabolism and animal eating, and therewith of life as such.

Let me introduce the question by reflecting grossly on the process by which we—and other multicellular animals—reach our maturity and by considering explicitly the relation between what we are and what we eat.

At first glance there is some reason to believe that one *is* just *what* one eats. We begin life as a single cell, barely visible to the naked eye. To reach our adult size, we must increase our bulk 120 billion-fold. We acquire this extra mass entirely from without, by ingestion. In addition, it seems certain that—no matter how diligently we search—we will never find any immaterial something that enters our bodies along with all that stuff. We are, from head to toe, altogether stuff-y. To be sure, we don't *look* like the food we eat. But appearance is deceiving. At bottom we are proteins, carbohydrates, fats, vitamins, minerals, and nucleic acids—and so is our food. No wonder food is so important to survival: Where it goes, there I am; where it goes not, there I am not; what it is, that too am I. We are identical, I and my stuff.

This plausible equation of what I am with what I eat, by means of the intermediate and even more plausible identifications of me and my stuff and of my stuff with my food, requires closer scrutiny. An obvious difficulty confronts us. Chicken embryos digest egg yolk and grow into egg-laying chickens; calves drink milk and grow into milk-giving cows; human children eat egg yolks and drink cows' milk but grow up only human. Yolk taken by the chicken becomes chicken; the same yolk taken by the child is humanized. How can this be, if one is what one eats? If we eat the same, why are we not the same? What is our distinctive being if we are materially the same? What is the relationship between what we eat and what we are?

Let us start again and proceed more slowly, taking nothing for granted. Let us begin simply and with the obvious, with what we—or any animals—eat: with food. What is food?

Food

If we begin grossly, and with the larger animals, food is other living things or their parts and products. Some animals are vegetarian: Frugivores like the squirrel or the cedar waxwing eat acorns or chokecherries, herbivores like the cow or the sheep eat grass, while the koala eats only the leaves of the eucalyptus tree. Up the so-called food chain are the carnivores, who, because they eat animals that in turn eat plants, are at least indirectly omnivores. Flies are food for frogs and phoebes, fish for crocodiles and cormorants, mice for snakes and owls, rabbits for falcons and foxes, zebras for lions and tigers. We omnivorous human beings, who transform much of our food by cooking, mixing, and seasoning it for tastiness or edibility, cannot fully hide from ourselves—or at least from our butchers and meat packers—that we eat cows, sheep, and pigs; chickens, fish, and shellfish; in addition to radishes, rhubarb, radicchio, raspberries, and rice and countless other roots, stems, leaves, fruits, and seeds.

Yet insofar as these other living beings are regarded as food, they cease to be treated as *what* they are, even before they cease to *be* what they are when they are ingested. From the point of view of the disinterested observer, a rabbit is a rabbit and spinach is spinach. Each organism is, in and for itself, a formed and determinate one of a determinate kind. Yet from the viewpoint of a hungry rabbit, spinach is lunch, and for a hungry fox, the well-fed rabbit is dinner. A mate for the zebra is just meat to a lion. The form of the object is finally unimportant to the eater; that it is potential material is all that matters.

It follows that something is *as* food only to another being—one that almost universally belongs to a different species. Food is a relational term. Yet the relation is not superficial: That which is appropriated as food is actually something other but (also and at the same time) potentially the same, at least in part. Strange as it seems and sounds, the zebra, in addition to being in fact a zebra, is also and at the same time capable of becoming (part of) a lion. Like all food it exists in the relation of desired unlike but potential like; through digestion it is transformed by the lion's living body from being something other into being just the same. Between being what it was as formed (and alien) and being what it becomes as formed (and one's own), food passes through the intermediate stage of being more or less formless, homogeneous elementary stuff. What was food to the mouth and the naked eye is unrecognizable when it becomes food to the intestine, as seen under the microscope.

Indeed the microscopic view provides us with additional reasons to think of food more as the *final* product of digestion—the chemical material just before absorption from the intestinal cavity into the bloodstream—rather than as the *initial* object of appetition or ingestion. For the microscope has also introduced us to simpler creatures, ones that lack mouths and intestines but that nevertheless take in food. The simplest organisms, bacteria, selectively absorb the simplest nutriments; for example glucose or other sugars and amino acids. Elegant studies have shown that even bacteria have preferences among foodstuffs—though obviously not conscious ones. For example, they will swim after and absorb glucose as their carbon source until it is exhausted from the medium; only then will they change over to pursuing, absorbing, and metabolizing a less-desirable sugar or some amino acid.

The amoeba, another of the simplest organisms, actually engulfs more complex foodstuffs. As they are engulfed, the food particles enter with some surrounding water to form little bubbles, called vacuoles, contained as discrete entities within the cytoplasm (the living cell substance) of the amoeba. There the food particles are broken down, and the simples (amino acids, simple sugars, fatty acids, and so forth) are absorbed into the cytoplasm across the vacuole wall in a process physically similar to the one that occurs across the intestinal wall in higher animals and men. Indeed the digestive tract of higher animals, though spatially located within the confines of the living body, is nonetheless—analogously to the vacuole—only a captured portion of the outside world, to which it is open at both ends. Topologically and digestively speaking, the bodies of higher animals are, in fact, highly complex variations of a simple plan: a thick-walled solid cylinder built around a hollow tube that runs through its center. In schematic cross-section, the organism is like a doughnut, nourished from its hole, here and there armed with appendages that work either to keep that hole filled or to keep the doughnut from filling some other doughnut's hole.

But the digestive cavity is not only a conduit, it is also a cauldron for transforming its contents. Along the extensive and extensively coiled tube through which the captured foodstuffs flow, the animal's digestive powers operate, so that, by the time the true orifices of ingress, the intestinal cells, are reached, the semipermeable membranes of each intestinal cell will be confronted with a feast of simples, to be absorbed by processes like those functioning in the bacterium or amoeba: diffusion and selective absorption.

Yet this reductive analysis, albeit illuminating, is not the whole story, and if we regard it as such it will prove misleading. True, every cell of multicellular organisms is nourished and is metabolically active in ways remarkably similar to microorganisms—for example the glycolytic and Krebs cycles (the chemical pathways for breaking down sugar) and oxidative phosphorylation (the process of capturing in usable form the energy released by breaking down sugar and other foodstuffs) are universally found. Yet the more complex organisms cannot be understood as mere aggregates or sums of their component cells, even with respect to nourishment: Complexity also brings with it genuine novelty. For example, the specialization required effectively to nourish the higher organisms means, among other things, that some cells and tissues must feed others as well as themselves, and one organ, the mouth, serves as a portal that collects all the fodder. This specialization gives rise to the two different views of food—one relative to the mouth, one relative to the gut (or, ultimately, to the individual cells). Furthermore the organ of ingestion acquires functions and pleasures of its own—biting, chewing, swallowing—as well as its own gustatory predilections and delights, which are logically, physiologically, and experientially separate from the ultimate goal of nourishment. Because it is such a long way from the taste buds to the true ports of call, food to the mouth need not be foodstuff to the intestine. The tasty or appetizing and the fitting or needful—each at the heart of one of two possible definitions of food—need not be identical, at least not for human beings (a fact to which we shall return). Speaking generally—and as we shall see more clearly later—these intermediate activities that serve to gain survival may become parts of the larger, well-working wholeness that an animal gets to enjoy by surviving. We begin to suspect that the "complex eaters" are not just simple eaters grown large, and that modern science's attempt to explain the activities of living animals in terms of interactions among "dead" chemicals may be not only incomplete but also distorting.

Eating

We began our look at eating by asking about what we eat, about food. But since food turns out to be that which is eaten (to nourish a nourishing being), the meaning of food falls back onto the meaning of eating (and nourishing). This is no illicit circularity. Such correlation of the activity and its object is captured in those languages that contain cognate accusatives for their verbs for eating. The Old English word *foda* and the Teutonic root *fôd*, meaning food, are cognate with the old Teutonic verb *fôdjan*, to feed, to be the source of food. Indeed, English has similar cognates: We feed food; we eat the edibles. Yet such formal correlation does not reveal concretely how activity and object are related, that is, how "feeding food" differs from, say, "smelling smells" or "thinking thoughts." In its transitive sense *to feed* means to give food to another, to supply someone else with fodder. A dog feeds her pups by suckling them; a bird feeds her young by putting food into their mouths; a farmer feeds his cattle by putting them out to graze and feeds his family by supplying them with grain, milk, and meat. Feeding in this sense is an act of nurturing assistance, even of generosity, and not only for human beings. Always a social act, it presupposes some communal relations between feeder and fed.

But reflexively *to feed* also means to take food for oneself. To feed (oneself) is to eat someone (or something) else. This usage is no longer applied, except colloquially, to human beings: animals feed, human beings eat. In the present chapter I shall use the term *eating* to refer to this common activity of both animals and men, the taking of food for oneself. Further on, we will consider the more specifically human features of eating, which distinguish it from mere feeding.

Eating has several aspects, linguistically distinguished. As an intransitive verb, *eating* is an activity of the animal, more precisely, the activity of the animal as eater ("First they eat, then they fall asleep.") Eating as an activity is thus one manifestation of animate being and is part of the animal's "being-at-work." But eating is not a pure and self-contained activity of the agent, like running or swimming or flying; the word *eating* is also, and always, a transitive verb as well. To be eating is necessarily to be eating *something*—something *other* and *in the world*.

Other vital activities also entail an encounter with correlative objects: To be at work thinking is to be thinking the thinkable; to be at work seeing is to be seeing the visible; to be at work copulating is to be fusing with the sexual complement, and so on. Yet the relations among agent, activity, and object in eating differ from all these other cases. In thinking the thinking mind seems to become one with the thing thought; the thinker is possessed by his thoughts, always "changing his mind" as the ideas that "fill it" change. (This, I trust, is now happening to you, in reading.)* In seeing we open our eyes and effortlessly receive the sights that "pour" in, mysteriously filling us with the appearance of visible things even as those same things remain undisturbed and in their place, unaffected by our activity of seeing them. In sexual activity, despite the longing for union, duality is never overcome; the lover does not lose himself in the beloved, the beloved does not become part of the lover, and the two do not become one flesh, except derivatively in the children that may issue from such sexual coupling. But when we are at work on the world in eating, we do not become the something that we eat; rather the edible gets assimilated to what we are.

---

*So powerful is this experienced coincidence between minding and the ideas-being-minded that ancient thinkers (like Aristotle) thought that the human so-called mind or intellect is basically a pure openness or receptivity, an immaterial "material," a capacity to be grasped and informed by the intelligibles. On this view mind is actually nothing except when it thinks, and when it thinks it is identical to the active being-at-work of the intelligibles.

Eating something means transforming it, chemically as well as physically. Eating comprises the appropriation, incorporation, and de-formation of a complex other, and its homogenization into simples, in preparation for their transformation into complex same. More precisely, in eating, another becomes one's own through specific stages. First it loses independence when it is seized or plucked or uprooted and grasped by hand or mouth. Next its own distinctive form is destroyed, beginning with ingestion and proceeding through the homogenizing process of digestion. Otherness is ultimately overcome by the incorporation of the homogenized simples that is absorption, followed by their re-formation and assimilation to sameness through biosynthesis. Whereas in seeing, the sight of the viewer is informed by the visible object, in eating, the edible object is thoroughly transformed by and re-formed into the eater.

The transformation is, of course, never complete; some of the ingested materials resist digestive breakdown; some of the simples produced by digestion are rejected for absorption. Even for the healthiest and most fastidious animals, there is digestive waste. A bacterium may absorb only glucose (and salts) and waste virtually none of it, but organisms with digestive tracts necessarily "have eyes bigger than their small intestines," excreting the unusables as solid waste. The conversion of other to same is thus only partial; for any complex organism there is no perfect food, completely incorporated without remainder, immediately active as part of the feeder. A crystal "grows" by addition and "waste-free" incorporation of units already directly identical to its own; an animal only by transmutation of another organism. That such conversion is possible at all is the wonder that is eating and metabolism.

Strange as it may seem, the necessarily wasteful character of metabolism is not necessarily a defect, for the need it creates turns out, as we shall see, to be the deepest cause of the richer forms of being available to living embodied organisms (compared to the "more efficient" crystals). As a thought experiment, one might ask, Why is there need for *new* food? Why does not nature favor the perfect recycling of materials? Why does not animal evolution tend toward the selection of organisms that effectively recycle, that waste less, that need less and less exogenous food? A physicist will point out that perfectly efficient recycling is impossible, a violation of the second law of thermodynamics. A physiologist will point out that the products of metabolic breakdown (like ammonia or carbon dioxide) are often toxic to the animal and therefore need to be expelled. But a philosopher will wonder whether these necessities are not, paradoxically, also *good* for the organism. For lack, experienced as desire, is the spur to all aspiration, to action and awareness, to having a life at all. Bodies as incorruptible as diamonds, or bodies lacking in nothing beyond themselves, would have no impulse or orientation toward the world beyond their borders. Waste makes need, and need makes for everything higher than need. Here, in the germ of hunger, is the origin of all the appetites of the hungry soul.

What Use Is Food?

What happens next to the material absorbed after digestion? What is foodstuff food *for*? Some of it will be used for energy, which in turn is needed for all bodily activities. In this sense food is to the organism what gasoline is to the automobile. No fuel, no performance. But the relationship between the fuel and the fuel-dependent performer differs markedly for an automotive organism and a mechanical automobile. In a car the combustion of fuel releases heat energy that expands the gases in the combustion chamber, and the expanding gases mechanically drive the pistons that, via a series of interconnecting rods, shafts, and gears, make the wheels go around. In the automobile (and the steam engine, the jet airplane, and the atomic-powered submarine) the motion is external to the site of fuel combustion, and the site of combustion is external to the mechanism that moves. The machine, though it houses the fire, is not itself altered or consumed by the combustion of fuel, except to be coated by some fraction of the unexpelled residues. Fuel goes in and combustion wastes go out, but the machine does not participate in the transformations; it remains unaltered, like the fireplace that hosts but escapes the transformation of the fuel-consuming fires.*

---

*The word "fuel," from the Old French *fowaille*, may be etymologically related to the Latin *focalia*, neuter plural of the adjective *focalis*, related to *focus*, which originally meant "hearth," "fireplace." Thus *focalia* are the things of the hearth.

In contrast the controlled biological combustion (or oxidation) of energy-rich carbohydrates for use in animal locomotion does not work through the use of released heat to expand physically an inert and external mechanism. Rather the chemical energy contained in foodstuff is trapped in the form of concentrated, transportable, and readily usable packets of energy still in chemical form (usually in the high-energy bonds of a carrier known as ATP), which bring about the contraction of the muscles, which in turn move the bones that move the body. Moreover—and this is the more profound difference—the oxidation that enables them to contract is housed (and conducted) by the muscles themselves. In the living animal fuel "burned" to permit motion moves and alters purposively especially the very "hearth" that burns it. (And, as will soon become clearer, the muscles are—indeed the entire organism is—not only moved but moving, actor as well as acted upon, in metabolic combustion as in all other organic activities.)

But animal nourishment differs still more profoundly from machine fueling. Food is, in fact, more than fuel, because it yields more than power. Food is needed also to maintain the "organic machine." All of the organism's constituent materials—that is, the proteins, carbohydrates, lipids, and nucleic acids and the complexes formed from these—are in constant flux, including also the materials that carry out these metabolic transformations. For example, the very enzymes instrumental (as catalysts) in the breakdown of sugar to produce useful energy are themselves regularly broken down and resynthesized from amino acids within the cell. Quite literally the organism that turns over foodstuff is itself constantly turning over its own stuff. No part of the cell is immune. But what is lost to degradation is regenerated by the cell itself, in part from the very foodstuffs brought from without. For the organism, unlike a machine, to nourish means to maintain as well as to fuel, and the organism is self-maintaining and self-repairing.

Organic self-maintenance not only preserves and restores the stuff of living cells; in multicellular organisms it also secures a stable internal fluid environment in which the cells live and function. All living cells and tissues are surrounded and sustained by body fluids, like blood and lymph, that not only bring nutrients and remove wastes but also make possible the optimum functioning of the cells by keeping roughly constant the physicochemical properties of their immediate habitat. The blood or serum concentrations of, for example, glucose, albumin, fatty acids, and various inorganic salts and ions (like sodium, potassium, calcium, phosphorus, and iron) are stably maintained—along with temperature and pH—within a narrow range. In higher animals elaborate neural and hormonal mechanisms help ensure this homeostasis* of the *milieu intérieur*, but the materials held in balance are constantly being supplied and replenished by nourishment, by food.

Nourishing provides not only for maintenance; it also provides, out of the same foodstuff, for increase and growth. But here a careful distinction is needed between mere increase in size and genuine growth. When a mature, full-grown adult eats more than he needs for activity and maintenance, that surplus stuff is turned into storage, largely as fat. Food is, in this sense, a source of quantity, of increased mass and bulk. Yet this surplus is not in principle essential for life and, except in animals that hibernate, may even be harmful—as we human beings know only too well. But even where spare bulk is useful insurance against a lean year, such an increase in quantity is not genuine growth.

True growth, in contrast, is *in-form-ation*—formation and organization, of and from within—not just increase. It is seen most clearly in the process of maturation. True, as an animal goes from a fertilized egg to a mature adult, as we already observed, its bulk increases enormously. But that increase is in the service of and subordinate to the development and differentiation of the various organs and their maturation to full functional capacity. Not as prospective storage bulk to be saved for the event of famine but as material to be reformed and transformed into the *essential* components of an organic, organized, and active whole is food the material of true growth.

What happens when the foodstuff is incorporated into the feeder? How are we to understand its transformation into the living flesh of the growing and active organism? What, precisely, is the relation between the nutrient part and the organic whole?

---

*The term *homeostasis*—meaning "staying the same"—was coined by Walter B. Cannon to describe the internal constancy that permits the remarkable persistence of the organism's bodily structure and function.[1]

Here we need to avoid some careless thinking about the meaning and relation of parts and wholes.* For not everything that is a piece or a hunk of something bigger is properly a part. A part, by its very nature, is always a part *of*. A part of what? A part of a whole. Only true wholes can have true parts. Not every larger entity, comprising subunits, is a whole. Everything depends on how the subunits and the larger unit are related, and on the kind of being each is and has.

The crucial distinction is between a composition and what I shall call a concretion. In a composition the so-called parts or elements are put together (*com + ponere*), "placed with" each other side by side, like bricks in a building or molecules in a crystal, *without losing their individual identity*. By contrast, in a concretion mutual interaction effects a transformation of the original subunits. The elements become "grown-together" (*con + cresco*) into a more intimate union, which submerges their original distinct identities into the larger whole. Curiously, when the elements are truly concretized into the whole, they are no longer *actually* what they were. They exist in the whole only *potentially*; that is to say, the original elements, now transformed and submerged, can be restored only by separation and only *if and when* the larger whole is broken down (as, for example, when a body decays after death or when scientists dissect and analytically destroy its integrity). A true whole is continuous and integral; even the internal so-called boundaries between the organic parts do not exist except as potential sites for future divisions of the whole. When a part is made to stand apart as an actual discrete something—like a hand or a liver or a DNA or protein molecule—it has ceased to be a true part of the functioning whole. A "hand" that cannot handle is in fact not a hand.

When foodstuffs like sugars and fats become material for organic growth, self-maintenance, or self-healing, their identity as discrete

---

*The philosophical questions of part and whole are among the most interesting and difficult: What is the relation of part and whole? What makes something a one, a unity, an integrity with its own identity, despite the presence of a plurality of parts or subunits? Though a powerful argument can be made that plants and animals are the clearest instances of natural wholes, the issue of part and whole crops up in many other realms: the electron within the atom, hydrogen within water (H_2O), lines within the triangle, notes within a song, bricks within a building, and so on. And then there is the overarching question of the relation of each thing or being to *the* whole. The reader may fruitfully ponder whether these part-whole relationships are all basically the same or whether (and how) they are at once both similar and different.

chemicals is submerged as they are incorporated into the larger units of life: cells, tissues, organs, organ systems, and, finally, the whole organism. (Indeed the identities of each of these progressively larger parts, as discrete entities, are submerged in the next larger organizational level.) True, the elementary foodstuffs are constantly being recycled in metabolic turnover, and they can be recovered as distinct chemicals on analysis. But as they exist when incorporated into the living being they exist concretely, not compositely; they exist grown-together in the integrated whole. This concretization and integration of renewable materials is the work of biosynthesis, a chief, if not *the* chief, use of nourishing.

Nourishing is thus the activity of self-renewal as well as self-fueling, self-maintenance, self-healing, and self-maturation. Its essence: the transformation of materials, from other to selfsame, by the organism itself—indeed by each of its cells, tissues, and organs, in well-coordinated and integrated processes of breakdown, biosynthesis, and concretization—to preserve and to serve the organism as a living, performing whole.

The Cause of Nourishing

Our reflections to this point have hardly broken new ground nor have they been especially controversial. The difficulty begins when we move from description to explanation, from stating the facts of nourishing to finding their cause. Here we begin to probe more deeply into the meaning of eating in relation to the being of animals.

Nourishing not only makes possible and sustains the performing whole; it is itself one of the whole's performances. As the many recent references to "self" imply, an organism feeds and nourishes itself. The impulse to feed, as well as all steps of ingestion, digestion, absorption, and regenerative biosynthesis, is an *accomplishment* of the animal itself. Though sustained by metabolism, an organism seems to be more than metabolism's product. It also appears to be its cause.

What is it *in* the organism that is *responsible* for these activities? This is, of course, the heart of the matter. At issue is the very nature and being of living things, a question once much debated by philosophers, but now virtually neglected even by biologists. Nothing less than a complete ontology can answer the question, and I am, quite frankly, unequal to the task. Nevertheless an attempt must be made, at least to clarify the question and to suggest the outlines of what seems to me the most reasonable answer.*

We ask "What is responsible?" because we are perplexed by change. Change of all sorts is puzzling, organic change peculiarly so. Organisms come into being and pass away; they grow, mature, metabolize, move, mate, decline, and die. We want to know *why* it happens; we want an "explanation." It is the aspiration of all explanation of change and activity to find something *beneath* the change, itself more stable or fixed, to which we refer, and in terms of which we explain, the activity. We seek, as it were, to arrest or capture the motion by identifying it with something simpler and more regular and predictable, something preferably permanent and immobile (or, if not absolutely unchanging, immobile in the sense that the character and quantity of its motions are not themselves changing). When we ask about responsibility† for metabolism, we are asking about such an under-lying cause, the stable something beneath or behind the flux.

When this question of responsibility or cause was first elaborated in classical antiquity,‡ a variety of meanings were distinguished, for there are many different kinds of responsibility, as many as there are meanings to the question Why? Consider, for example, the chair in

---

*The ensuing difficult but necessary discussion of causation and of form and material, like that just concluded about part and whole, will be insufficiently rigorous for the sophisticated. Yet I fear it may also be too dry or tedious for those impatient with philosophical argumentation, despite my strenuous efforts to avoid technical terms and jargon. Such readers may derive some comfort from knowing that I too find these matters very hard to sort out; thinking about the true being of familiar things is never easy.

†I deliberately lead with the phrase "what is responsible for" rather than the more common "what is the cause of." For, as will soon emerge in this discussion, the notion of "cause" carries the weight of 2,500 years of philosophical dispute; moreover, in its contemporary use, it generally means at most something like "moving agent," that which propels or pushes the motion or change. Yet there are a variety of answers to the question "why this motion?". What, for example, is responsible for your present activity of reading? Among others, the physical existence of the book, the intelligibility of its contents, your desire to learn, the physiological health of your eyes and brain, and your capacity to receive the units of intelligibility mysteriously carried by the words on the page.

‡The term entered classical philosophy from its ordinary usage in the Greek law courts, where an *aitios* was the guilty party, the one responsible for the crime. Hence *aitia*, cause, became that which bore responsibility for some happening or change or for some being's existence. A cause is that which is "guilty" of and for the deeds—and misdeeds—of Being itself.

which you are sitting: Why is it the way it is? More than one thing is responsible. Responsibility for its being precisely the way it is lies with the carpenter-upholsterer who made it, and also with his art and tools (responsible as source of its coming-into-being); with the wood or springs or cushioning out-of-which it is made (responsible as its material); with the shape or structure it displays (responsible as its form or idea); and also with the use it serves, sitting (responsible as the that-for-the-sake-of-which or purpose-for-which it was made). In short, the from-what, the out-of-what, the what, and the for-what are all modes of responsibility.

With the coming of modern science, the notion of causation shrank to mean only the moving cause or the efficient cause, the source of the effect, that which puts something in motion. In the Newtonian world of inert matter in motion, the true cause would be the force that pushed or pulled from the outside, overcoming inertia to produce a change. Yet it proved easier to describe and quantify these changes than to identify the sought-for underlying substantive cause. (What kind of being, for example, is gravity?) Thus, today, abandoning altogether the search for a true cause or for an underlying being or substance whose properties explain the phenomena, scientists often content themselves with finding instead the regularity and permanence of so-called laws of change and motion, which express descriptively the relations of variables, usually in mathematical terms. Contrary to common opinion, the laws of motion—like Newton's famous expression $f = m \times a$, which defines the quantity of force as a constant product of a body's mass times the acceleration it experiences—do not explain motion or address its cause; they merely relate certain measurable external quantities of the motion and the thing moved, quantities defined in terms of preconceived parameters of space and time.

Nevertheless, despite these epistemological difficulties, scientists are by orientation drawn to materialism, to a belief in the primacy of matter and its necessary movements, to a faith that responsibility for natural phenomena resides ultimately with atoms and molecules and their autonomous attractions and repulsions, unions and divorces. Biologists are no exception. Though there are some nonconformists, nearly all contemporary biologists tend to explain the vital phenomena of feeding, nourishing, and metabolism in terms of the structure, motions, and relations of the material parts of the organism (and of its food). Not since Descartes broke with his philosophical ancestors to present his doctrine of the "animal machine" and a purely mechanical explanation of vital phenomena has any philosopher or scientist of the first rank thought to argue that some notion of form or soul or purpose was required to understand metabolism or, indeed, any activity of life with the possible exception of consciousness. One can well understand why, for modern biology has made enormous progress precisely by eschewing all such speculation.

Modern biochemists have made great strides in identifying the pathways of intermediary metabolism and biosynthesis, in defining the chemical fates of all absorbed nutriments, in describing the structure and mechanisms of action of the enzymes that catalyze bioorganic reactions, and in working out the genetically controlled regulatory mechanisms that keep the process running smoothly. Physiologists have analyzed the numerous elements of digestion and absorption and have defined the autonomic nervous system's control of these processes. And neurobiologists are presently searching out the "chemical basis" of appetite. In short the whole is treated in terms of its "parts" and the activities of the living being in terms of the motions of inanimate matter, of that underlying stuff more durable, long lasting, and regular than any living thing it frequents. The great successes of our analytic and reductive biology seem to most scientists to vindicate their mechanistic and materialistic presuppositions, not only as heuristic but as ontological hypotheses. Most biologists are, tacitly if not by explicit profession of faith, philosophical (as well as methodological) corporealists, firm believers in the primacy of the material: Understood in this sense, "You are what you eat" might well be their motto.

Against the stream I want here to argue for the necessary supremacy of living form. There is, of course, no doubt that our corporealist science has taught us much that is both illuminating and useful about the *how* of metabolism, but understanding the *what* and the *why* requires attention to organic form and its special properties. For, as we shall see, the relation of living form to its own material differs markedly from the form-material relation in inanimate things. In order to show this, we first need to gain greater clarity about our terms, *form* and *material*.

Form and Material

Every tangible object or being, whether of natural origin or made by human beings, both *is* a something and is *made-out-of* something. Provisionally let us call the latter its "material" and the former its "form." Form and material are, in the first instance, relative and correlative terms: Form *is* the something made of certain materials; materials are, as materials, materials *of* and *for* the thing as formed. In fact to *be* material means to be potential, to be able to receive a certain form or forms, to be capable-of-being-worked-on by some process or operation that would trans-*form* it—that is, form it into that something whose material it then becomes. Wood is, by itself, just wood; marble is marble; cholesterol is cholesterol. But marble becomes also material for Michelangelo only because and when its capacity to be the marble David or Moses is realized through the workings of the sculptor's hand. And cholesterol becomes material for a cholesterol-requiring organism when its capacity to interact intimately with other membrane materials is realized as it is incorporated by the organism as a component of its living cell membrane. Without ceasing altogether to be or to manifest properties of marble or cholesterol, these "things" are transformed and altered by their subordination to the activity of "information." The materials, though following their own nature, are at the same time constrained by their new arrangements, which constitute a nature of a higher order.

Form and material are interdependent not only in definition but usually also in fact; though distinct as ideas and separable in speech, they are, especially in living things, grown-together in the enmattered form or the informed matter that is the given thing; the dog and its flesh, the oak and its roots, no less than the desk and its wood, are each as inseparably related and as mutually interdependent as the concave and the convex. The relativity and interdependence of material and form persist also at multiple levels of organization: The oak wood that is material for the table is itself a special form, say, of xylem and phloem, which are in turn special formations of cells, which are special formations of carbohydrates, lipids, and proteins, and so on and on. At the "lowest level" some least or ultimate material would be reached (if any such there be) that could not be analyzed further into its form and material (and whose parts, if it had parts, would be homogeneous with the whole). Such an ultimate "material" would be more than material relative to some other form; it would be *matter*. It is, of course, one of the aspirations of a corporealist science to explain the formation, organization, and workings of all complex wholes in terms of the dispositions, motions, and interactions of their parts or materials, and, ultimately, of such ultimate matter. Form, on such an account, would be at all levels but an accident, or at most a result, of the necessitated bumpings and joinings, in stages, of the ultimate matter. It is this view that we are here challenging.

If material is material relative to a form, what then is a form? Form is often connected with shape and figure. But when we think of form with regard to living beings, we mean more than shape or figure, and more than an aggregate of corporeal parts. A pile of rocks has shape but not form; it is a heap, not a whole. Form is what makes a being a unity and a whole, in the world and through time. Form is that order or ordering that makes a one of the many components, giving it an integrity the components by themselves do not have. It is, I confess, extremely difficult to say just what this unifier is (if it is a distinct "what"). It cannot be the outside surface or skin; although the boundary defines the limits of the organism against everything it is not, it does not define what it is. The boundary is not the cause of unity but rather one of its manifestations. We begin to suspect that form is not primarily something visible or tangible—in short, that there is, in this sense, some immaterial "thing" that unites and informs the absolutely corporealized organism—but what it is we cannot define. Yet we may continue to discern its meaning and its work.

Form provides not only unity but also specificity and identity; each being is both a particular *one*—that is, a singular whole being, distinct from all others—and also a one *of* a particular species or kind. Although form is more than its visible aspect, these unifying and specifying properties of form are immediately evident in an organism's surface appearance or *gestalt*.[2] Both the hidden ground of its unity and the distinctive character of its being are attested to by its visible looks. Indeed the word *looks* has been suggested (by the late Jacob Klein) as the best translation of the Greek word *eidos*, central to the thought of Plato and Aristotle, which is usually translated as "form," "idea," or "species." (*Eidos* is derived from a root meaning "to see.") "Looks" preserves the etymological insight that both the *fact* of a thing's wholeness and, more important, the distinctive *kind* of whole that it is are generally evident in its visible appearance. The "invisible looks" or form or nature of an organism is announced eidetically, in the language of visibility. Indeed our word "species," from the Latin *species* (again literally "looks"), also carries this double sense of form: form as contrasted with its own material, and form as distinctive kind, contrasted with other kinds.

This way of approaching animal forms accords well with our ordinary (that is, prescientific) experience of the world. It also fits with human speech, which acknowledges the manifest species character of animal form by the use of such general nouns as *lion, tiger, cardinal*, or *eagle*. Despite what some critics might say, this recognition of species does not commit us to so-called typological thinking, to a belief in the permanence of species, or to any particular ontological teaching regarding form. In such ordinary speech we do no more than acknowledge what any healthy rabbit recognizes—without metaphysical prejudice and without deception attributable to language and its reliance on general nouns—when it flees from all hounds, finds all carrots to its taste, and mates only with other rabbits. Not philosophers but living nature is responsible for the existence of natural kinds, distinctively and recognizably formed after their kind.

Living things are not only visibly ordered, they are also internally organized. Organization—literally, the division of the whole into instrumentally active parts (the word *organ* means "instrument" or "tool," and *organization* means "the condition of systematic coordination of distinct instrumental parts or organs")—is, in a sense, the distinctive form of organism. Organs are genuine and heterogeneous parts, each with useful activities crucial to the life of the organism as a whole. One organ breaks up the food, another pumps nutrient-carrying blood throughout the body, a third filters the blood of toxic wastes; some organs of sense help locate the food; other organs of motion help capture it. Each organ in its own way contributes something useful to the whole. Indeed the very being and meaning of an organ is always given by its relation to the whole of which it is a useful part; to be useful is, necessarily, to be useful *to* something or someone, in this case to the whole organism. Utility, like the things that are useful, is a subordinate and subservient matter, always pointing to something that is being served.

To be sure, complex machines also have organization and comprise organs. But one of the chief differences between an organism and a machine is that *organisms are self-organizing*. They are organized—that is, they acquire their organs—developmentally and from within, realizing an innate plan or program. There is a second chief difference: The organized machine serves its owner; the *organized animal, to begin with, "serves" itself.*

Some animals are, of course, more highly formed—that is, intricately organized—than others. It is sometimes difficult, all the more so in lower organisms, to discern the boundary between one organ and another, and organs often have or can acquire more than one useful function. Yet organization, the special and coordinated arrangements of the necessary material, with the coincident emergence of new powers or capacities and new activities or functions, is an indisputable fact. And it is also a fact that many, if not all, of the interesting vital powers and activities of any organism depend absolutely on the arrangement of the suitable materials, rather than on the materials alone.

Our frequent references to animal activity remind us that, in living things, form is not a static notion. The looks of animals are often mobile, like the mobile animals that bear them, and the motions of the looks are generally recognizable and true to form. Most fundamentally, living form *is* generally *functioning* form or organization, that is, form in its work or activity. To be a something, to be a particular animal in the full sense, is to be that animal-at-work: Really to be a squirrel means to be actively engaged in the constellation of activities we can call "squirreling." The true squirrel is a bushy-tailed fellow who not only looks but also acts like a squirrel

> who leaps through the trees with great daring; who gathers, buries, covers but later uncovers and recovers his acorns; who perches out on a limb cracking his nuts, sniffing the air for smells of danger, alert, cautious, with his tail beating rhythmically; who chatters and plays and courts and mates, and rears his young in large improbable-looking homes at the tops of trees; who fights with vigor and forages with cunning; who shows spiritedness, even anger, and more prudence than many human beings.[3]

The dead squirrel or the sleeping squirrel or the squirrel-in-utero do not fully manifest the squirrel form.

Two further observations follow: Form-at-work in all its aspects can be said to be the distinctive way of life of an animal. And since every way of life is related (or adapted) to a particular place in the "outside" world—not just a geographic or climatic place but one filled also with other life forms—animal form-and-activity often shows itself in, and in turn bears the marks of, active reference to place and to relations beyond its border. The being of animals is not limited by their apparent visible boundaries; they live, thanks to the special powers of their peculiar forms, in and in relation to the larger world, as it were, "outside themselves" (a point to which I will return). Second, form manifests itself inwardly as well as outwardly, not only "spatially" in the internal arrangements of organs but also "psychically" in "inner" experience, that is, in feelings, moods, appetites, and so on. Sometimes, especially in the higher animals, this inwardness manifests itself on the surface, gaining outward expression in the changing patterns of visible form; in the higher animals, facial expressions and gestures make possible genuine communication of mood or emotion from one formed being to another. Form can thus be a conveyer of meaning, including some aspects of what it might *mean* to be *this* particular formed being.*

---

*From a philosophical point of view this discussion of form has but scratched the surface. It leaves many large and important questions unaddressed. For example, it ignores the vexing question of the origin or coming-into-being of the forms; for if the forms (or species) of living things change, as evolutionary doctrine teaches us that they do, we face the challenge of understanding how that is possible, especially if we insist that form is not just an accident of matter—that material receives and does not determine form. My discussion also ignores the difficult question of whether the form of an given animal is always the same or whether it can be present more or less. Is the form of the frog embryo the same as the form of the tadpole, and is either of these the same as the form of the mature frog? If form in the emphatic sense means form-at-work, then the early frog embryo does not have the full form of frog; yet it has the form of frog rather than the form of cockroach, it will remain the *same* frog from fertilized egg to full maturity, and the full form of frog is somehow "present" to the embryo as a potentiality toward which its growth is directed. What does it mean to say that the form is "present" in the embryo as a potential? Can the potential form be alone responsible for its own coming into full and actual presence? Since the frog egg does not contain a miniature preformed "froglet" (a "frogunculus"), but does contain the full directions and inclinations for producing such a frog, how exactly is that "absent" frog "present" and efficacious in its own coming-into-being? What is responsible for the emergence of such "emergent form"?

I am aware of these questions and know they cannot be avoided. But they are, I insist, *secondary* questions that arise only after one has discovered the distinction of form and material and, as I shall argue in the next section "The Primacy of Form," once one has discerned the superior responsibility of the form for all the activities of living things, metabolism included. For the purposes of my present inquiry, these secondary questions can be left hanging. My purpose is to begin close to the ground, with the phenomena, and to show why we need notions like *form* and *form-at-work* simply to make sense of what appears before us. I trust my more metaphysically inclined readers will be tolerant of my refusal to tackle here their favorite questions.

The Primacy of Form

After this preliminary exploration of form and material, we are at last prepared to argue that the activity of nourishing is the work more of an organism's form than of its matter. In the course of showing the supremacy of form, we shall necessarily be indicating also the ways in which the relation of living form to its own material differs from the form-material relation in inanimate things.*

Though we are partisans of the primacy of form, we do not reject the importance of material. Matter must be given its due, and one must even acknowledge the initial attractions of materialism. The classical argument for the primacy of matter began from the fact that all living beings die and that, after death, their bodies decay into lifeless stuff. The persistence of matter, against the perishability of life and living things, seemed to attest to its greater causal power. As Adam Schulman has observed:

> From the latter evidence (organic decay into lifeless matter) early Greek thinkers like Empedocles concluded that what truly exists are the materials earth, air, fire, and water, and that organisms and other putative wholes are merely aggregates of these immutable elementary bodies. There are therefore no genuine wholes, but only complex systems, all of whose properties are attributable to the spatial organization of their material components. In such a world nothing is ever truly generated or destroyed, just reorganized. . . . Empedocles said, "Of all mortal things there is no birth nor any end in baneful death, but only a mixing and a separation of things mixed." The Empedoclean viewpoint in physics proved persuasive to Galileo and Newton, and finds modern expression in the eighteenth century's "man the machine," as well as in the implicit reductionism of much of modern natural science.[5]

Yet, paradoxically, it is the activity of metabolism itself that should make it clear that the materials do not *by themselves* even begin to account for the phenomena of life. Yes, the organism is perishable. Yes, the properties of its materials are in part responsible for its workings and character. But, as we ourselves know best from the in-

---

*My argument here is much indebted to the late Hans Jonas's penetrating essay "Is God a Mathematician? The Meaning of Metabolism," in his splendid book, *The Phenomenon of Life: Toward a Philosophical Biology*.[4]

side and precisely because of our constant need to eat and to replenish our bodily stuff, the living animal has a unity and a self-identity that in fact outlast its ever-shifting material.

Over the course of a lifetime of metabolizing, the *organism persists, though its materials do not*. Metabolism means the continuous exchange of stuff between inside and out, and no molecule in the organism is immune to turnover. Thus the organism is never the same materially, yet it persists as the same being, and indeed precisely by means of exchanging its materials. But *what*, then, *is* it that persists? Among other things the organism's boundedness and separation from all else beyond its border, and its wholeness and identity (both species-specific and individual) within. Persisting too is the internal organization and the functional harmony among the parts. Most important, persisting are the organic powers and activities, including the powers and the activities of self-persistence (that is, metabolism) itself—maintenance of the self, by the self, and for the self—always exerted and directed against a largely indifferent world of otherness and against the impending negation that is death. In short, what persists is form: integrated, specific, individuated, empowered, and efficacious organization.

Second, the persistence of organization or form, despite and indeed because of the interchange of material, implies a certain independence of the form from its own materials. True, any organism's form is absolutely dependent on, and always inseparable from, material and precisely on such and such kinds of materials, but not on these and these individual molecules. True, the organism is, always, coincident with its materials at any moment, but it is independent of—not tied to—any one collection of stuff over time. Indeed, if organic form ever coincided for any length of time with the exact same collection of molecules, it would have ceased to live. The organism would have become a thing, with exactly the same form-material identity as seen in such inanimate bodies as rocks and crystals.

Third, and most crucial, this "persistence" and "independence" of form or organization is itself an achievement of form. The form of a given organism is a certain organization-in-action, whose first activity is to keep the enmattered organization-in-action (that is, itself) both organized and acting. The organization is not a mere outcome or heap or aggregate *caused* by the motions and joinings of the material parts. On the contrary, the joinings and motions of the material parts are caused and governed by the organization. Organization organizes, at each stage guiding the activities of the next. To be sure, the energy for organic activity is chemical energy, trapped in elementary molecules and always transferred from molecule to molecule. And no chemical molecule reacts in the organism contrary to what would be predicted for it by the laws of thermodynamics. But the reactions of the molecules are constrained by their organization in the cell, which in turn is constrained and directed by the overall organization of the animal. Only *as organized* do the materials conduct the orderly and directed metabolic exchange of stuff that provides the cell and the animal with energy, with materials for maintenance and growth, and with the wherewithal to respond to changes in the environment. Even at the cellular level and even in the simplest organisms (for example, a bacterium or an amoeba), the sequence of chemical reactions is ordered and directed by structural and functional arrangements uniquely provided by the living cell: enzymes that catalyze the reactions; highly intricate three-dimensional intracellular structures (organelles), such as mitochondria or endoplasmic reticulum, that link chemical processes together and that channel intermediates in functionally useful directions; positive and negative feedback mechanisms, which regulate the metabolic activity in keeping with the physiological needs of the cell and changes in its external environment; and so on. Moreover, the functional arrangements of molecules—in cell organelles, cells, tissues, organs, and organ systems—is the work not of the molecules as such. The living organization directs the comings and goings of molecules and all their interrelations, as the legislative guides the executive or a musical score the musicians. And organization, legislation, and harmony, I remind you, are not themselves material.*

None of this is altered by the marvelous findings of biochemistry and molecular biology, claims of molecular biologists or biochemists

*Form or organization is, as has been noted, absolutely dependent upon material. One never finds the form of lion separated from its leonine flesh. But, unlike the flesh, the form cannot be held in your hand. Neither can one touch or see the *powers* inherent in living form. One can point to or hold the eyeball, but one cannot point to or hold its power (sight) or its activity (seeing). These aspects of its form are themselves intangible because they are immaterial.

to the contrary notwithstanding. We cannot here present a full argument. But suffice it to say that even DNA—the genetic material, the so-called molecular basis of life—functions *not* as a chemical material but as *information carried by material*. True, the information carried in DNA is borne by its material elements—that is, by the nucleotide bases (adenine, guanine, thymine, cytosine)—though here too the preservation of the same *kind* of base, not of this particular nucleotide molecule, is all that is required. True, the nucleotides of DNA are chemically well suited to act as the coded letters of legislative messages for protein synthesis. But the medium is *not* the message. Call it a plan, a program, organization, whatever—this ruling principle is itself immaterial. Proof: One can hold DNA *molecules* in a bottle, but one cannot physically hold or grasp the *messages* they carry.

We must not allow ourselves to be deceived by the materialistic counter-claims of scientists who, to be blunt, are philosophically rather naive. With a little careful thought we can see through their materialistic interpretations of experiments, which they (wrongly) believe demonstrate that it is the chemical materials that bear primary responsibility for the doings of living things. Such proof they find, for example, in experiments that have achieved the synthesis of fully active DNA—say of a functioning virus—from simple inorganic nucleotide precursors. The synthesis takes place according to chemical principles, of course, and no vitalist ghost jumps into the flask. But form is still dominant and rules over the synthesis. The order in which the chemist adds the nucleotide bases, one to the next, is dictated not by the bases themselves or even by the chemist. It is prescribed by the natural order—that is, by the form—of the virus itself. One might say that here the hands of the chemist substitute for intracellular mechanisms to execute the legislation carried in the sequence of the DNA for replicating the same organized whole. DNA *is* a material molecule, but the *information* it carries as the *genetic* material is no more material than are the meanings of words carried by visible letters. And although the information carried in DNA is in a form utterly different from the visible looks of the mature organism, the developmental and physiological processes DNA directs are orchestrated to generate the organic, self-maintaining whole that appears visibly as just this-here individual and just this-sort of animal.

Fourth—returning to the main argument—because the persistence and independence of form through metabolism are themselves achievements of the form, which guides the animal's traffickings in materials, feeding and metabolism necessarily entail for living things a new and distinctive relation to the world. Unlike nonliving things that persist inertially as what they are—immediately self-identical and without any need to maintain their self-identity through their own efforts—living things must constantly work to maintain both their existence and their self-identity in the face of ever-present dangers of going out of business. Metabolism is a full-time occupation from which only death provides release. The organism's ability to endure as an able-bodied being means that nourishment—newly gathered or retrieved from storage—is a *continuous* necessity. An organism's ability to metabolize is inseparable from its absolute need to do so. The organism's *in*dependence as a self is inseparable from its absolute *de*pendence on what lies beyond its borders.

Thus, with the emergence of life, even in its most elementary forms, comes the emergence of a genuine "self"—a distinct and separate being, potent but perishable, which persists by its own performance in metabolism and self-nourishing—pitted against but in active commerce with a correlative "world," in which, from which, and against which it acts to maintain itself. The neediness of living things, not shared by self-sufficing inanimate matter, drives the organism into genuine relations with its surrounding environment, for which there are no precedents among nonliving things. Indeed, it is only living things that have—and have a relation to—an environment, a world, and not merely contiguous, adjacent, and neutral space. This need-inspired relation to the world entails—necessarily—all the essential powers of life, powers present to an organism here and now but exercised always in relation to what is beyond and not yet. All animals—even the simplest or lowest—possess (even if only as rudiments) the great powers* of action, awareness, and appetite.

---

*By "power" I mean "ability," "capacity," "potency," "faculty," (in Latin, *potentia*; in Greek, *dynamis*), in all cases, the requisite organized strength and facility for performing a specific activity or activities. An organic power is more than a mere possibility; it is a readied and available capacity that inheres in already existent cells, organs, or organ systems.

The Three Great Powers of Organic Form

The need for outside material means that organisms must be capable of reaching out to obtain it—to find, appropriate, and transform it. They must be able to act in and on the world. In mammals the distance-effacing and world-altering character of chasing, capturing, and devouring are self-evident, as are the innate powers to move, grasp, bite, and crush, which are manifested in these activities. But simpler animals are also agents of change and worldly transformation. Barnacles and other filter feeders do not chase their victims, but they hold and destroy them nonetheless. By means of pseudopodia, an amoeba approaches, surrounds, and then engulfs its food. Even inanimate food can be actively pursued; some species of bacteria propel themselves along concentration gradients, seeking and consuming those sugars (or other carbon sources) that are most efficiently metabolized. Granted, these "actions" are performed and these powers are exercised "automatically," without deliberation or conscious intention; one could argue, rightly, that we do not here have action in the full sense. Still, the doings of living things are spontaneously done, exercising immanent powers adapted for such exercise, and the transformations wrought are real and large—in the aggregate, massive. In order to live every living animal disturbs and alters its surrounding world, each in its own characteristic ways, though it seeks in fact not "world alteration" but only its own persistence.

Actions on the world in food seeking are generally fairly specific; only some parts of the environment are regarded as edible. Discriminate action implies discriminate awareness.* And awareness, too, is present—if in only rudimentary form—even in the simplest forms of life. Specific nutrients are actively transported even in single-celled animals and bacteria. Such active transport involves the presence of specific proteins, located at the cell boundary, that recognize, selectively bind, and carry inside the desired nutrient. And again, even at

---

*I use the broad, nonspecific term "awareness" to encompass all forms of openness and receptivity and sensitivity, from the barest irritability to the richest intellection. Sensing, perceiving, imaging, cognizing, minding, intellecting—all these are species of awareness. There can also be internal awareness (kinesthesia) and self-awareness. Awareness need not be self-conscious or even conscious to be awareness.

these lowest levels, awareness is awareness of form: Bacterial transport systems can discriminate between D and L stereoisomers (structural mirror images) of the same sugar, which differ not at all in their chemical composition but only in their three-dimensional geometrical form. Biological *trans*formation of the world presupposes *in*formation about the world; powers to alter the outside world necessarily coincide with powers to perceive it, and both are born with life itself.

Needless to say there is enormous structural and functional variation in the means animals use to recognize and to pursue food. Some rely more on sight, others on smell, still others on hearing, whereas animals with less-developed external sense organs locate their food by following, say, temperature gradients or chemical traces given off by the edible object. But of just *how* awareness guides food-securing action, even in the higher animals who hunt by sight, we are still largely ignorant. We know that we human beings depend very much on the visual image of the desired object, and, as we shall see (in Chapter 2), our imagination works with images available to it even when the objects are long absent. But when the fox chases the rabbit, does it follow a visual image? Does such an image depend on the presence—or the very recent presence—of the rabbit? Is there memory of previous chases, and does it function in the present one? That animals learn from experience suggests that some sort of memory plays a role, but, lacking direct access to animal awareness and inner life, we may never really know how. Nevertheless awareness they have, whatever its precise form; they are discriminatingly receptive to the world beyond their borders.

Here, perhaps, it is worth a moment's interruption to note the obvious fact—often overlooked because it is taken for granted—that organic powers of nourishing, including powers for active transformation and receptive information, require complementary possibilities of and in the surrounding world. Animal need is met by the (at least partial) hospitality of the world. The animal's need for food is answered by its availability; his ability to transform other into same is matched by the other's transformability; and his power to sense and to be informed about the world is made possible by the world's articulated, formed, and sensible character. Our world need not have been thus hospitable—other planets, as we know, cannot support life. It is only a partial explanation to say (correctly) that if the world were not hospitable to life in the first place, living things would not have arisen at all. The world's original receptivity, in a sense reenacted for every new organism that sees the light of day, is itself unexplained, a given—and, to all that lives, an unmerited gift.*

But, to return to the vital powers implicit in metabolism, simple awareness of some outside edible is insufficient to account for the action of self-nourishment. Something must "take an interest in" the perceived edible object; something must energize the animal into action. In short, something like "felt need" or "appetite" is also required. In higher animals awareness of an edible being or object leads to eating only because—and if—hunger or felt lack is present. To be sure, the experience of lack *as* hunger, in the full sense of the term, presupposes a nervous system sufficiently advanced to allow for the self-experience of inner states of being. But the essence of what, in such higher beings, comes to be manifest to feeling or conscious experience is already (unconsciously) present to the simplest forms—albeit unknown to any mind. What moves an organism to feed is not merely the sensed and registered presence or absence of a certain chemical or edible being in its environment but the *inner needy state* of the organism, for which such an absence is a lack, an absence to be overcome or remedied. Bacteria do not measure the concentration of glucose in their environment in the indifferent and detached way of the biochemist who prepared their growth medium. Not the numerical measure itself but the immanent "perception" that it represents a potential fulfillment of a *lack* leads to the activities of "chasing" and selective absorption. "Lack" need not be conscious to be "felt"—to be efficacious. Here we see a refutation of the impoverished and faulty explanation of stimulus-response theory, which attempts a strictly mechanistic account of behavior: The organism would not "respond" to perceived food "stimuli" were it not an "interested" or "appetitive" being, were it not already internally ordered toward the necessary activities of self-nourishing. As with action and awareness, the seeds of appetite are

---

*I return to this topic in the last chapter.

copresent with life. Indeed the germ of appetite governs, guides, and integrates awareness and action: Appetite or desire, not DNA, is the deepest principle of life.

The attentive reader, reflecting on the immanent powers of appetite, awareness, and action I claim are coextensive with animal form itself, will recognize that we are now speaking about the inner or *psychic* meaning of animal embodiment. To repeat, animal form turns out to be internally capacious, empowered to sense, to move, to want. Somehow—and I would say mysteriously—animal organization means "animation," means "inwardness," means the presence of what the ancients called *psyche* or *anima*, soul. By this they did not mean a disembodied spirit, a ghost in a machine, a vital force superadded to an otherwise "dead" body, a separate being that flees the body on death. Rather, *psyche* referred to and comprised all the integrated vital powers of a naturally organic body, always possessed by such a body while it is alive. Not the property of the materials alone but of the materials as species-specifically formed, the species-specific psyche might be said to be the vital form or ruling-beginning of each animal, when the animal is regarded as a unified center of awareness, action, and appetite. When soul is thus understood, we should not be reluctant or embarrassed to recognize that animals— all animals—indeed have soul.

Thanks to the psychic powers of action and awareness, energized by need and appetite, living things exist in the world differently from nonliving things. All living things in some degree transcend their confinement to the here and the now. Though isolated from and precariously poised in opposition to the world, they live effectively in that larger world. The organism's boundary is open for traffic with the world, in principle with the whole. Organisms are all able to appropriate and transform material beyond their borders. They are all able to receive information from outside themselves and to discriminate among the things received. Just as they impress themselves on their surroundings, so, in varying degrees, aspects of the surrounding world impress themselves upon (and within) living animals. The rudiments of action *in* and *on* the world and of perception *of* the world, born with life itself, give the living being a certain transcendence of the space it physically occupies. The powers of life transform the surrounding territory into "lived space" or "action space," which, it should be stressed, is *not* the homogenous, neutral and mathematized space of the physicists.

The animal lives not only beyond the here but also beyond the now. As we have seen, its new world-relations grow out of a self-concern with persistence and are driven by a rudimentary inwardness or subjectivity, which orders present needs to actions that may bring future satisfactions. To be sure, the existence of the present powers of an organism is decisively the result of past performance and successes (especially those of its ancestors from whom these powers are inherited). But when they are actually at work and exercised in the here and now, these powers imply and point forward toward the "not yet." The self-concern of the organism, manifest in appetite, means that the future moment of satisfaction of need is always implicit in the present moment of want and in the activities to which want gives rise. Appetite and its ministerial actions are, by definition, always forward looking and purposive. As Hans Jonas puts it:

> With respect to the organic sphere, the external linear time-pattern of antecedent and sequent, involving the causal dominance of the past, is inadequate: while mere externality is, at least can be presented as, wholly determined by what it was, *life is essentially also what it is going to be and just becoming*: in its case, the extensive order of past and future is intensively reversed.[6]*

This forward-looking character of organic activity is most obvious in the doings of whole animals: the chase points to capture, ingestion points to satisfaction. But the same directedness is manifested at all levels, down to the intracellular. The transcription of a gene into messenger RNA points toward the translation of the message in protein synthesis; the protein as synthesized points toward its subsequent use

---

*Jonas also shows how the organism's transcendence of the here follows from the need to transcend the now, and also how biological time and biological space differ from the neutral time and space of modern physics: "[I]t [the organism] faces outward only because, by the necessity of its freedom, it faces forward: so that spatial presence is lighted up as it were by temporal imminence and both merge into [future] fulfillment (or its negative, disappointment). Thus the element of transcendence we discerned in the very nature of metabolizing existence has found its fuller articulation: both horizons into which life continually transcends itself can be traced to the transitory relation of organic form to its own matter. The internal direction toward the next impending phase of a being that has to continue *itself* constitutes biological time; the external direction toward the co-present not-itself which holds the stuff relevant to its continuation constitutes biological space. As the here expands into the there, so the now expands into the future."[7]

in transporting, from without to within, the sugar newly present in the environment; the transport of the sugar derives its meaning from the utilization of the sugar that follows, providing needed energy for all future reactions and activities. Without any trace of conscious intention, in metabolism all organisms face forward in time and engage in self-directed purposive behavior aiming at a future goal. Even lowly metabolism, mindlessly conducted throughout the animal kingdom, is unintelligible save as a purposive, goal-directed activity.

Animals face purposively forward in goal-directed activity not only in the self-interested and self-preserving functions of eating and taking nourishment. They do so in most everything, and nowhere more than in the activity of reproduction. The fact and necessity of reproduction remind us of the intrinsic limit on the future-serving power of eating: No amount of self-preservative feeding can provide the indefinite preservation of the feeder. Eating sustains the life of the living but only for a finite time; sex provides a partial answer to this finitude. But whereas eating serves the good of the being that eats, sexuality—however pleasurable to the animal participants—serves mainly the good of those beings that issue from this sexual union (and, indirectly, the "good of the species"). In sexual activity animals necessarily serve an end that goes beyond them; indeed quite literally so: In the very act of reproducing, animals—even if mindlessly—ratify and acquiesce in the necessity of their own mortality. (Salmon going upstream to spawn and die provide only the most vivid example of what is, in fact, a general truth about all sexually reproducing animals.) Thus, because of built-in limits on the power of metabolism to maintain individual life, animals—unbeknownst to them—live bifurcated and divided lives: Self-servingly they eat to secure their own existence, self-sacrificingly they reproduce—and, with the higher animals, also feed the young—to secure the existence of their descendants.* The complex relations between individual and group well-being, between self-love and other-regard,

---

*The world-relation of animals that reproduce through sexual union is thus not adequately characterized solely by the distinction between self and nonself, some of which non-self is edible. Certain other "selves"—sexual partners or mates and, in some cases, the young they generate—stand out for the animal and are of special interest. Here is the germ of animal sociality, of that special transcendence of individual isolation that is part and parcel of the necessarily selfish business of staying alive (and of thus facing one's inevitable "self-ish" death).

between independence and sociality, all have their origins in this ubiquitous biological fact.

The Hierarchy of Living Forms

All these essential aspects of life—needful freedom; selfhood set against otherness; relation to the world through the activities of perception, appetite, and reaching-out in action; purposiveness (all present rudimentarily even in bacteria and amoebae)—become more developed and rich as organisms become more complex. To the rudimentary ability to discriminate the shapes of sugars and other chemical nutrients, still retained by individual cells of higher organisms, are added the abilities to perceive the temperature, hardness, shape, color, and motions of outside objects and, relevant to our topic, the looks, sounds, smells, and tastes of the edible ones. To the amoeboid or ciliate motion of single cells, still retained by certain white blood cells in mammals, are added the somatic power and psychic direction for locomotion—for the hunt, the chase, and the capture; and to the catabolic capacities of single cells are added the powers to gnaw, bite, tear, grind, chew, and swallow, as well as elaborate mechanisms for digestion, absorption, and transport of nutrients. The inner perception of lack is gradually transformed into the genuine experience of hunger, which is simply one aspect of the emergence of a more pronounced sense of selfhood. Eventually, consciously felt and even deliberately set purposive actions supervene atop the mute and mindless—but at the same time perfectly rational and intelligible—goal-directed food-gaining behavior of simple organisms. With greater powers of awareness, mobility, dexterity, and self-perception, with greater internal bodily control over the essential conditions of life, and with greater social interaction, higher organisms attain greater freedom and a richer way of life.

The richer life of higher animals is, in a way, implicit in the way they get and take their food. Unlike simple organisms and plants, whose relevant environment is largely only the immediately contiguous, higher animals (including all vertebrates and the higher invertebrates like bees, spiders, and squids) live and meet their needs over greater distances. They both can and must perceive at a distance and move to reach their food. Animal appetite, which entails experiencing a distant object as a goal, persists throughout the time of absent satisfaction and drives the animal's motion toward his food. Nourishment—calories for the energy bank and materials for biosynthesis, repair, and growth—is still the bottom line, but it is now attained only through intermediate activities. In a bacterium the need for sugar and its proximate availability translate immediately into active transport of sugar into a cell. But in a lion metabolism is detached from, and must await the successful result of, many prior acts: the lion must first see, smell, stalk, chase, attack, and finally conquer the zebra, whose flesh he then tears, tastes, chews, and swallows. All of these activities are *voluntary*: They are performed by the action of striated (voluntary) muscle under the control of the voluntary nervous system, unlike the subsequent digestive processes, which are performed by the action of smooth (involuntary) muscle under the control of the autonomic (involuntary) nervous system. These larger activities of the whole animal are distinct from the metabolic goal they serve; they even have their own inherent pleasures (and pains). Indeed some of the intermediate activities, which were originally adapted to serve nutrition and mere survival, eventually even acquire a life and fulfillment of their own; they become part of the goal—as well as the means—of surviving.

Special kinds of mediated nourishing are found among those higher animals—especially birds and mammals—that feed their own young. Here getting food ceases to be simply self-ish: Not only does one animal (an adult bird, a lactating female mammal) put food into the mouth of another; the food-gathering activity is itself often socialized (for example, the pack-hunting of wolves and lions). In the very special case of mammals, where the young are fed out of the mother's own substance—first, "intravenously" while the young are *in utero*, then after birth by suckling—intimate "social" ties are established around the activity of feeding, with pleasures in those mediating interactions that go beyond the mere satisfaction of hunger, pleasures that anticipate the social enjoyments of human eating-together. In the higher animals, the hungry soul wants more than food.

With regard to our subject of eating, several implications of the mediated nourishing of the higher animals deserve emphasis. First, the feeder, though ultimately interested in the nutritional value of his food, acts seemingly for different reasons. The lion pursues the zebra, as meat to be sure, but the zebra nonetheless. The lion in fact sees and chases and kills—and is by his form empowered to see, chase, and kill—the formed zebra, however much his processes of digestion will then automatically turn zebra into the necessary biochemical simples, themselves to be worked up into lion. Indeed, in most of their voluntary food-gathering activities, higher animals engage other ordered and formed living beings or their products. Though we cannot know what the inner experience of eating feels like or means to the lion, it seems reasonable to suggest—from evidence provided by examining ourselves and by observing animals, including a cat's playing with a captured mouse—that the lion's satisfactions in eating come mainly from the pleasures of capture, tasting, and devouring and from relieving the pains of perceived hunger, not from the restoration of intracellular nitrogen balance or the availability of extra sugar to replenish the glycogen stores. Anyone who has for a time been forced to take nourishment intravenously or via stomach tube, or who has been restricted for a time to pureed foods, knows first-hand how welcome and enjoyable it is at long last to sink one's teeth into something solid and to chew it up. Eating comes to satisfy appetites for more than nutrition, and not only among human beings.

Second, the higher animals—with fully developed powers for living with and over distance, and with intermediate activity in part dissociated from the continuous vegetative activity of metabolism—increasingly display a more comprehensive relation to the world, and this in several aspects. In the realm of awareness, powers of distance perception and locomotion disclose much more of the world; the higher senses—notably sight and the sense of forms—eventually provide an awareness of whole beings in their wholeness and specificity, not merely (as with smell or sound) of their mere presence. The diverse and plentiful forms of life eventually become known to life itself; in fact, by means of facial expressions, postures, and gestures, the looks of the higher social mammals are even capable of communicating something of an animal's inner life to members of the same species.[8] In the realm of action, locomotion and speed also enlarge the animal's arena in which it can act. The travelers, in many cases, are more exposed to risks than, say, the barnacle or clam, which stay put indoors and filter. But they also enjoy many more possibilities, including possibilities for food. The most varied diets belong mainly to those beings who most vary their place and who can perceive more clearly and accurately the variety of things among the possibly edible. The biggest transformers of the world are generally those who are also most receptive to its many-splendored forms.*

This observation brings us back to that great paradox of life, clearly embodied in the necessity of eating: Living form, to preserve life and form, threatens life and form. Eating is at once form preserving and form deforming. What was distinct and whole gets broken down and homogenized, in order to preserve the distinctness and wholeness of the feeder. In the case of predatory meat eaters, what was alive is killed in order to preserve life. This tension in eating is emblematic of the ambiguous relationship between life and form in general. Although the vital powers of metabolism exist only in specific, formed beings, these powers as exercised threaten the existence of specific, formed beings. Nature manifests both variety and vitality; in living things vitality presupposes, conserves, but also threatens variety.

Life, though an advance over nonlife—indeed, *because* it is an advance over nonlife—is in tension with the articulated character of the world. True enough, on the side of awareness, only animals are capable of recognizing and appreciating the multifarious forms of the ordered world. But at the same time, on the side of action, animals threaten the survival of that order and those forms. Forms that need to transform other forms are, in principle, a threat to the stabil-

---

*Several of the points of the last few paragraphs are beautifully made by Hans Jonas in his essay, "To Move and To Feel: On the Animal Soul," in which he defends the hierarchical character of life and demonstrates that survival is an inadequate standard for evaluating life's success:

> If mere assurance of permanence were the point that mattered, life should not have started out in the first place. It is essentially precarious and corruptible being, an adventure in mortality, and in no possible form as assured of enduring as an inorganic body can be. Not duration as such, but "duration of what?" is the question. This is to say that such "means" of survival as perception and emotion are never to be judged as means merely, but also as qualities of the life to be preserved and therefore as aspects of the end. It is one of the paradoxes of life that it employs means which modify the end and themselves become part of it. The feeling animal strives to preserve itself as a feeling, not just a metabolizing entity, i.e., it strives to continue the very activity of feeling: the perceiving animal strives to preserve itself as a perceiving entity—and so on . . . The rift between subject and object, which long-range perception and motility opened and which the keenness of appetite and fear, of satisfaction and disappointment, of pleasure and pain, reflect, was never to be closed again. But in its widening expanse, the freedom of life found room for all those modes of relation—perceptive, active, and emotional—which in spanning the rift justify it and by indirection redeem the lost unity.[9]

ity of the world—and ultimately even to their own survival. The danger and the glory of living forms is writ large in the fact of eating.

Let me summarize the argument to this point:

1. The animal world is articulated into formed and recognizable kinds, distinctive individuals belonging to distinguishable species yet depending for survival on their eating—that is, on their de-forming and homogenizing—other individuals belonging to other kinds. Indeed, the evolutionary differentiation into new kinds—speciation—is in part a consequence of the pursuit of survival through feeding, as mutations giving selective advantage in obtaining food or in avoiding being eaten gradually give rise to new living forms; conversely, new varieties of food appear with the proliferation of new kinds of living beings.

2. Though there is, for every organism, a constant need for new material, what persists despite and indeed as a result of the transformation of material is the selfsame formed organism in its characteristic and recognizable form.

3. The primacy of form is most evident in the fact that the formed organism is not the result of metabolism but rather its cause, for persistence through nourishing is an *achievement* of the organism as *organized*, not of its materials alone. Yet the possibility of success depends on the partial hospitality of the world—namely that food is there to be taken. (In this dialectical relation of power and dependence, we can see the seeds of both pride and gratitude.)

4. Though their neediness makes their being more precarious, living things have "more being" than nonliving things. They *are* more in, and are *in* more of, the world. Because of their need of sustenance from the world, they participate in genuine relationships with the world beyond their borders, in some ways transcending their confinement to the here and now: open to recognizing and acting on what is spatially outside, pointed purposively always to the future to satisfy present need, while bearing also the marks of ancestors both proximate and remote.

5. This openness to the world and this relation to the world increase as one goes up certain evolutionary paths, as seen in increased powers for and pleasures in receiving (and discriminating accurately among) the distinctive presences of the world as articulated, and in

increased powers for and pleasures in acting upon and altering that world to suit the animal's needs and its increasingly complicated and subjectively felt desires. Finding and taking nourishment are more genuine accomplishments for the mobile than the sessile, for the carnivore than the grazer, for the intelligent than the dumb. Yet, though growing omnivorousness (direct or indirect) seems to correlate with—and perhaps to require—growing awareness of the limitless variety of the formed world, omnivorousness means, in principle, the willingness to homogenize and destroy the world as formed and ordered, to put it all to use for oneself, or rather, to swallow and to turn it *into* oneself.

These thoughts lead directly to the question about man.

2

The Human Form

Omnivorosus Erectus

And, though all other animals are prone, and fix their gaze upon the earth, he gave to man an uplifted face and bade him stand erect and turn his eyes to heaven.

—Ovid

Metamorphoses (1. 84–86)

The theme of the last chapter was living nature in general, especially animals. Its thesis, that living form has an independence from and superiority to its own material, and therefore that the corporealistic ontology—expressible in the maxim "One is just what one eats"—is incorrect. Beginning phenomenologically, with discussions of "What is food?" "What is eating?" and "What *use* is food?" we moved to questions of cause and responsibility; I argued for the primacy and the efficacious responsibility of organization, of form, as an explanation for metabolism—on the grounds of the persistence, independence, and efficacy of empowered organization and of the different form-material relations in living things that drive them into active commerce with the world and with other beings beyond their borders. In considering these new world-relations, I stressed three kinds of psychic powers, integral to the meaning of organic form and present, even if only in rudiment, in all living things: powers of *action* in and on the world, powers of discriminating *awareness* of the world, and powers of *appetite* for particulars in the world. Finally we discussed the hierarchy of living forms, in terms of the emergence of pleasurable intermediate activity, inserted between need and its satisfaction, that characterizes life lived at ever-greater distances: heightened externally pointed powers to overcome distance—that is, locomotion and distance perception, with sight at the peak; heightened internal powers to sustain interest as distance is covered, that is, lasting felt need, experienced as appetite and desire, looking forward to future satisfaction. The discussion of hierarchy, and the problems connected with it, lead directly upward to the subject of man. Human nature now claims our attention. We expect to encounter here, in full-blown form, both the promise and the danger inherent in life as such, already advertised in the purchase of preservation of life and form through destruction of life and form, constitutive of the activity of eating.

Human beings are animals, both in their nature and in their origins. Though it is the theory of evolution that finally establishes our genealogical ties with all the other animals, knowledge of human animality is nothing new or surprising; indeed the truth of our animality is quite independent of the question of human origins. Even those remote sources of our tradition that emphasize the difference of man teach also of his likenesses to the rest of living nature. For example, Aristotle, no evolutionist, stresses repeatedly that if man is rational he is also animal, as needy and as mortal. Conversely, soul, according to Aristotle a principle of more than consciousness or mind, is not confined to human beings: all animals (and even all plants) have soul (*psyche*), understood as the form of a naturally organic body or as the integrated vital powers for self-motion and awareness, powers that in all living things include the capacity for self-development, growth, self-maintenance, self-healing, and reproduction, and in the fully formed animals, also the powers of sensation, memory, imagination, desire, and locomotion.[1] And in our biblical tradition, according to Genesis, God Himself thought the animals sufficiently similar to man to have fashioned them as his possible companions;* and subsequent parts of the biblical story (for example, the expulsion from the Garden; the Noah story) emphasize the common vulnerability and neediness of all that lives, human beings no less than others.

To be sure, other strands of Western thought sharply divorce man from the animal world. Some do it by raising the human, others by lowering the animal. For example, Christian beliefs in the immortality of individual human souls, said to be denied to animals, or Marxist beliefs in man's radical freedom to make himself what he becomes, elevate human beings to a more-than-animal, and even supranatural, status. On the other side, mechanistic views of the nonhuman living things, as beast-machines devoid of inwardness—views present in Western science at least since Descartes—make the animals, paradoxically, *in*animate, even unnatural, and worlds apart from man. These dichotomies, advanced by theory, condition and reinforce the ordinary prejudices of urbanized people woefully igno-

---

*This is the account given in the second of the so-called creation stories (Gen. 2:4ff). The accents of the first story (Gen. 1) fall differently: Here man alone is said to be created in the image of God and he is given dominion over the other animals. These texts have been credited with and/or blamed for the belief in man's radical separation from the rest of the living world; and, as they have been interpreted and used, there is some justice in these claims. Yet even while pointing out man's distinctiveness, Genesis 1 shows also man's kinship with the animals: man is created on the same day as the other terrestrial animals (verses 24–27); man and the animals share in the blessing to be fruitful and multiply (verses 22, 28); the needs of man and animals for food are addressed together (verses 29–30); and the food offered man and the beasts is both similar and different, like the creatures themselves. (For a fuller discussion of the Bible's view of eating, see Chapter 6.)

rant of animal life and (for this reason among others) overly impressed with their own singular place in the world.

These separatist notions are no longer tenable; they are permanently embarrassed by the theory of evolution. By showing conclusively the common natural origins of human and animal life, it reintegrates man into the realm of living nature. The first word about man—never to be refuted, not even by the last word—is that he is a natural being and, speaking naturally, an animal. There follows, of course, a corollary, equally true but less often noted: Darwinism, by its linking of man to the animals, links the animals to man, and thus necessarily invites the overthrow of the purely mechanical and corporealistic view of animal life:

> In the hue and cry over the indignity done to man's metaphysical status in the doctrine of his animal descent, it was overlooked that by the same token some dignity had been restored to the realm of life as a whole. If man was the relative of animals, then animals were the relatives of man and in degrees bearers of that inwardness of which man, the most advanced of their kin, is conscious in himself.[2]

As we argued in the last chapter, to be an animal is to have special being and dignity; thus that man counts as one of the animals is no disgrace, for animals are far from contemptible beings.

The point was not lost on Darwin himself. Indeed, in *The Descent of Man* and also in *The Expression of the Emotions in Man and Animals*, Darwin is at pains to show that the many traits, powers, and activities thought to be peculiarly human are, in fact, shared by the other animals, from whom man is thus said to differ only in degree. True, Darwin argues vigorously—and, to this reader, not successfully—that animals possess *all* the moral and intellectual powers frequently attributed to man alone;* only on this basis did he believe

---

*Darwin does, however, allow for at least one exception, namely, blushing: "Blushing is the most peculiar and the most human of all expressions. Monkeys redden from passion, but it would require an overwhelming amount of evidence to make us believe that any animal can blush."[3] Unfortunately, he does not sufficiently explore the significance of this singularly human expression and its psychic companion, shame, a full understanding of which could lay bare much of what is essentially and especially human. (See the chapter "Looking Good: Nature and Nobility," in my *Toward a More Natural Science*.) As we shall see later in Chapter 4, shame—and the aspiration to dignity that it protects—plays a large role in the humanization of eating.

that one could establish without doubt man's community of descent, by purely natural means. It never occurred to Darwin that certain differences of degree—produced naturally, accumulated gradually (even incrementally), and inherited in an unbroken line of descent—might lead to a difference in kind (or at least its equivalent),* say, in mental capacity or inner life. Nevertheless many of Darwin's observations stand confirmed by contemporary students of zoology and animal behavior. An unprejudiced examination of the evidence shows that animals and human beings share not only common ancestry but also many similarities in form and powers. Among all the vertebrates there is a common body plan, with bilateral symmetry, distinct head and tail poles, external sense organs, and appendages for locomotion and, developmentally, progressive modifications of a primordially segmented body scheme. And, especially (but not only) among the higher mammals, there is clear evidence of the activities of sensing, remembering, desiring, enjoying, dreaming, playing, learning, and socializing, along with the experience of hunger, thirst, fear, anger, spiritedness, lust, and affection. Animals display intelligence and the possibility of some self-control, and the social birds and mammals exhibit forms of communication, cooperation, and (albeit innate and largely fixed) decent and generous conduct toward their kin; conversely, we human beings possess many of the animals' powerful and deep-seated instinctual urges, as part of our animal legacy.[4]

Nevertheless, when we contemplate the human form we also must acknowledge our distinctiveness, for among the many strange, wonderful beings, none goes stranger than man. He alone goes on four legs in the morning, two in the afternoon, and three in the evening. He has upright posture and bipedal locomotion; fully formed hands with fully opposable thumbs; a proportionately large head, unusual jaw, and distinctive dentition; a fully developed, highly plastic face, with penetrating eyes and with a mouth that lets in almost anything as food and lets out articulate, intelligible sounds as speech, which bespeaks almost everything. Reflections on upright posture, the face, and the mouth can illuminate most clearly the spe-

---

*In other words Darwin was unaware of the distinction between a *superficial* and a *radical* difference in kind. See Mortimer Adler's useful discussion of this distinction in his book, *The Difference of Man and the Difference It Makes* (New York: Holt, Rinehart & Winston, 1967).

cial features of the peculiarly human way of being-in-the-world. They will also reveal the connections between human rationality and human omnivorousness and will thereby expose the inescapable moral dimension and dilemmas of human life.

The Upright Posture: Special Standing in the World

The peculiarity and significance of human upright posture was a favorite theme in antiquity, commented on by authors as different as Aristotle and Ovid. In modern times few have been interested, but the subject was recently revived by the late German American neurologist-psychologist Erwin Straus. In his remarkable essay, "The Upright Posture"[5] (from which I draw extensively), as in his other writings, Straus sought a biologically oriented psychology and anthropology that would take seriously the special features of the human form and, accordingly, of man's peculiar posture in the world. Not content with a biology or behavioristic psychology that levels all ranks and homogenizes all differences and that therefore treats man on all fours with the other animals, Straus was at the same time also sharply critical of a psychology that interprets human experience in terms only of thoughts, percepts, wishes, and feelings in a sequestered mind or consciousness having little connection with the body that carries it. Rejecting thus both corporealism and mentalism (as well as dualism), Straus takes seriously the meaning of human embodiment and marshals the evidence that man is a psychophysical unity, remarkably both like and unlike the other animals. He shows how human capacities and activities are both intensifications of life as such, continuous with the rest of living nature, yet, at the same time, also unique and apart. By showing the close correspondence between human physique and certain basic traits of human experience and behavior, he is able to connect our rationality and our sociality with our bodily uprightness. Upright posture is thus not only peculiar and unique but also essential to our humanity:

> The shape and function of the human body are determined in almost every detail by, and for, the upright posture. The skeleton of the foot; the structure of the ankle, knee, and hip; the curvature of the vertebral column; the proportions of the limbs—all serve the same purpose. This purpose could not be accomplished if all the muscles and the nervous

system were not built accordingly. While all parts contribute to the upright posture, upright posture in turn permits the development of the
forelimbs into the human shoulders, arms, and hands and of the skull
into the human skull and face.[6]

Human uprightness is nothing superficial; our peculiar form is reflected in every detail of our deep structure, somatic and (as we shall
soon see) psychic.

Upright posture is a matter not merely of static shape, of flat-foot-
ed two-leggedness or mere verticality. It also conditions all our relations to the world and colors all our experiences of ourselves acting
and suffering in the world.

> Men and mice do not have the same environment, even if they share the
> same room. Environment is not a stage with the scenery set as one and
> the same for all actors who make their entrance. Each species has its
> own environment. There is a mutual interdependence between species
> and environment. The surrounding world is determined by the organ-
> ization of the species in a process of selecting what is relevant to the
> function cycle of action and reaction. . . . Upright posture *pre-establishes*
> *a definite attitude toward the world; it is a specific mode of being-in-*
> *the-world.*[7]

To be sure, the human mode of being is in many respects only an in-
tensification of that of the higher terrestrial animals; like them facing
outward in space and forward in time, man stands as a singular,
needy, interested self who lives also outside himself, and in relation
to other selves, near and far. But in the human being special and
novel features emerge, already foreshadowed in the efforts required
to attain and maintain our upright standing and gait.

Though upright posture characterizes the human species, each of
us must struggle to attain it. Our birthright includes standing, but we
cannot stand at birth. Feral children who have survived in the wild
were not found upright but were able to become so. As with other distinctively human traits (speech, for example), human beings must work
to make themselves do or become what nature prepares them to be or
do. Upright posture is a human, and humanizing, accomplishment.

> While the heart continues to beat from its fetal beginning to death
> without our active intervention and while breathing neither demands nor

tolerates our voluntary interference beyond narrow limits, upright posture remains a task throughout our lives. Before reflection or self-reflection start, but as if they were a prelude to it, work makes its appearance within the realm of the elemental biological functions of man. In getting up, in reaching the upright posture, man must oppose the forces of gravity. It seems to be his nature to oppose nature in its impersonal, fundamental aspects with natural means. However, gravity is never fully overcome; upright posture always maintains its character of counteraction.[8]

Effort does not cease with rising up; it is required to maintain our uprightness. Automatic regulation does not suffice; staying up takes continuous attention and activity, as well it should, inasmuch as our very existence is at stake. Awakeness is necessary for uprightness; uprightness is necessary for survival. Yet our standing in the world is always precarious; we are always in danger of falling. Our natural stance is, therefore, one of "resis*t*ance," of "with*st*anding," of becoming cons*t*ant, *st*able.

Standing thus becomes a model of the unpremeditated natural human relation to nature: It requires effort, expended against certain undifferentiated and homogenizing tendencies of natural necessity (in this case, against gravity); it is made possible by certain powers and impulses naturally given; and it yields a natural and energetic attainment of special *st*anding, crowned by the delights of self-fulfillment attained through our own activity. (Recall the self-satisfaction of the child and the thrill of his parents when he or she first succeeds in standing erect, and even more when he or she does so without holding on.) Standing, understood as *with*standing, is pregnant with the possibility of full humanization: "Considering man in his upright posture, we do well to envisage the possibility that [it is] not society [which] has first brought man into conflict with nature, but that [it is] man's natural opposition to nature [which] enables him to produce society, history, and conventions."[9]*

Our instituted and oppositional yet precarious posture introduces an ambivalence into all human behavior, a function of new kinds of

---

*This opposition to nature is necessarily incomplete, and our failure to recognize this fact is likely to lead to disaster. The clue is contained in standing itself: Though an effort against gravity, it is also a gift of gravity. Absent gravity—and other naturally given constraints—human life can have no standing and no home.

distances from things, physical and (hence) psychic. "Upright posture removes us from the ground, keeps us away from things, and holds us aloof from our fellow-men. All of these distances can be experienced either as gain or as loss."[10] We enjoy the freedom of motion that comes with getting up, but we miss and often sink back to enjoy the voluptuous pleasures of reclining and relaxing. We miss the immediate commerce with things given to animals and crawling infants, but we enjoy instead the pleasures of confronting a true and distant horizon, as interested seeing becomes detached beholding. As upright, we enjoy our dignity and bearing and the opportunity to encounter one another "face-to-face"; yet this very rectitude makes us distant and aloof—verticals that never meet. To meet, we must bend or incline toward one another, or express our intentions to one another in some departure from strict verticality (for example, in leaning forward or recoiling, in nodding the head or extending a hand, and in other gestures of so-called body language).

Distance between self and world is, of course, a property of all living things—as we saw in the last chapter. The higher animals especially have acquired powers to overcome distance, through distance perception, wide-ranging locomotion, and lasting appetite, together enabling them to cope with the greater distances relevant to their lives. Thus the new kinds of "distances" implicit in the upright posture may be regarded as intensifications of the greater mediacy of animal life as such. Yet, as we shall gradually see, the improved or newly developed and accompanying human powers for overcoming distance—including powers of seeing, imagining, speaking, understanding, pointing, grasping, embracing, handling, fingering, planning, making, and acting-at-a-distance—make possible, perhaps for the first time in the story of life, a new kind of world relation, one that admits of a knowing and accurate encounter with things, of genuine and articulate communion and meaningful action between living beings, and of conscious delight in the order and variety of the world's many splendored forms— in short, a world-relation colored by a concern for the true, the good, and the beautiful.* We approach this conclusion slowly, beginning with the human arm.

---

*A skeptical and alert reader, suspicious of ascribing so much meaning to upright posture, will perhaps be thinking of embarrassing counterexamples. I once heard one such fellow, a smart undergraduate at St. John's College, Annapolis, ask Erwin Straus, after his lecture on "body schema,"

The Human Arm and Hand

In upright posture, the upper extremities, no longer needed to support and carry the body, are free to acquire new tasks. Much has been made of the significance of the opposable thumb and the prehensile hand, which becomes the tool of tools. But this is a small part of the story. The free swinging of the arms is crucial to the psychological experience of what Straus calls "action space." Action space is not the neutral homogeneous space of objective Cartesian science, but lived space, my space, a sphere of my action, which somehow both belongs to and gives rise to my sense of myself and to which I am related through body, limbs, and hands. In relation to action space, created by the arms, the hands develop into a true sense organ, a tool of "gnostic touching," ranking with the eye and ear in powers of discrimination.* Moreover, the hand—in which the

---

"What about penguins?" but I don't remember Straus's answer. Quite clearly, mere two-leggedness and vertical posture are not by themselves the sufficient sign of rationality. Uprightness that supervenes on the mammalian form, with mammalian powers for a life lived firmly grounded in a place on terra firma, will no doubt have a different meaning. It involves, as we shall see, a remodeling of the mammalian face and mouth, a reordering of the relation between sight and bite, a reorientation of the direction of locomotion, and the genuine liberation of the forelimbs—which birds, no less than tetrapods, are compelled to use for locomotion (that is, wings for flight). Birds are two footed, but their verticality is no great achievement; when they fall asleep at night they don't drop out of the trees. The birds' real achievement is flight, and they need to work (and often to receive instruction) to master it. They take flight from the earth; we stand up against it. They attain a bird's-eye view only by fleeing the scene and only while their forelimbs are compulsorily aflutter; we can contemplate, and deeply, while solidly planted on the earth and with arms (at least) at rest. (Penguins, though at rest, cannot see a "world," for they lack stereoscopic vision; to see you with each eye they must cock their head first this way, then that.) The birds do not really have the same kind of uprightness, for human uprightness is much more than simple verticality. This should become clear through the subsequent sections on arm and hand, head and face, and eyes and mouth.

*Straus uses this observation to show the limitations of the present biological approaches for truly understanding the activities of living things:

Anatomy that describes the eye and ear as sensory organs does not grant the same privileged status to the hand. Anatomy dissects. It divides the hand into different layers and, "in a systematic order," describes the skin as a part of the integument and places the bones in the osteological, the muscles in the myological, and the vessels in the cardiovascular system. Not to call the hand an organ seems strange in view of the fact that "organ" originally meant "tool." For Aristotle (432a 12–14), the hand was "the tool of tools." Anatomy has good reasons for its procedure; they are not, however, simply of a pragmatic order. The hand is a tool in relation to the living, experiencing being—to the man who stretches out his hand, touches, and grasps. The anatomical description that attributes the tissues of the hand to different systems is an analysis of the dead body. The wholes that function as frames of reference differ widely.

The hand as an object of anatomy and the hand experienced as a part of my body are not exactly the same object. The moment the anatomist takes up his scalpel, he behaves, in regard to his own hand, like anyone who has no knowledge of anatomy. . . . The anatomist, like everyone else, does not

individual fingers function as an integrated sensory-motor unit, by moving together over and around the object—gives us the shapes and forms of things (or, at least, of small things) and permits their re*cognition*. This cognitive function of handling—like every act of cognition—requires an inner or psychic distance from the object, a detachment experienceable even in this case despite the actual proximity of physical contact. This inner "experienced distance" (which, Straus shows, cannot be expressed in geometrical terms) implies a relation to things of "disinterested interest," in which we seek neither closeness nor remoteness, neither unification (or appropriation) nor separation, but in which we are simply *open* to things the way they are. The curiously discriminating receptivity of the open hand contains and expresses our curiously *theoretical* and contemplative attitude.

The arm and hand also function, again thanks to the upright posture and again in cooperation with eye and ear and mind, to form new kinds of *practical* world-relations as well. The arm, joined in the most flexible manner at the scapulohumeral articulation (the shoulder joint), and held in position mainly by muscle action, is capable of the greatest variety of movements—up and down, forward and back, round and round—over the widest angle of excursions. The accessibility to lateral space (space to the left and right of us)—generally denied to the quadrupeds, who need forelimbs mainly for support or for simple grasping or digging—provides the room for the exercise of the human crafts:

> Hammer and ax, scythe and sickle, the carpenter's saw, the weaver's shuttle, the potter's wheel, the mason's trowel, and the painter's brush all relate to lateral space. . . . [L]ateral space is the matrix of primitive and sophisticated skills: of spinning and sewing, stirring and ironing,

---

innervate the opponens, the interossei, the flexores digitorum. He does not use *the* hand but *his* hand. . . .

. . . Adding part to part does not give a full reintegration of the whole. The parts have to be understood from the beginning as parts of that specific whole to which they belong. With attention focused on details, the human arm and hand appear as just one other variation in the development of the forelegs. For every part, one can find a homologue in other species. However, "homologue" means difference as well as similarity. If one gives due respect to both and considers the arm in its entirety within the entire framework of upright posture, one can hardly deny that, through the peculiar structure and function of arm and hand, a new relation between the human organism and the world has been established.

Only in relation to action space, then, will the hand be understood as a sensory organ.[11]

sowing and husking, soldering and welding, fiddling and golfing, batting and discus-throwing.[12]

Throwing reminds, too, of the arts and weapons of war, displaying yet another form of action at a distance—say with bow or spear or sling—made possible by the arm and hand, in turn a part of the upright posture. Thanks to upright posture, man is naturally armed for virtually any action. In action no less than in awareness, the arm itself takes on the character of human openness—openness, this time, in the sense of unspecified possibility*—the badge of man's place atop the evolutionary tree.

Yet, in another sense, not all the actions of the arm are simply indeterminate and subject to our arbitrary will. In at least some cases—for example, with gestures such as shaking hands or embracing or cradling or shrugging one's shoulders—our arms and hands participate in expressions to one another, expressions that are, one might say, solicited by or expressive of the given human meaning of the interpersonal encounter. Holding hands expresses affection, outstretched arms betoken desire; a forward-thrust open hand, palm skyward, bespeaks need, palm forward commands halt; the embrace of lovers (and the face-to-face sexual intercourse it makes possible) embodies the differences between human lovemaking and animal sexuality. And there is at least one new function of the arm and hand that brings together practice and theory, sociality and contemplation: pointing.

When we point, we quite literally constitute a relation with another human being, a relation based on our mutual openness to the world. We point to things that invite our attention; we point them out to our fellows, whom we take to be equally invited to attend:

> In pointing, also, man's reach exceeds his grasp. Upright posture enables us to see things in their distance without any intention of incorporating them. In the totality of this panorama that unfolds in front of us, the pointing finger singles out one detail. The arm constitutes intervening space as a medium which separates and connects. The pointing arm,

---

*The interrelation of the two kinds of human openness—receptivity (in awareness) to forms of things, unspecified possibility (in action), including the freedom to destroy the forms of things—will become a crucial theme in the sequel, when the account turns ethical: How can and should the first openness influence and guide the second?

hand, and finger share with the intervening space the dynamic functions of separating and connecting. The pointing hand directs the sight of another one to whom I show something, for pointing is a social gesture. I do not point for myself; I indicate something to someone else. To distant things, within the visible horizon, we are related by common experience. As observers, we are directed, although through different perspectives, to one and the same thing, to one and the same world. Distance creates new forms of communication.[13]

Pointing points ultimately to both friendship and philosophy. Pointing expresses the peculiarly human openness to and powers for communion, both with other human souls and with the truth about the world.*

Head and Face, Eyes and Mouth

Pointing to the remote but common visibles implies the power to see and to recognize what can be pointed out. We are not disappointed. With upright posture come major changes not only in the hand and arm but also in the head and face, and, with them, a reordering of the rank and relation of the senses. Sight replaces smell as the dominant sense, and in so doing is itself transformed, finally coming into its own as the sense which recognizes forms and wholes:

> In every species, eye and ear respond to stimuli from remote objects, but the interest of animals is limited to the proximate. Their attention is caught by that which is within the confines of reaching or approaching. The relation of sight and bite distinguishes the human face from those of lower animals. Animal jaws, snoot, trunk, and beak—all of them organs acting in the direct contact of grasping and gripping—are placed in the "visor line" of the eyes. With upright posture, with the development of the arm, the mouth is no longer needed for catching and carrying or for attacking and defending. It sinks down from the "visor line" of the eyes, which now can be turned directly in a piercing, open look toward

---

*These two communions are in fact connected. The best friendship is widely held to be the one devoted to sharing speeches and thoughts, in search of understanding of the world. C. S. Lewis distinguishes it from companionship: "In this kind of love, as Emerson said, *Do you love me?* means *Do you see the same truth?*—Or at least, 'Do you *care about* the same truth?' The man who agrees with us that some question, little regarded by others, is of great importance can be our Friend. He need not agree with us about the answer."[14]

distant things and rest fully upon them, viewing them with the detached interest of wondering. Bite has become subordinated to sight.[15]

Whereas smell, like taste, with which it is intimately connected, is a chemical sense indifferent to the forms of things, sight—especially in higher animals—brings awareness of wholes. Things, as distinct, formed, and whole, are given all at once and effortlessly to the external senses only in sight. Thus, when sight is liberated from its subordination to the mouth, it is open to become interested in forms as such, apart from the utility of such perception for feeding and defense:

> Eyes that lead jaws and fangs to the prey are always charmed and spellbound by nearness. To eyes looking straight forward—to the gaze of upright posture—things reveal themselves in their own nature. Sight penetrates depth; sight becomes insight.[16]

Man's philosophical prospects are foretold in his gaze.

Though man remains a nourishing being, we now see clearly that his being-in-the-world is oriented not solely or even primarily as eater. He is, by natural attitude, a being whose eyes are encouraged to be bigger than his stomach.

> Animals move in the direction of their digestive axis. Their bodies are expanded between mouth and anus as between an entrance and an exit, a beginning and an ending. The spatial orientation of the human body is different throughout. The mouth is still an inlet but no longer a beginning, the anus, an outlet but no longer the tail end. Man in upright posture, his feet on the ground and his head uplifted, does not move in the line of his digestive axis; he moves in the direction of his vision. He is surrounded by a world panorama, by a space divided into world regions joined together in the totality of the universe. Around him, the horizons retreat in an ever growing radius. Galaxy and diluvium, the infinite and the eternal, enter into the orbit of human interests.[17]

As with upright posture itself, the contemplative gaze—or the transformation of seeing into beholding—requires maturation, and especially inner or psychic growth; small children do not have it and remain largely interested only in things that lie within their grasp. Eventually, as adults, we are able to organize the visible world into things near and far or, alternatively, into those visible and even remote things we are interested in prehending (by bringing them near) and those we are content to let be and to comprehend, at a distance and in their place, against a background totality, a world. Embedded in such detached beholdings, we encounter and experience, without any deliberate effort on our part, the distinction between form and material; in seeing we see or receive the looks of things without their stuff. Whatever the physics of the process, our psychic experience of seeing attests to this description: The lion I see is, as embodied form, over there, but his looks are somehow also here with me. Moreover, we experience each form as belonging to a "kind" or "species," as we recognize many a "that there" also as a "one such." The human form embodies the psychic power to notice, discern, and appreciate all other forms—and also its own.

This eidetic character of human vision has momentous implications, of which we can here give only the barest suggestions.[18] In ordinary seeing (which we probably share with other mammals) we experience the reality of the objects we see as coexisting with us here and now. Regarding each object, we are aware through its looks not only that it is "one such" being; we also are simultaneously aware of its immediate and self-giving presence. Yet the experience of encounter with the other is partially neutralized by two kinds of integrative abstraction, unconsciously and effortlessly performed in the activity of sight: we experience only the visible object, and do not feel any of its multiple effects on our eyes and brain that give rise to our seeing of it; and we integrate the multiple and varying visual impressions we receive from a single object into a single percept, so that we recognize the identity and unity of the object despite and through its changing aspects and movements. The form or *eidos* received in each visual sensation is thus at best a *partial* likeness of its object. Each view is, in fact, exactly like an *image*: It is both like and unlike the object of which it is a likeness.

Mysteriously the human viewer—unlike his animal forebears—is able to grasp and exploit this distinction between image and original. Perhaps because he is upright and hence best built for the detached surveying of the entire scene, he is able detachedly to include his own experience of seeing within this panorama. He is able to look reflexively on the difference between what appears to him and what is. Stepping back to examine what he has in appearance, he recognizes that the form present to sight is not the concrete reality of the enmattered form that is the visible object. Further, he comes to see that each of the multiple appearances are at best partial and incomplete likenesses of the object. This discovery of the detachability of image from object—an extension of the detachability of form from matter implicit in sight as such—is the key to the human imagination, itself the key to our decisive difference. For we can recall eidetic images at will, in the absence of their objects, and we can alter them, group them, dwell with them. A duplicated image world, whose existence and character are largely under human control, grows up between the self and the real world (not, to begin with, under our control) and ultimately alters that world and our relation to it. Images seen internally can be externalized and re-presented—in drawings, paintings, and ideographic symbols. As externalized, they become sharable, communicable, and subjectable to judgments about their accuracy: in discerning the difference between image and original lies the peculiarly human discovery of truth and falsehood. And the recognized general or species character of visual images comes to be the basis for the generality of names, for rational speech. But images freely conjured can be freely changed; through them the world can be not only reproduced but altered. Under the guidance of the *productive* imagination, human action also takes a decisive practical step beyond that of animals: Our external makings and doings come under the control of freely chosen, internally represented, purposefully projected forms, from a child's crudest stick-figure drawing to the blueprint for a spaceship, from the plan for a vegetable garden to the dreams of a human world beyond war and poverty.

The productive mental capacities of human beings for abstraction, image making, representing, and picturing, and the receptive mental powers of discerning, appreciating, admiring, wondering, and theorizing follow in the train of the ascendancy of sight; all of them are manifestations of the aesthetic or theoretic attitude implicit in the upright posture itself. As a consequence, such living-at-a-distance can bring us most fully back to ourselves. Distance is mediated first by imagination and then by thought, each of which duplicates the given world in image and idea. The distance is closed when the wondering eye or mind returns to look at itself and, with an inward gaze, sees through the surface into the heart of our existence. Now what was lost in foregoing the immediate contact or union with things is made up for by the possibility of *reflection*, of returning to ourselves, now consciously perceived in relation to an articulated and ordered world. (The alertly self-conscious reader of this sentence may here recognize that he or she is experiencing its truth firsthand—and has been throughout this reflexive book.)

This may be as good a place as any to emphasize that these implications of the distinctive character of human vision are entirely independent of the question about how our sight or mind came to be the way it is. Human seeing, discerning, and reflecting are without doubt human seeing, discerning, and reflecting, whether man emerged by chance and necessity ultimately from the primordial slime or whether he was directly created by God. Should scientists someday manage to construct a human being, molecule by molecule, who looked and saw and thought and did exactly as you and I, the fact that it was made from scratch would in no way alter what it means to be a human being or to have a human life—abstracting, of course, from the absence of natural ties to mother and father. By explicating the meaning of upright posture and its prospects for human openness to the world, I in no way mean to imply that man's peculiar powers of awareness and reflection are necessarily part of some peculiar purpose man was put on earth to serve. Nor when I say (loosely) that man is *built* for uprightness, or that he exercises *given* powers, am I implying that God or nature consciously and deliberately built him this way or gave him what he has, or that evolution has built-in goals or purposes that have been given to man to fulfill. (However, neither am I, by these present disclaimers, implying the contrary.) Rather, I am taking human nature as we find it and as each of us has received our share in it; in this sense, to us it is *a given*, whether or not there is or was a giver. I adopt here a neutral stance on the great metaphysical questions not only of causation but also of whether form or structure precede function or inwardness, and I am not claiming that the specialness of human being is caused by or reducible to man's upright form. Rather, accepting the view that man came from nonman, God knows how, I am concerned to understand the nature of our being and the meaning of our difference; and I find in our visible gestalt—and in the human face, eyes, and mouth—revealing manifestations of our human essence. Anyone who wants to know our nature must always take his bearings from what we are, looked at both directly and in comparison with other animals,* and much less from whence we came. Being or meaning is one thing, coming-into-being another; the first is not reducible to the second. Protected, I hope, against such misunderstandings, we can return to the psychic implications of the distinctively human face.

The prospects for wonder and thought—and for a sociality founded on and conducive to thought—are supported also by striking differences in the mouth itself. Animal jaws, previously equipped to grasp and crush, are extensively remodeled, as are the snout, teeth, tongue, and muscles of the face. The human mouth—still the organ of ingestion, taste, and mastication—has acquired the flexibility and subtle mobility to serve the expression of emotions and especially the articulation of speech. Where sight once served the mouth, now the mouth gives utterance to what mind through eyes has seen. The mouth not only homogenizes form to capture its matter, it helps now to preserve and communicate perceived and intelligible form through articulate speech. What enters the mouth nourishes—that is, supplies *material* for—the body; what departs the mouth nourishes—that is *informs*—the mind.

The dumb human body, rightly attended to, shows all the marks of, and creates all the conditions for, our rationality and our special way of being in the world. Our bodies demonstrate, albeit silently, that we are more than just a complex version of our animal ancestors to which a little dab of rationality has been added, and, conversely, that we are also more than an enlarged brain, a consciousness somehow grafted onto or trapped within a blind mechanism that knows only survival. The human body form as a whole impresses on us its inner powers of thought (or awareness) and action. Mind and hand,

---

*Everyone seriously interested in human nature, whatever his philosophical prejudices, has tried to learn about it by seeing the human over against the nonhuman animals, regarded both as kin and as alternatives. Thus, when one sees in the mammalian world a near universal subordination of sight to bite or no independent possibility for forelimbs beyond weight bearing or stuffing the mouth, the human difference stands out against these (submerged? rejected?) alternatives, regardless of how it came to be.

gait and gaze, breath* and tongue, foot and mouth—all are isomorphically part of a single package, suffused with the presence of intelligence. We are rational (that is, minding and thinking) animals, down to and up from the very tips of our toes.†

Rational Animal, Questionable Animal; Questionable Animal, Ethical Animal

Yet to be a rational animal is no simple matter. As we have already seen in explicating the meanings of upright posture, our form—that is, our given nature—points in a variety of directions and all at once, even before these directions are explored, pursued, and shaped by culture. In some cases, such as our native capacities for wonder and thought, for appreciative beholding of the looks of things, and for sociality based not only on need but also on shared speech about the world around us, we are prepared by our nature for rich and genuine "meetings" with the world and with one another. Face to face with one another and with the articulated world, we are open to discovering what is true or beautiful, and we are able to share these discoveries in friendship with fellow human beings. In other cases, such as our capacities for the useful arts, for self-conscious recognition of our neediness (and mortality), and for highly individuated self-presentation, -expression, and -experience, we are prepared by our nature for greater freedom and independence from the world. Solitary verticals withstanding temporarily our absorption into "mere nature," and small centers of self-concern poised against the vastness of the world disclosed to us as largely indifferent to our existence, we experience also—and more intensely than any animal—our

---

*Human respiratory patterns undergo marked changes during speech, and without conscious effort or awareness. More air is inhaled, the time of inspiration is shortened, and the time of expiration is prolonged, the number of breaths per minute decreases markedly, chest and abdominal muscular activity differs, and so on. We tolerate these modifications of breathing for almost unlimited lengths of time, without suffering respiratory distress. Special inherited anatomical and physiological adaptations in breathing enable us to talk for hours. They constitute a crucial part of the composite package that is "rational animal," the animal having *logos* or thoughtful speech.[19]

†I leave out of the present account other ways in which the gestalt of our entire form shows forth what and who we are. I also neglect the various bodily marks of our *individuality*, from obvious things like face and gait and gesture to fingerprints and, even on the cellular level, the unique cell-surface antigen patterns, which are responsible for such things as our unique blood type and our immunological rejection of alien material, including organ transplants.[20]

uniqueness and apartness, and especially ourselves as sources of self-generated actions in and on our world. Animal life's inherent possibilities for both need and independence, for mutuality and separation, for engagement and detachment, for commonality and distinctiveness, for harmony and opposition, and for the readily sharable and the intensely private all reach new heights in humankind, thanks to our heightened powers of mind and self-consciousness. As we shall soon see, human self-consciousness makes manifest and efficacious the tacit ethical dimension of animal life as such, as human beings must knowingly face the tensions implicit in the unavoidable conjunctions between self-concern and world-relation, rivalry and cooperation, holding back and reaching out, individuality and community, the life of awareness and the life of action. These natural, animal bases for the content of an ethical life—a life that is, however, contingent on choice—are finally realized once they are illuminated in human self-awareness.

The ethical aspect of human life follows not only due to mind but also due to necessity. For, needless to say, man is not a simple metaphysical success story. His heightened powers live alongside the lower ones—fear, hunger, thirst, and lust. Partly for this reason, mind and especially self-consciousness are a mixed blessing, for some of their discoveries are hardly cheering. For example, in the revealing story of primordial man and woman in the Garden of Eden, the first discovery of our newly conscious humanity is the painful and shame-filled knowledge of our sexual nakedness; we learn, in embarrassment to our aspiration to godlikeness, that as sexual beings we are neither self-sufficient nor capable of full self-command. Each of us, as male or female, abjectly needs the other even to fulfill our own sexual nature; each of us is possessed of demanding powers that resist efforts to govern our own life. To satisfy the demands of our sexual nature, we abandon our distinctively human upright posture and lie down to meet necessity (though we can do so humanly, face to face). These marks of our lowliness make us ashamed, so we artfully (via the productive imagination) cover up our nakedness ("the fig leaf"). Here, in the concern with self-esteem, is a major engine of the ethical life. As a result of the emergence of a *judgmental* self-consciousness, which compares our image of what we would like to be with what the stares of others compel us to admit to ourselves that we are, we human beings enter upon a new plane of existence: We must live as beings faced with ethical choice.* Human beings must live consciously, judgmentally, and concerned with the opinions of others; they must also live tentatively, trying out first this and then that, seeking a way freely to become the persons they think they would like to be, in light of the competing offers of their nature and with no guarantee of success. The rational animal is an ambiguous animal, indeed often a highly questionable animal, even with respect to his own good.

Well before the emergence of those moral complications that stem from society and from our need to attend to the needs and wishes of others, the human animal faces the ethical difficulty of balancing and adjudicating the claims of the competing stirrings in his own human soul. For the anthropological account we have just presented raises many deep questions, regarding both the relations among the diverse human possibilities and their import for the ordering of human affairs. True, these questions become accessible for us only through speech and within society; but their *substance* or content is deeply embedded in our nature. For example, which fulfills more the central aspirations of the human soul, community or autonomy, world relation or independence, the receptive openness of awareness or the indeterminate openness of freedom? How possible or likely is genuine communion, either with the beings of nature or with other human beings? Can human freedom, understood as will exercised in opposition to nature and instinct—or, eventually and more radically, as that display of selfhood that molds and masters nature by its own godlike creation and imposition of order—provide an adequate basis for human life, individual or social? Or must this freedom seek and take guidance from some standard or measure not of its own imaginative and free invention? Can we successfully guide our *indeterminate* openness (in the realm of action) by some of the discoveries of our *receptive* openness (in the realm of awareness)? Can our actions be improved with the aid of self-knowl-

---

*"Now the man is become like one of us, knowing good and bad." This is God's final observation on the meaning of the human transformation following the eating of the fruit of the forbidden tree. In God's own words, it sounds like a rise, not a fall, albeit a bittersweet, not to say unhappy, rise. For fuller discussions of this episode, see my essay, "Man and Woman: An Old Story," in *First Things*, November 1991; and for its implications in relation to the upright posture, see my "Thinking About the Body," in *Toward a More Natural Science*.

edge, including the sort we are seeking here? Is there any clue in man's embodied uprightness for finding and securing man's moral uprightness?

We human beings, unlike other animals, have no choice but to face these moral questions. Man has no choice but to be a passionately questioning—and questing—animal, precisely because he is such a perplexing—indeed questionable—animal. Let us pursue these large questions more carefully and concretely, albeit somewhat indirectly, as they emerge in considering the special features of human eating.

Rational Animal, Omnivorous Animal

What is the meaning of the human form for eating? Though man as a beholder of nature is capable of a disinterested relation to the forms of things, he is, as much as any other animal, in need of their material for his persistence. No matter how much he fancies himself free and independent, he remains forever needy and dependent on the world for his sustenance. Yet it would be strange if human eating failed to show the marks of human rationality and the accompanying peculiarities of the human form. Biologically considered, how has the advent of the new (or intensified) human powers of awareness, action, and appetite affected the activity of eating?* Revealing clues lie, quite literally, on the tips of our tongues, and, more generally, in the wonderful features of the human mouth.

Let us first consider the human mouth. Even looking only at the mouth's activities in eating, we see specializations for intermediate activities that are suffused with human freedom. In the front, the mouth's most tactile and sensitive part, the surface of the lips and the tip of the tongue touch and examine the food. Exploration is possible and judgment is rendered. If it meets with approval, the food is bitten off with the front teeth (the incisors) and taken into the center of the oral cavity proper. Here the food is thoroughly chewed and tasted: The rhythmic chewing remains under voluntary control and yields the pleasures of muscular exercise working our will on submissive ingesta; and, as we shall soon see, the chemicals

---

*Cultural modifications of eating are treated in the subsequent chapters.

released are detected and savored, generally with full human self-consciousness. The processes that follow become more and more unconscious and uncontrolled, as the voluntary yields to the autonomic: The chewed and ensalivated food is moved back to the region of the posterior tongue and the soft palate, automatically inducing the act of swallowing; thereafter the food descends into the fully unconscious part of the body, where digestion and metabolic activity proceed without our noticing them.*

But it is the multiple activities of the mouth—speaking, ingesting, tasting—that are truly emblematic of the peculiarly human; the conjunction of the functions of articulate reasoning and nourishing in one organ is a sign of their possible interaction, as well as a reminder that the rational remains precariously animal. The quasi-independent function of tasting, to be discussed later in this chapter, can be seen as an intermediate between minding forms and transforming materials: As discriminative, it is a species of awareness and receptivity, but because it perceives chemicals forcibly expressed from the object by grinding or crushing, and because it is itself intimately connected with metabolism, it is a species of transformation. The aesthetic turns out to be that aspect of life where the somatic and psychic most fully fuse.

The multiple functions of the mouth are also expressed in the extraordinary versatility of the human tongue, a truly remarkable little organ that gives virtuoso performances in masticating, tasting, swallowing, and speaking. Some ingesta it presses and crushes all by itself; some it maneuvers to and from the appropriate teeth; everything it feels and tastes; everything it handles and moves for swallowing. Articulate speech depends on its precise positioning in the formation of most of the consonants (the dentals, palatals, nasals, sibilants, *l*, and *r*). A voluntary muscle (actually comprising many different muscles, both intrinsic and extrinsic), the tongue moves in myriad ways: not only in and out, up and down, and side to side, but also curling up its edges to form a troughlike receptacle for

*Wolfgang Schad sees a deep significance in this tripartite division of the mouth. He ties it to three distinct poles of life: "Thus the three parts of the oral cavity are arranged as follows: in the anterior part, the conscious nerve-sense pole is predominant; in the rhythmic chewing and tasting, the middle system [tied to circulation and respiration] prevails; in the unconscious throat area, the metabolic system predominates."[21]

food, drawing down its sides and flattening its thickness to cover the mouth's floor, sweeping in a circle to clean food from between teeth and cheeks, simultaneously protruding and rotating to lick the lips, elevating and retracting the tip or the center to form sounds, and so on. The tongue is also the seat of taste, its entire surface covered with papillae that house the taste buds; in addition it is generally sensitive all over to touch and temperature. The richness of its talents is seen in the richness of its neural supply: Five different cranial nerves go to the tongue, mediating general sensation and taste and supplying its musculature. And its intimate connection to speech and language is honored by nearly every language: We learn at home to speak the mother tongue; things hard to say are tongue-twisters; those who are speechless are tongue tied. The ambiguities of speech and speaker are metaphorically assigned to the tongue: duplicity and lying (forked tongue), verbal assault (tongue-lashing), disrespect ("Hold your tongue"), humor and irony (tongue in cheek), eloquence (golden tongued), mystery (speak in tongues), diffidence or surprise ("Cat's got your tongue"). The human tongue, like the human mouth, bespeaks all aspects of our rational animality.*

The tongue and mouth need not have acquired all these functions. Nature might, after all, have evolved two distinct orifices for eating and speaking (and breathing), and there are good reasons to believe that fully separate pathways would be biologically advantageous (for example, choking on food would become impossible). These two functions live warily side by side, and not without moments of tension or frank opposition.† While it is possible to converse in the midst of eating—that is, with food in one's mouth—eating and talking are ultimately incompatible: One cannot talk while biting, chewing, or swallowing; conversely, one cannot swallow while

---

*The comparative anatomy of the tongue bears out our difference:

The *primary tongue*, found in fishes, is simply a part of the buccal [mouth] floor demarcated anteriorly by a fold. It contains no muscles or glands. In amphibians a crescentic *gland field* develops in front of the primary tongue and fuses with it to form the *definitive* tongue. In amniotes [reptiles, birds, mammals] . . . the definitive tongue is invaded by voluntary musculature . . . and is richly supplied with glands and taste organs. . . . The tongue exhibits numerous adaptive variations in form and use. Very long, mobile tongues are seen in some lizards, in snakes, woodpeckers, and ant-eating mammals.[22]

In contrast to these narrow specializations, the human tongue acquires enormous flexibility and plasticity of use—far and away the greatest in the animal world.

†Cultural attempts to address and resolve this tension will be considered in Chapter 4 and especially Chapter 5, in the discussions of conversation at table.

in the act of speaking. Not only fools but even geniuses cannot literally speak and chew gum at the same time. Usually human beings can freely orchestrate the successions of speeches and swallowings, but there are limits even to this self-control: The body sometimes "revolts," for example, in hiccoughing, destroying the easy flow of both words and food.*

The (partial) control over the functions of the mouth is but one manifestation of the (partial) control reason enables human beings to exercise over what, when, and how they eat. Greater control by deliberate decision means less control by fixed instinct. The decline in the dominance of smell and snout and the rise in the power of sight (and with it imagination, and so on), already mentioned, are in fact the external marks of the decline in the hegemony of instinct over human affairs. The power to see other beings at work is part of the power to imitate what they do and to learn from them—and not least about food. The point was already well made by Rousseau, describing protoman in the state of nature:

> Men, dispersed among the animals, observe and imitate their industry, and thereby develop in themselves the instinct of the beasts; with the advantage that whereas each species has only its own proper instinct, man—perhaps having none that belongs to him—appropriates them all to himself, feeds himself equally well with most of the diverse foods which the other animals share, and consequently finds his subsistence more easily than any of them can.[23]

Such an appropriation of all instincts would amount, in fact, to the absence of any ruling instincts or appetites, or, in other words, to the freedom of complete indeterminacy. Rousseau, of course, exaggerates: Human beings do not appropriate the instincts of *all* other animals. Some we cannot imitate, others we would not imitate if we could. Moreover, it is not true that human beings have no instincts

---

*For a famous example of such bodily insubordination, see Plato's *Symposium* (185C–D), in which Aristophanes is prevented from speaking by a bout of hiccups, brought about "by a surfeit or some other cause." Jacob Klein once suggested that Plato here dramatizes nature's anticipatory "objection" (in the form of a fitting punishment) to Aristophanes' speech, in which he will deny the importance of speech and mind in human aspiration and will characterize human *eros* as an unsatisfiable longing for mute bodily union. A man who would speak to deprecate speech and the soul's quest for truth contradicts himself when he makes such an argument; he deserves to be silenced, and by an uprising from his own mute body. Here, ironically, the body's revolt against speech turns out in fact to be not rebellion but "rational" defense. Plato, like Erwin Straus, sees that even the silent human body comes to the aid of reason.

of their own: Considering only diet, there is, for example, an inborn instinct for suckling and milk, and a lifelong and innate enjoyment of things sweet. Nevertheless, with the necessary qualifications, the major point stands: Man is far more free—that is, less strictly ruled by instinct—than are the other animals.

This freedom is in some respects an outgrowth of the germinal transcendence of space and time present to all animals (discussed in Chapter 1), but it is also something genuinely new. Correlated with the rise of intelligence and the attendant openness to the world, it provides hitherto impossible opportunities for action in and on the world. The latter is guided by the former: What mind discerns and imagines, will can attempt.

This new world relation is reflected also in human diet and appetite. The correlation of human freedom and human appetite is emphasized by Rousseau in a second (and somewhat later) passage in which he begins to consider natural man no longer only physically but now "from the metaphysical and moral sides." This shift of perspective is probably responsible for the less than celebratory treatment of man's new powers, for greater freedom of appetite is not an unmixed blessing:

> In every animal I see only an ingenious machine, to which nature has given senses in order to revitalize itself and guarantee itself, to a certain point, from all that tends to destroy or upset it. I perceive precisely the same things in the human machine, with the difference that nature does everything in the operations of a beast, whereas man contributes to his operations by being a free agent. The former chooses or rejects by instinct and the latter by an act of freedom, so that a beast cannot deviate from the rule that is prescribed to it even when it would be advantageous for it to do so, and a man deviates from it often to his detriment. [N.B.: Rousseau here admits that man does have his own instinctive rules, but that they do not simply bind him.] Thus a pigeon would die of hunger near a basin filled with the best meats, and a cat upon heaps of fruits or grain, although each could very well nourish itself on the food it disdains if it made up its mind to try some. Thus dissolute men abandon themselves to the excesses which cause them fever and death, because the mind depraves the senses and because the will still speaks when nature is silent.[24]

Freedom (and the human difference) is demonstrable in diet. Whereas instinct guides the senses of animals generally to "choose"—which is to say, to take—foods that are salutary and to "reject"—which is to say, to leave—foods that are not, the human imagination presents to the will as attractive foods (and quantities of food) neither naturally (that is, instinctively) desired nor healthy. Rousseau rubs our noses in the fact that the consequences for human well-being are not necessarily good. After demonstrating the often deadly inability of animals to deviate from their fixed diets (and just when we expect him to praise our greater dietary adaptability), Rousseau points out the possibly worse than deadly consequences of human flexibility and omnivorousness, ambiguous gifts of freedom and reason. We shall ourselves develop and extend this thought in the following pages.

Human omnivorousness is a known fact, but how men came to be omnivorous is a matter of dispute. In particular, the question of human meat eating is widely controverted, some claiming that the biological route to man is intimately connected to his becoming carnivorous, others arguing that meat eating is a latter-day and inessential addition to an already highly humanized ancestor. At stake in this dispute is more than diet, for what animals eat does in fact reveal much about what they are and how they live. Carnivorousness generally goes with ferocity and with the disposition to fight and slash and kill; those who stress the centrality of meat eating in human evolution have claimed that man is largely as he is because he was once a killer and that various central aspects of his being are adaptations to his need to kill—for example, uprightness for greater speed, strong desires and crafty intelligence for stalking and trapping, hand and tool use for weapons, language and sociality for communication and cooperation to facilitate the chase and capture. In this view, humanization becomes inseparable from spiritedness or aggressiveness, rooted in (or, at least, correlative with) meat eating, which aggressiveness extends also toward members of one's own species.*

Other scientists believe otherwise. They deny that aggressiveness and meat eating are *originally* natural to man. They stress the largely vegetarian diet of man's nearest relatives, the higher primates, and note the progressive reduction in the size of the canine teeth in the existing fossils of our prehuman ancestors; both are presented as ev-

---

*I return to this topic in Chapter 3, where I consider not the origin but the significance of human meat eating.

idence that man was originally vegetarian. Increased cranial capacity, making possible new forms of communication and adaptation, or, alternatively, special features of human sexual and reproductive behavior (for example, no periodicity of female sexual receptivity, prolonged periods of gestation and lactation), have been proposed as necessary and/or sufficient conditions for the evolutionary step toward humankind. In any of these views, carnivorousness turns out to be a later and inessential addition to human behavior; so, too, the accompanying ferocity and disposition to fight and kill. Indeed, in some views, when man finally became a meat eater, he did so without first becoming a killer but instead merely scavenged what the killers (or natural death) had left behind.

The truth regarding the origin of meat eating, and its bearing on the origin of man, may very well remain beyond our reach, inasmuch as the evidence is necessarily so sparse. But once again doubt about the coming-into-being cannot cast doubt on that which has come to be. Plain facts of present human anatomy and physiology clearly suggest that man is—and therefore has long been—biologically and not only culturally prepared for omnivorousness. For one thing his digestive tract is well adapted for handling meat, even uncooked meat, whereas it lacks the cellulose-digesting powers needed to utilize many raw vegetable products, such as those consumed by the browsing and grazing mammals. But even more impressive evidence for the unspecialized character of the natural human diet is found in our dentition, especially when it is compared to that of other mammals, both living and extinct.

Teeth and Jaws: Omnicompetent

The basic (and original) mammalian dentition comprises 44 teeth, eleven teeth on each ramus ("branch," that is, right or left half) of the upper and lower jaw: three incisors, one canine, four premolars, and (after change of teeth) three molars. The incisors are generally best adapted for cutting or gnawing, the canines for slashing and tearing, the premolars for shearing, the molars for grinding. This pattern was present in the primitive insectivores that became the ancestors of the entire mammalian line; it is still present in modern insectivores like the tree shrew. But in most mammals the pattern has been altered, often markedly, in relation to various specializations of diet.

The teeth of mammals show three basic kinds of specialization. Rodents, for example, show marked development of the anterior incisors: They possess two pairs of chisellike teeth, well suited to gnawing, especially on nuts and seeds; their canines are absent and their molars are reduced in size, number, and function. Second, typical carnivores, such as the big cats, show accentuation of the canines and other adaptations for killing and eating meat; even the neighboring incisors and premolars have become pointed, and one of the premolars is in fact called the "tearing" or "shearing" tooth. A third group, the grazers, such as the hoofed animals (ungulates), have accentuated the molars, which often show highly complicated patterns of cusps and crescents that permit efficient grinding of grasses and other foods rich in cellulose; most ungulates lack canine teeth, and some even lack incisors. The cow, for example, has incisors only on the lower jaw, which function as a flat shovellike plate useful in tearing grass but useless for biting. The ungulates (and also many rodents) have a large gap between incisors and molars, usually much larger than the space the missing canines would occupy.

These differences in teeth, tied obviously to differences in diet, are naturally correlated with many other differences of form, somatic and psychic. Compare, for example, the jumpy, nervous manner of the mouse; the bold, confident movement of the tiger; the serene, languid ways of the cow. In the teeth are telling marks of animal—and human—being.[25]

Human dentition, in contrast to almost all mammals, shows no specialization. All four tooth forms are present (though the number is reduced to 32, in keeping with the retraction and shrinkage of the jaw discussed earlier; the pattern on each ramus is 2:1:2:3). Furthermore, no one type is larger than or dominant over the others. And there are no gaps, but rather a progressively modified and continuous sequence in which the diverse types maintain their distinctive yet balanced forms.* The human teeth are omnicompetent and ready for almost any kind of fodder.

---

*The pig, a primitive ungulate yet, like man, an omnivore, retains the original 44 teeth, but in this case all three types are exaggerated in form. "The incisors are elongated and protrude from the mouth, the canines have become large tusks, and the molars are conical in shape and covered with numerous cusps. No animal has a complete set of teeth in balanced form."[26]

The unspecialized and multipotent character of human dentition is paralleled by the unspecialized and versatile character of the human jaw movements:

> Three main directions of moving the jaws against one another differentiate the carnivores, rodents and ungulates: the vertical, or up and down; the direction along the length of the head, forward and backward; and finally, laterally from side to side. They are all combined in man, who is almost equally capable of them all.[27]

The multiple competences of the jaws fittingly support the multiple competences of the teeth. Both stand open to welcome the extremely broad human diet.

A broad diet goes with a broad environment, with highly developed curiosity about foods and with highly diversified behaviors of exploration—searching, examining, comparing, and appropriating. Some meat may be had by scavenging, but for the active hunter there are also diverse behaviors of prey location, stalking, attacking, and killing. All these activities are manifestations of the higher psychic powers essential to the emergence and flourishing of the human form—powers of awareness, powers of action, and, of course, powers of appetite.

Taste and Appetite

The desire for food, the first of the human appetites, is, to be sure, an extremely complicated subject, physiologically as well as psychologically. One aspect is especially relevant to our present focus on human omnivorousness: the matter of taste. *That* one eats is governed internally by felt lack, that is, by hunger, and externally by the presence of food, which also conditions to a large extent *what* one eats. But what one eats is also governed internally by specific appetites, for this rather than for that. Appetites are, in turn, intimately connected with taste: To desire is, as we say, to have a taste for. Human omnivorousness is also in part a matter of taste.

Food, we have previously noted, may be seen relative to the intestine or relative to the mouth, to absorption or to taste. Though sound or smell may alert us to the presence of the edible, and though sight and touch may guide us toward it, it is in taste that we truly encounter the edible as food. Taste, defined by the early-nineteenth-century French gastronome Brillat-Savarin as that sense "by means of which we approve the sapidity [tastiness] and esculence [edibility] of things,"[28] is in fact physiologically bound up with smell and with touch. Like smell, it is a chemical sense; like touch, it depends on intimate contact with its object. The psychic experience of taste, a complicated blend of flavor, texture, and odor, along with hot and cold, dry and wet, is virtually indescribable: There are a limitless number of savors but only a handful of descriptive terms, and many of these refer to the elementary tastes of salty, sour, bitter, or sweet.

Taste, at least to begin with, is intimately connected with the needs of nutrition. Brillat-Savarin distinguishes its two principle uses:

1. It invites us, by way of the pleasure derived, to make good the losses which we suffer in the activities of life.
2. It helps us to choose, from the various substances offered us by nature, those which are proper to be consumed.[29]

Nature leads both animals and man by means of pleasure to do the needful and to choose the fitting; but in human beings, as we shall see, the pleasures of the palate can be pursued as ends in themselves, detached from the nutritional goals they were first meant to serve—another instance of the progressive rise and partial independence of intermediate activity. Be this as it may, what gets eaten must first be tasted—and approved.

> Thus man's omnivorousness will also be mirrored in his taste. Animals are limited in their tastes: some live on vegetables, others eat only flesh, others again feed exclusively upon grain; not one of them has any notion of composite savors.
>
> Man, on the contrary, is *omnivorous*; everything eatable is at the mercy of his vast appetite; hence, by immediate consequence, he must command powers of degustation proportionate to the normal claims made upon them.[30]

Never mind, for now, the question of whether these broad powers of taste are fully inborn or largely acquired—taste, we know, is notoriously subject to influences of eye and mind, and, of course, to habit. Either way we are naturally prepared for "omnigustation." For even if our tastes are largely acquired, we must by nature have the *capacity*—thanks to reason and imagination—to acquire them.* The acquisition of broad tastes presupposes an inborn plasticity or indeterminacy of taste, which is progressively filled in and further expanded. Learning to *eat* all things must be reflected in a broadening *taste* for all things, or at least a latitude or openness of taste. To be sure, the entire digestive system needs also to be adapted to omnivorousness. But it is the relaxed and polymorphous gatekeeping of taste that allows in such varied fare.

The latitude of taste and its educability have significance not only for nutrition. As mind and imagination can affect taste, increasing the variety of its experiences, so can appreciating the variety of tastes affect the mind and the soul more generally. Attention to flavors increases the capacity to make qualitative distinctions; conversely, a refined palate implies, at least in some respects, developed powers of discrimination. Much of the pleasure of taste is, in fact, intellectual: There is delight in the recognition of the distinctiveness of the various flavors and pleasure even in their positive identification. To be sure, taste is the most subjective and self-serving of senses: It depends on physical contact with, and the destruction of, its object; what is tasted is never a being but only some of its chemical materials, that is, the "wholes" and forms of taste are not wholes of nature or the forms of plants and animals; therefore, taste (in contrast with sight) can reveal almost nothing about the nature or way of life of the beings being eaten. Nevertheless, to savor implies a psychological distance between the taster and the tasted: Witness the difference between the child's immediate enjoyment of her ice cream and the gourmand's semidetached delectation of his grasshoppers. Tastes and flavors are both recognized and appreciated for themselves, quite apart from the quenching of hunger or the subsequent usefulness of the food. In short, like aesthetic experience generally, the delight in the distinctions made and savored stirs the soul be-

---

*In the paradigmatic story on this subject, it was the freedom-yielding activity of human reason (the conversation with the serpent) that broke down the human beings' adherence to the strict diet prescribed for them. The woman's imagination liberated and stimulated, she then looked upon the forbidden tree with fresh eyes, finding it attractive: "And the woman *saw* that the tree was good for food, and that it was a delight to the eyes, and a tree to be desired to make one wise, and she took of the fruit thereof, and did eat, and gave also to her husband with her, and he did eat." (Gen. 3:6) This story will be discussed more fully in Chapter 6.

yond concern for the merely necessary, transcending the preoccupation with survival, indeed, in the very activity whose main purpose is to promote survival. However fleeting, partial, or self-indulgent, the experience of taste manifests an openness to the world, tinged with wonder and appreciation.*

Whatever our final verdict on those who seemingly live to eat, there is, psychically speaking, at least something to be said for the gourmand. He is not, as some would have it, a slave to his belly, a glutton with brains. On the contrary, he is an aesthete whose need to eat is made to serve a more refined and higher aspiration, the desire to know and appreciate. Here is how one gourmand said it for them all:

> The machinery of taste attains a rare perfection in man; and to be convinced of the fact, let us watch it at work.
>
> As soon as an exculent [edible] substance is introduced into the mouth, it is confiscated, gas and juices, beyond recall.
>
> The lips cut off its retreat; the teeth seize upon it and crush it; it is soaked with saliva; the tongue kneads it and turns it over; an indrawing of breath forces it towards the gullet; the tongue lifts to start it on its slippery way, its fragrance is absorbed by the sense of smell, and down it travels to the stomach, there to undergo sundry ulterior transformations; *and throughout the whole operation not one particle, no drop nor atom, escapes its fate of being thoroughly appreciated.*
>
> It is this perfection which makes man the sole gourmand in nature.[31]

Not for nothing do we call those connoisseurs of the subtleties and refinements of things "men of taste."

Yet we must not get carried away by gourmandism and the kind of "knowledge" it provides. Unlike the contemplative enjoyment of illuminating ideas or even of beautiful sights, the pleasures of taste are radically ephemeral; the enjoyed savor disappears almost immediately with its tasty cause, for destruction is here the inescapable price of delight. For this reason the ultimate gourmand is ever seeking new and different pleasures; we might call him the Casanova of food. True, he lives the truth about the fleetingness of things and knows how to savor the immediate and to take delight in the now.

---

*An instance of the transcendental possibilities of taste will be presented in Chapter 5.

But for this very reason his way of "knowing" is closed to the permanent or the eternal. He dances lightly on the stage, loving every particularity. His epicureanism distracts him from his implicitly tragic view of life: Taste and be merry, for all else is vain; eternal are only the atoms and the void. Whether he is to be simply admired or even pitied depends in part on whether he is ultimately right—and this book argues that he is not—about our human standing in the world.

Be this as it may, and leaving the gourmand to his exquisite gustatory delights, there remains another, also less celebratory, way to consider both the openness of taste and the separation between the tasty (the free) and the nourishing (the necessary). For, truth to tell, the plasticity and freedom of taste—which, for human beings, turns out to be greatly influenced by upbringing and culture, custom determining what instinct has left blank—is a mixed blessing. For one thing it opens a possible gap between the tasty and the healthy, or more generally between the pleasant and the good. True, among small children (as among animals) this gap is probably rather small; their uneducated tastes generally lead them toward decent nourishment, provided only that it be available. Still, even for them, the correlation between the appetizing and the nourishing is not perfect; sometimes poisonous or other harmful things are ingested with gusto. And, in any case, the pleasing and the nutritious are separate principles that do, in fact, diverge in many a cultivated human diet. Moreover, the openness of human taste, its partial emancipation from instinct, and, therefore, its susceptibility to cultivation or adulteration testify to the natural ground of the difference between that which pleases and that which is good for us, as well the human importance of this difference. The good is not simply given, or, if given, it is neither obvious nor easily seen and embraced by human beings. Left by nature dangerously open ended, man acquires at once both the need and the capacity to concern himself with the questions of good and bad. Even his uninstructed appetites for food reveal that man is by nature the ethical animal; that is, the animal that necessarily "goes in for ethicizing,"[32] the animal who knows that there *is* good and bad and who lives his life in the shadow of this distinction. But—and here's the rub—there is no *necessary* link between the concern for the good and its correct apprehension. Knowledge that there is good and bad is not yet knowledge of *what* they are. And human pride leaves most of us often unimpressed with—indeed even ignorant of—this, our most crucial lack of knowledge. We eat, as we act, either confident that we know what is best or, rationalizing our preferences, insisting that what we like cannot really hurt us—or anyone else.

Omnivorosus Erectus: The Best and the Worst

The point, once generalized, goes very far: The expansion and indeterminacy of human appetites—reflected in human omnivorousness—is greatly problematic, as is man himself. If eating means always homogenizing some portion of the formed world, then omnivorousness is the ultimate in homogenization. Human omnivorousness is the bodily mark of man as homogenizer, as deformer and transformer. It is the unpremeditated, strictly natural sign of our dominant and mastering posture in the world, a posture of great danger as well as great promise, not only for the world but also for man himself. For it turns out that this easily recognized, highly distinctive, singularly upright and mindful being is free—and indeed invited—to alter, battle against, disguise, and corrupt not only the given world but even his own unique form—so much so that it sometimes seems (wrongly) as if he has no natural form at all. He is protean, polymorphous, and quite likely perverse—even from the point of view of his own interests.

The problem was noted long ago by Aristotle, in the very passage famous for celebrating man as the rational animal:

> For just as man, when he is perfected is the best of animals, so too separated from law and justice he is worst of all. . . . Without virtue he is most unholy and savage, and worst in regard to sex and eating.[33]*

Man's rationality lies behind his potential savagery, no less than his excellence, because it lies behind his broad, open, and undetermined appetites. The capacity to *discern* opposites—implicit in the ability to separate and combine, the distinctive power of reason—makes possible the *desiring* of opposites, by means of an imagination

---

*Aristotle does not explain what he means by this last remark; one surmises that he is speaking about incest (or bestiality) and cannibalism.

open to opposites. The capacity to think almost everything makes possible the capacity to do almost everything, by means of the desire to appropriate or control whatever is alien. Whether man becomes the best or worst of animals depends, to begin with, it seems, on whether or not he comes under law and justice; that is, on whether his protean and indefinite appetites receive delimitation and definition by custom. But Aristotle implies that law or custom as such is insufficient; virtue or excellence is required. Though man by nature lives by convention, not all conventions, it seems, conduce equally to his improvement or perfection. Some laws and customs seem to encourage virtue, others vice—in regard to eating no less than other matters.

How to think about better and worse customs? Here we again take cognizance of perhaps the most distinctive mark of the difference of man: self-consciousness. Reflection on our nature and on our situation within nature differentiates human intelligence from the intelligence of animals that precede man evolutionarily. We alone are capable of thinking through and appreciating the relations between the feeder and the food, form and material, self and other, the animal in man and the human in man. We alone are capable of contemplating the variety and power of the many forms of life, including our own distinctive "open" form. We alone are capable of understanding and feeling the weight of the meaning of eating, at once form and life preserving and form and life destroying, including the meaning of our own omnivorousness. How should life's becoming self-conscious affect how it is lived? How can or should our awareness of our nature and our place influence our practices, our customs, and our laws? What difference can or should knowledge of life, living form, and the peculiar features of human aliveness make for how we relate to the world and to other men? How, for example, ought our insights *into* eating affect *what* and *how* we eat?

The natural, and especially the humanly natural, have led us naturally to the brink of the ethical. Can they also guide its content?

3

Host and Cannibal

From Fressen *to* Essen

*Be not forgetful to entertain strangers: for thereby some have
entertained angels unawares.*

—Hebrews 13:2

*For the son of Chronos has ordained this law for human beings,
that fishes and beasts and winged fowls should devour
one another, since right is not in them; but to human beings
he gave right, which is far the best.*

—Hesiod
Works and Days 276–280

Nature was the theme of the first two chapters; first, animal nature in general, second, human nature in particular. The theme from now on is ethics: Here the legal and the just; later the noble and the holy.

The idea that connects nature and ethics is man: Man is, by nature, that animal which goes in for "ethicizing." He alone among the animals self-consciously considers the question of how to live; he alone either pretends or aspires to knowledge of good and bad, in light of which he deliberately lives his life. This he does not only because he can, but also because he must: as Mark Twain put it, "Man is the only animal that blushes. Or needs to."

In the last episode we left our hero on the threshold of the ethical. The possibility and necessity of crossing this threshold were prepared by reflections on the human form and on human eating and, in particular, by thoughts about omnivorousness. In human beings, as we saw, the powers of animal life—powers of locomotion in and action on the world, of awareness of the beings and becomings of the world, and of appetites and desires for particulars in the world—reach new heights. We human beings are uniquely prepared, in physique and psyche, for openness: We are open in awareness and appreciation, receptive, with pleasure and without constraint, to all the world's forms, both sensible and intelligible; we are open in action, freely able to enact vast and indeterminate possibilities and projects; and we are open to one another, face-to-face (thanks to upright posture), and capable of going hand in hand and of sharing thoughts and speeches about the one world—in which we have special standing, toward which we point and are pointed, and about which we are moved to speak. With man life and the world become self-conscious: Man is that part of the whole that can think the whole; that part that in thinking (and acting and desiring) can reflexively feel and experience its own special being-at-work-in-the-whole.

The problem of man parallels his promise. It can be seen already in his eating. As we learned in Chapter 1, eating as such reveals the paradoxical and problematic relationship between any living being and the rest of the world; for in eating, each living form homogenizes other forms and denies other life, appropriating them solely for its own use and purpose. The ultimate in eating is omnivorousness, and the ultimate in omnivorousness is man. Man is, by his inborn nature, *der grosse Fresser*—the great devourer and glutton—who stuffs his face and gorges his belly with the widest variety of fodder. Possessed of indeterminate and potentially unlimited appetites, willing and able to appropriate and homogenize nearly anything in the formed world for his own use and satisfaction, man stands in the world not only as its most appreciative beholder but also as its potential tyrant. If he is not to become the worst of the animals, he must be restrained by law and justice. And if he is to become the best of the animals, he must be perfected by rearing in customs that bring out and complete what is best in his nature.

As with the ethical in general, the primary need is for restriction, for nay-saying; if too much latitude is the problem, then a prohibition is the beginning of the civilizing process. Holding down is the precondition of drawing up. In the first place, man's protean and indeterminate appetites need to be delimited and constrained. But custom will not only restrict and constrain. It will also embellish and dignify, shaping virtually every aspect of human eating; it will determine what, when, where, how much, with whom, and in what manner human beings eat. We should not be surprised to find that the negative restraints and the positive adornments are mutually and deeply related: At bottom both share and spring from a view of human flourishing that informs, even if only tacitly, all the particular customs, whether negative or positive. What is held to be disgraceful or disgusting necessarily points to—and is informed by—what is held to be honorable and humanly fine. You may not *be*, literally, what you eat. But what and how you eat reveals who you are, humanly speaking.

To be sure, much of the particular content of the cultural forms will be a matter of human agreement—that is, strictly conventional—and relative to time and place. But this does not necessarily mean that there cannot be better and worse customs. Some customs—including customs about eating—might be more conducive than others to human flourishing. Some customs might be more fitting to the truth about the world.

Consider, for example, our insights about nature, eating, and human nature. Could they not help provide something of a standard for judging customs about eating? As self-conscious eaters we can know about both the supremacy of living form and its absolute dependence on newly obtainable material; we do know about our own form, with its special possibilities for community and understanding (or, as I put it in the last chapter, for friendship and philosophy); we know about vulnerability and necessity; we know about both the indispensability and the ambiguity of all eating, which deforms and destroys as it re-forms and preserves; and, finally, we know that such knowing about feeder and food, about form and material, about self and world, and about the upright and omnivorous animal that can know all these things is a knowing that is available, in principle, to every member of our own, uniquely self-conscious species. Might not these insights into life, eating, and man guide our thoughts about what and how we human beings should eat?

I think one can go very far in suggestions for conduct that are fitting to these physiological and anthropological insights. To begin with let us consider some of the most elementary customs: conventions, both positive and negative, regarding what we eat and whom we feed—specifically, conventions regarding hospitality, cannibalism, and certain forms of vegetarianism. These conventions and mores embody, at least tacitly, certain opinions about who and what one is and about the proper relations to whom and what one is not. In these customs, as in the natures they shape and clothe, we see again that eating is a crucial—even paradigmatic—instance of the relation between what is one's self and one's own and what is not one's own but other. Let us look at the customs governing eating in relation to the customs governing strangers.

This may seem an odd place to begin, especially if the question is how to limit human omnivorousness and voracity; that is, if, as was argued, the first steps in ethics are matters of saying no. Anthropologically and morally it might therefore make more sense to begin with the nearly universal taboo against eating human flesh, especially because, as we shall see, the taboo against cannibalism clearly reflects a certain human understanding of the human, albeit in its negative form: The human being is not food. One can even argue that this one interdiction, rightly understood, tacitly entails the full development of civilized morality: Seen formally, as an absolute prohibition promulgated without explanation, it establishes the principle of self-restraint and self-command; seen substantively it pays homage both to the superior dignity of the human being and to each person's

full share in that dignity. But I believe that the meaning of this interdiction will be clearer still if we first present the correlative *positive*
ethical teaching, as it is tacitly present in the customs of hospitality
toward strangers.

Strangers and Hosts

The mention of strangers reminds us of an obvious but terribly important fact about human beings. Man, considered biologically, may
be a singularity—or perhaps a heterosexual duality—but considered
socially or politically he is a multiplicity. Naturally homogeneous and
universal mankind is always and everywhere divided into culturally
heterogeneous and parochial groups. Human beings live always and
everywhere organized into exclusive groups—familial, tribal, social,
religious, civic, national, political—each with its own beliefs, customs, and practices. Birth into one group rather than another may
be a matter of chance, but the existence of groupings that distinguish who's in and who's out seems to be a matter of necessity. Indeed it is precisely necessity itself that is the mother of the most fundamental of such groupings, the family. Among human beings the
prolonged period of dependence, neediness, and vulnerability of the
young necessitates a fairly stable social unit whose first business is
the care and feeding of its own members. Cooperation between
families and within large clans, accelerated eventually by the division
of labor and backed by shared customs and beliefs, extends the network of necessity and the bonds of "one's-own-ness" to larger and
larger groups. But even today, within the massive nation-state and
our advanced technological society, the household remains the primary place for meeting the daily necessities, especially for food—
notwithstanding the fact that very few households now produce
what they consume. People nurse, nourish, and nurture their own,
usually exclusively. It is a rare mother who will feed needy strangers
by taking food out of the mouths of her own hungry children.

Given our so-called enlightened and cosmopolitan tendencies, we
sometimes sneer at the provincialism and xenophobia of those strictly loyal to their own. But preferential care and love of your own and
distrust of the alien are in some sense natural and fitting. It is perfectly appropriate—even just—for parents to care first and most for

their own children, for whose presence in the world they are in large measure responsible. And, sharing a common origin, all branches of the family tree can with right feel the claims of connections to one another, connections that are absent toward strangers.

But how far should this go? What are the limits on the love of one's own? What is the proper treatment of the stranger? In the extreme case, shall you feed him or eat him? These are the questions answered by customs of hospitality, governing relations between hosts and guests.

The problem of the stranger, whose solution is hospitality, is embedded in our very terminology. The outsider who enters a household is, most obviously, a stranger; but so, too, from his point of view, are the household members. Both guests and hosts are, to begin with, strangers—not kin—to one another and, for this reason, under some suspicion of possible ill will. The English word *host*— one who lodges and entertains another in his home—stems from an Old French word (*oste, hoste*) that means *both* "host" and "guest," primarily because it also means "stranger" or "foreigner." (The original Latin root, *hostis*, from the Indo-European *ghostis*, means "stranger" and "*enemy*"; this meaning lies behind our use of *host* to mean an armed company of men, presumably *host*ile to us.) A similar dual meaning of "host" and "guest" (and also "stranger" and "foreigner") attaches to the Latin root *hospes*, source of our words *hospital* and *hospice* (originally "a house or *host*el [italics added] for the reception and entertainment of pilgrims, travelers, and strangers"), *hospitable* (originally "affording welcome, entertainment, and generosity to strangers and visitors"; now "disposed to receive or welcome kindly"), and *hospitality*, the practice of welcoming and tending generously to the needs and desires of stranger-guests. Much of the transformation of *host* from stranger and would be enemy to provider of hospitality is the work of often-elaborate custom. But such custom in fact gives expression to the natural human ability and willingness to recognize natural sameness despite and beneath conventional otherness. Let us consider what this might be.

Though we easygoing Americans are, especially when we travel abroad, disinclined to view strangers with suspicion, we are, at home, at a relative disadvantage in understanding what is involved in hospitality. Hospitality has not quite died among us, though it is certainly in decline. Our way of life does not support it. How many of us make sure to keep extra food in the house just in case someone drops in? How many of us would be embarrassed at our failure to offer food—and not only drink—to a visitor in our homes, invited or not? And who in his right mind in urban America lets unknown strangers into his house, let alone offers them food, before being assured about their name, character, and purpose?

Although one suspects that there are yet places where stranger-guests are generally welcome, one knows this was true in the past. The ancient Greeks, for example, had an elaborate network of relations based on offering hospitality. The guest-friendship, based on received hospitality that obliges reciprocity, was a crucial part of the Homeric culture, and Zeus himself, as the god of strangers, Zeus Xenios, watched over these relations. In the *Odyssey*, which Fielding called "Homer's wonderful book about eating," we are given numerous examples of "eat first, talk later":

> But when they had put aside their desire for eating and drinking, first to speak was the Gerenian horseman, Nestor: "Now is a better time to interrogate our guests and ask them who they are, now they have had the pleasure of eating. Strangers, who are you? From where do you come sailing over the watery ways? Is it on some business, or are you recklessly roving as pirates do, when they sail on the salt sea and venture their lives as they wander, bringing evil to alien people?"[1]

What understanding of life and human relations informs a hospitality that would unhesitatingly feed strangers before discovering who they were and whether they bore you good or evil intent?

Offering hospitality could result from calculation. One good turn lays claim to another, and among frequent travelers generosity might be the best policy, because it pays. Aristotle, in his own subtle discussion of friendship, considers these guest-friendships as friendships only of utility and ranks them rather low.[2] But even if they fall short of true friendship, guest relations between strangers rest on much more than calculation.

Offering hospitality could rest instead on piety, because the gods demand it. Zeus is protector of strangers, suppliants, and beggars, and guards all proper relations between host and guest: It was Zeus Xenios, according to some accounts, who sent Menelaus, Agamem-

non, and the Achaian host against Troy in order to avenge the violation of guest-friendship—in this case, a violation of host by guest
and in matter of wife-stealing, not food. Further, given the powers of
Greek gods to assume any shape or form, hospitality toward
strangers would make prudence the better part of piety: The
stranger, one whom you have never seen before and may never see
again, might in fact be a god. The Homeric poems are filled with examples of gods and goddesses appearing in the guise of beggars and
suppliants. More often than not it is only those who treat them kindly who are able to penetrate their disguises.

To us this belief of the Greeks about their gods probably seems
silly. Yet, if properly understood, it embodies a profound insight, one
that leads to the true ground of hospitality. What might it mean that
the divine takes the form of the stranger or the beggar? Strangers,
and even more suppliants and beggars, are exposed and unaccom-
modated. Isolated and homeless, they are stripped of most of their
own powers to provide for themselves. They are abject creatures of
necessity, not in command of their survival. That they continue to
exist at all is a matter of fate and good fortune or, if you prefer, of
the unmerited generosity of nature or divine grace. Curiously it is
the vulnerable stranger who reminds us of providence, who makes
us acutely aware of our own (relative) blessedness, who inspires us,
in gratitude, to imitate and improve on nature's beneficence with
our own gracious deeds of hospitality. When the stranger comes, his
very mode of being can teach everyone of all these matters.

The possibility that the stranger might be a god in disguise also
prompts the host to remember and recognize the god-like possibilities in all human beings, and not only in those who are near and
dear. The sight of possible god-like-ness in the other inspires in the
host god-like acts of generous beneficence, and the offering of food
and drink sanctifies both the meal and the human relationship. In
this way sharing food with any stranger is like offering sacrifice—
sacrum facere, doing the sacred thing—to a god.

These insights and discoveries are not only Greek, they are also
biblical. (They are, in fact, shared also by, many cultures, Eastern
and Western—including India, China, and Japan; the Arab world;
and many parts of Africa.) The adventures of Father Abraham teach
him and, through him, all readers about proper relations not only to

one's own but also to strangers. Sometimes, as in the case of the War of the Kings (Gen. 14), one must have courage and fight against strangers in order to save one's own (in this case Lot, who had been captured). But Abraham is never allowed to forget that the stranger—and even the sworn enemy—shares a common humanity. Indeed Abraham's education begins with his trip to Egypt, where he learns what it feels like to be a stranger in a hostile country. Sometime later, the roles reversed, Abraham receives stranger-guests—who are (we later learn) not men but angels—in a most beautiful manner:

> And the Lord appeared unto him by the terebinths of Mamre, as he sat in the tent door in the heat of the day;
>
> and he lifted up his eyes and looked, and, lo, three men stood over against him; and when he saw them, he ran to meet them from the tent door, and bowed down to the earth, and said: "My lord, if now I have found favour in thy sight, pass not away, I pray thee, from thy servant.
>
> Let now a little water be fetched, and wash your feet, and recline yourselves under the tree.
>
> And I will fetch a morsel of bread, and stay ye your heart; after that ye shall pass on; forasmuch as ye are come to your servant." And they said: "So do, as thou hast said."
>
> And Abraham hastened into the tent unto Sarah, and said: "Make ready quickly three measures of fine meal, knead it, and make cakes."
>
> And Abraham ran unto the herd, and fetched a calf tender and good, and gave it unto the servant; and he hastened to dress it.
>
> And he took curd, and milk, and the calf which he had dressed, and set it before them; and he stood by them under the tree, and they did eat.[3]*

Abraham sits at the opening of his tent and *runs* to meet the three strange men. In speaking to the men, he upholds their dignity by graciously understating or even denying their neediness (he implies that they are just passing by and that they need at most a *little* water

---

*This episode is the immediate sequel to the covenant of the circumcision, enacted by Abraham, Ishmael, and all the men of Abraham's house, the covenant that defines and separates the people of Israel. The juxtaposition of these two tales shows that the separation of Abraham's people is perfectly compatible with—indeed requires morally—the continued recognition of the common humanity of those outside the fold.

to wash their feet and a shady place to rest). Moreover, he belittles
the fare he offers to provide ("a morsel of bread") and makes it appear as if they would do him honor by pausing at his home and accepting his (modest) service. But though measured in speech, he is
quick and open handed in deed: He organizes Sarah and his entire
household to the task of preparing food; he provides a lavish feast of
fresh cakes of fine meal, a tender dish of dressed veal, curds, and
milk; and he serves his guests himself—all with energy and dispatch.
In the immediate sequel the guests announce the long-wished-for
(and now forthcoming) birth of a son to Sarah: Abraham's guests
reciprocate his generosity in divine measure. The strangers show
themselves to be agents of grace.

The excellence of Abraham's conduct is made absolutely clear
when it is compared with Lot's treatment of the same strangers later
on their journey, when they come to the city of Sodom (Gen. 19). An
important clue to the difference: When they come to see Lot, the
men are called "angels" and appear to him directly as such; Lot apparently would not be able to penetrate their disguise—that is, unlike Abraham, he would not have been able to see the divine "within" the human. Lot is hanging about the gate of the city, does not
rush forth to meet them, insists with unseemly urging that they enter
his house, makes a much less gracious and generous offer, prepares
a less adequate meal, ("unleavened bread") all by himself (Mrs. Lot
is not in evidence, and the entire house is poorly organized to receive strangers). In the end, when the Sodomites come menacing his
guests in the most explicit contempt for the dignity of strangers, Lot
offers his own daughters to protect his guests from violation. He and
they are saved only when the visitors pull Lot inside, shut the door,
and blind the attackers "so that they wearied themselves to find the
door." From this episode we see that in a place where strangers are
improperly treated, finally not even one's own kin are safe.*

Let us try to make explicit what is merely implicit in these stories.
To begin with, hospitality recognizes simultaneously the neediness

---

*Through these two juxtaposed stories and their contexts, the Bible invites us to discover the
problem of justice and injustice, to begin with evident in attitudes toward the stranger, and to see
why the city—not just Sodom, but the city as such—is a breeding ground for injustice. For the city
has walls to protect it against hostile outsiders (access limited, through the gate), yet its houses
come to need doors to protect them against predatory neighbors (compare Abraham's tent opening, freely communicating with the world). Paradoxically, the city in its quest for self-sufficiency is

and vulnerability and also the humanity of the stranger. Sympathy and fellow feeling are aroused by the sight of another human being away from hearth and home, without the sustenance and nurture they provide. Moreover, unlike animal neediness, ours is self-conscious and understood to be such. The stranger knows that we know that we both know what it is to be estranged and necessitous. To feed the stranger is to make him feel less his absence from his own; yet to treat him as a *guest*, only *temporarily* at home with us, is to acknowledge the importance of his *own* home. In this way hospitality also recognizes simultaneously the importance of the love of one's own and the insufficiency of loving and being loved *only* by one's own. Hospitality springs from these common perceptions of our common elevated yet necessitous humanity; it reflects this mutually shared and self-conscious recognition of mutual vulnerability and dependence, awareness of which is embodied in the first institution men establish to meet necessity, the home.

Hospitality recognizes not only necessity and the meaning of home. It also recognizes nature's beneficence. In their acts of generosity hosts imitate and improve on the hospitality—albeit only partial—of nature, which "provides" us with food and not because we merit it. But whereas nature's beneficence is silent and (perhaps) unintended, human hospitality is deliberate and self-aware.

Indeed, by being self-aware, hospitality connects generosity and neediness. The perception of necessity faced by another human being provides the occasion for our own nobility, for rising above ne-

---

more likely to forget human vulnerability and our dependence on powers not under human control: The city is blind to the meaning carried by strangers and beggars. Sodom, perhaps the paradigmatic city, is notorious for injustice, for that unqualified love of one's own and that unqualified hatred and mistreatment of strangers, exemplified in the attempted homosexual rape of the men-angels visiting Lot (*all* the men of Sodom, young and old, came to abuse the strangers). Sodomite injustice is epitomized in the very acts of sodomy (practiced by the citizens) and incest (practiced by Lot's daughters on their father), each of which is an excessive embodiment of the principles of love of like, aversion to unlike, principles in fact not peculiar to Sodom, but to some extent native to all cities. For every city defines itself by magnifying the importance of the distinction between who's in and who's out; it will tend to injustice unless its regime is informed by the teachings of hospitality, of the sort taught through Abraham—and Homer.

The similarity of Greek and biblical teaching is evident from the following story. When Abraham, in the next episode of his adventures, travels to Gerar and *receives no hospitality*, he fears for his life and passes Sarah off as his sister. The reason he gives is the same as that given by the Greeks: "Because I thought: 'Surely there is *no fear of God* in this place; and they will slay me for my wife's sake.'" (I owe this last insight to Michael Fishbane.)

cessity. Feeding oneself is obligatory, but feeding *another* feeder is liberal, that is, free. Necessity is thus the mother also of virtue. The host rises above his own necessitous scrambling, not by ignoring the importance of scrambling, but by doing it justice. Hospitality is at the same time an assertion against and a recognition of the given dog-eat-dog character of the world. Just as upright posture pays tribute to gravity as it rises against it—for in the absence of gravity, we could not stand—so hospitality pays tribute to necessity, for necessity is necessary for nobility. By facing and going beyond necessity, the hospitable host elevates both it and himself.

Insofar as he is just an animal, man is by nature *der grosse Fresser*. But in his thoughtful encounter with an-*other Fresser* who comes along, he recognizes himself in the other and allows him to remain *another Fresser*. A host's inclining from aloof verticality to meet and serve his fellow feeder, even silently, speaks volumes and so humanizes the merely animal act of *fressen*. As host feeds guest, *essen* replaces *fressen*; eating supplants feeding.

Hospitality thus recognizes necessity and generosity, needy vitality and human self-consciousness, and, above all, the importance of preserving yet moderating the distinction between same and other, between one's own and the alien. Hospitality is one of the civilized and civilizing customs at the foundation of most if not all political communities. It may seem strange to suggest that exclusive and sectarian communities, if they are to be civilized, depend radically on acknowledging the existence and dignity of the broader and universal human community, most of which they exclude. Yet if civilization is to be civil, the otherwise arbitrary and largely conventional division of mankind into heterogeneous and multiple sects or associations must pay homage to the nonarbitrary and natural sameness of the human species and its dignified place in the natural whole. Failure to recognize nature and the naturally human leads one to treat as respectable and worthy only what is merely *familiar* and *one's own*. Cannibalism is perhaps the radical embodiment of such a mistake.

Cannibalism: Hospitality Inverted

The subject of cannibalism, or anthropophagy, to use the more technically correct term, is complicated by the existence of several different kinds, distinguished either by purpose or by the social identity of the persons eaten. In gastronomic cannibalism human beings are eaten primarily as a source of food; in ritual cannibalism eating serves a variety of nonphysiological ends, from taking revenge on or humiliating one's enemy, through incorporating the remains of one's beloved ancestors, to propitiating or imitating one's god. Sometimes the eaten belongs to the same social group as the eater (so-called endocannibalism); sometimes he is an outsider or perhaps more explicitly an enemy (so-called exocannibalism). To some extent, but by no means entirely, these differences in the meaning of the act to the participants must affect our judgment of the practice. Indeed I would be prepared to argue that all forms of anthropophagy are an affront, both to the truth about the world and to any notion of decency, even in those possibly forgivable—perhaps even justifiable—cases where it appears as a unique event in the face of starvation (for example, with the Donner Pass survivors in California in 1847 or, more recently, with the Uruguayan football team whose plane went down in the Andes in 1972).* But for present purposes, our subject being hospitality and its perversions, let us think only about gastronomic exocannibalism, eating strangers just for food.

The taboo[†] against such eating of human flesh is both nearly universal and extremely powerful. Just imagining the deed not only out-

---

*These rare and exceptional cases have been used in arguments that seek not only to refute the absoluteness of the prohibition against eating human flesh but to suggest thereby the utter irrationality of the prohibition itself. Such arguments hold it to be not merely excusable but obligatory, even praiseworthy, for people in desperate straits to save their lives by eating the remains of *already dead* fellow travelers. (*Killing* them for food would be another matter). The dead, being dead, cannot be further harmed; why should not their flesh be used to save life? (This argument has already won the day for organ transplantation, which is, as I have somewhat luridly argued elsewhere, an elegant if sanitized form of cannibalism. See my "Thinking About the Body," in *Toward a More Natural Science*, and "Organs for Sale? Propriety, Property, and the Price of Progress," *The Public Interest*, Spring 1992, pp. 65–86.) But what is done, justifiably, under the gun of necessity is no measure of what is justifiable simply. On the contrary these exceptional cases prove the rule by showing the true horror of eating human flesh. Those forced to partake will no doubt experience—even as they push past—the horror; and I expect a person of normal sensibilities to feel terrible about the grim necessity of his deed for the rest of his life. As I try to show in the sequel, the taboo here set aside embodies a reasonable and proper respect for the dignity of the embodied human form. To be human is, for a human, to be not-food.

†Perhaps because the old taboos have lost their grip on modern man, the very idea of taboo has lost its force—and even its meaning. A taboo is more than a "no-no," more than a strong, even unexceptionable rule. It is a rule conveyed less by speech, more by horror-preventing revulsion. It operates not only on the mind but also and especially on the viscera. For these reasons modern ratio-

rages our sense of right; it revolts and horrifies our sensibilities, which seek to purge the abominable picture from our mind. Though the taboo is clearly a humanly instituted, self-imposed restriction on human omnivorousness, its near-universal presence leads one to suspect that it has a natural grounding. What might this be?

One possible natural ground has been suggested by some evolutionary biologists. They posit the likelihood of a sound biological reason for the origins of the cannibalism taboo, namely, some (as yet unidentified) selective advantage afforded those who refrained from eating human flesh or disadvantage to those who indulged. If ingesting human flesh seriously undermined, say, reproductive fitness (a biological equivalent of the curse on the house of Atreus), natural selection would reward those who were powerfully nauseated at the prospect. But until such selective advantage can be specified and documented, this could be just an overconfident prejudice of Darwinian orthodoxy. Indeed studies of other animal species suggest that there might in fact be some selective advantage to eating members of one's own species, provided that one refrains from eating one's own *kin*. For example, growing tadpoles of the spadefoot toad (which lives in the Arizona desert) eat other spadefoot tadpoles, but not their brothers and sisters, which they recognize by taste! The hungry tadpole nips its neighbor and tastes it: If it tastes like his siblings, he lets it go; if the victim tastes strange, he devours it. This behavior fits with the theory of kin selection, which explains the evolution of certain social behavior in terms of advantages to the survival not of individuals but of close relatives—which, of course, are genetically closely related to one another. Cannibalism of unrelated "stranger" rivals is, at least in some cases, an evolutionarily successful way of life.

But the taboo on cannibalism may be natural in another sense: It may represent the near-universal-yet-uninstructed—that is, natural—intuition of human beings, independently arrived at in whatever place civilization begins to flower, of the *difference* of human beings (from other animals) and therewith also of the importance of honoring this difference if the promise of human nature is to be realized.

nalists have attacked many taboos as mere atavisms, rooted in religion and superstition, fundamentally irrational. But though they may work by nonrational means, they are not thereby irrational or unreasonable. They may indeed be reason incarnate—like the human being whose dignified *embodied* life they are meant to protect.

The taboo might be natural both because it rests on a proper under-standing of our nature and because it is necessary for the perfection of that nature.

We will probably never know the real story of the origin of this taboo. But we are not thereby prevented from understanding it. For the meaning of a custom or practice, as understood by its adherents, can be discerned independent of its origins. It might be perpetuated self-consciously by human beings for their own reasons, reasons that have nothing to do with natural selection. Thus, in suggesting that cannibalism is based on an error of understanding, I do not mean to imply that I am giving a historical or genetic account of the taboo against it or that I can account thereby for the great revulsion we feel for cannibalism; rather, I am suggesting that anthropophagy embod-ies, in principle, a false view of human life.

(I feel compelled to apologize to my readers for speaking about cannibalism, and not only because it is revolting. Some things should perhaps not be spoken of at all, for, especially in democratic times, familiarity breeds tolerance more often than contempt. Our sensibil-ities are blunted by frequent mentioning of the unmentionable, and the force of revulsion is weakened should an argument to defend the reasonableness of such revulsion fail to persuade. Still, unlike other once-upon-a-time horrors such as abortion, adultery, infanticide, sui-cide, sodomy, pederasty, incest, and bestiality, cannibalism is not an American temptation, and I doubt if my speaking about it can make it one. Moreover, we liberals ought to ponder the prohibition against eating human flesh—an act that, if the victim is already dead, is what we would call a "victimless crime." For we might thereby learn the insufficiency of our liberal belief that one does evil to a man only in violating his will or in not respecting his autonomy (read "mind"). Thus, by thinking about what's wrong with cannibalism, we might be able to re-discover the indispensable foundations of liberalism which are not themselves liberal.)

I again draw help from Homer. In his wanderings Odysseus comes to the land of the Cyclopes and is a stranger-guest in the cave of the giant Polyphemos. The Cyclopes are a lawless, savage, impi-ous, uncivilized race of men who live in caves widely separated from one another, devoid of community or council, poor in speech, and without agriculture, shipbuilding, or most other arts: "Each one is the law for his own wives and children and cares nothing about the others." Like a mountain peak in size and shape, the Cyclops has a single round, immobile eye in the midline; he thus lacks a horizon, all depth of perspective, and can see only what is immediately before him, here and now. His one eye, lined up directly over his mouth, seems to serve the mouth (like a telescopic sight for capture) rather than the mind, as a window for the wondering beholding of the articulated world—from these features alone, we learn that Cyclopes still dwell among us. Each Cyclops herds sheep and goats for milk and meat yet lives with them in the same cave. He shows compassion and affection for his own sheep but not for a strange man. His barbaric treatment of strangers is central to his ways, and reveals his defective understanding of, and relation to, the world.

On first encountering Odysseus and his men, the Cyclops immediately interrogates them, in the familiar Homeric manner, but before and, as we shall see, without the customary hospitality: "Strangers, who are you? From where do you come sailing over the watery ways? Is it on some business, or are you recklessly roving as pirates do, when they sail on the salt sea and venture their lives as they wander, bringing evil to alien people?"[4] Recognizing the danger implicit in the lack of hospitality, Odysseus answers, concluding with a supplication, and reminding Polyphemos of the gods and their support of strangers: "Therefore respect the gods, O best of men. We are your suppliants, and Zeus the guest god, who stands behind all strangers with honors due them, avenges any wrong toward strangers and suppliants."[5]

Polyphemos responds pitilessly:

> "Stranger, you are a simple fool, or come from far off, when you tell me to avoid the wrath of the gods or fear them. The Cyclopes do not concern themselves over Zeus of the aegis, nor any of the rest of the blessed gods, since we are far better than they, and for fear of the hate of Zeus I would not spare you or your companions either, if the fancy took me otherwise."[6]

Hospitality denied foreshadows hospitality defied. Within moments Polyphemos catches up two of Odysseus's men, dashes them mortally against the ground "like killing puppies," and then cuts them up limb by limb, "and like a lion reared in the hills, without leaving anything, [eats] them, entrails, flesh, and marrowy bones alike." A little later, unsoftened by Odysseus's pleasing—albeit cunning—gift of the divine wine, Polyphemos ridicules Odysseus's request for reciprocity: "Then I will eat Nobody [that is, Odysseus] *after* his friends, and the others I will eat first, and *that* shall be my guest present to you."[7]

The Cyclops is exactly that beastly human type spoken of by Aristotle who is, because separated from law and justice, the worst of all animals, "most unholy and savage, and worst in regard to sex and eating." Not so much his killing but his eating of Odysseus's men arouses our revulsion and horror. These feelings bespeak a crucial insight: Cannibalism is that extreme of inhumanity regarding eating, more beastly than anything found among the beasts. Let us try to make sense of this judgment.

To begin with, the Cyclops, though he has but weak relations with and no concern for his neighbors, is hostile only to strangers but gentle, even affectionate, to his own dumb animals. For him not nature or the divine but "one's-own-ness" is supreme. He respects no order, natural or human, save the order of his own making, reflected in his utter indifference to the bounty and beauty of his immediate environment and in his marked preference for the things he owns: He sups with his own rams and sheep but eats outside members of his own species. The human stranger he regards as meat, mere material for consumption. He denies, therefore, the importance and dignity of the human form, and therewith—though he does not know it—also his own dignity as human. Though he goes on two legs, there is nothing upright in his posture and attitude toward the world. One-eyed, without perspective, he is confused about what is truly near and far, about what is superficial and what goes deep, indeed, about that which is truly his own—the human soul and its openness to learning and loving. Odysseus's subsequent blinding of Polyphemos thus accomplishes physiologically what has long been true of him, humanly speaking.

The Cyclops is blind not only to natural form and, in principle therefore, to his own humanity. He is also, paradoxically, blind to the meaning of necessity. He plants no crops, thinks nothing of past or future, and seems oblivious to his own mortality. He eats because he is hungry but knows not what it means. His lack of pity—he is often called pitiless and merciless—stems from his inability to understand that he too might one day suffer similar evils. Having denied the dignity of the human form, in turning men into meat, he denies also death by swallowing entirely its evidence, "without leaving anything . . . entrails, flesh, and marrowy bones alike."

In denying both natural form and natural necessity, the Cyclops stands in the world as tyrant. Everything in the world is appropriable and appropriate for his voracious, limitless appetites. No natural form or given order elicits his respect or reverence. He lives believing nothing to be stronger or higher than himself, looking down even on Zeus and the blessed gods, those idealizations of the human form, the remembrance of whom in turn sanctifies and elevates human life. Like all tyrants, who make *themselves* the measure of all things, the Cyclops lives in folly no less than in wickedness, *for he lives in contradiction with the truth about himself.*

The same charge can be sustained, I believe, against those (actual) cannibalistic cultures, for example, the Aztecs, which—unlike the (merely fictional) Cyclops—practice *ritual* cannibalism, though this goes beyond our present subject, the meaning of the nearly universal prohibition against eating human flesh. These cannibals don't appear to ignore the distinction of the human form, for it is crucial that it be a human being whom they offer up to their god and whose flesh they share with the divine in a sacramental meal. One could even try to argue that they appreciate more than the mind-body dualists the unity of body and soul (for which I argued in the last two chapters), and that their act of human sacrifice proves their appreciation of the incarnation of spirituality, which they make manifest symbolically in the sacramentalizing of the victim's body in this holy feast. They may even be mindful of the special human powers of the chosen victim, which they seek to gain by eating him. But their way of noticing the human form and its powers is, in fact, perverse and is based on a profound misunderstanding. For one thing, although they see the victim in some sense as human—that is, as human rather than as animal—they do not really know what that means, for they neither respect that visible humanity in the victim nor see it as the same as, or as the equal of, their own. For how else could they believe that they serve the spiritual longings of their own heart by offering up someone else's? Also, they err "philosophically" in mistaking the dead body for the enlivened whole; they treat the dismembered "parts" as if they still carry vital powers. Ironically their practices implicitly deny the difference between the living and the dead; like the Cyclops, they ignore both the dignity of the integrated human form and the brute fact of its irreversible disintegration in death. Curiously, not unlike the corporealists whose views we criticized in Chapter 1, they do not know that the powers they seek to incorporate inhere only in the materials *as formed* and whole, and that ingestion (not to speak of the ritual killing) is form destroying. Ritual or no ritual, to treat human beings as food is perversion.*

Vitalism: Hospitality Parodied

Cannibalism is one antithesis of hospitality that denies the worth of the human form by treating men as food, and that denies the importance of nature by exaggerating the importance of one's own. But there are seemingly opposite customs that, in an apparent excess of hospitality, equally undermine human dignity by indiscriminately feeding all men without question and by utterly denying the importance of one's own. Such men, too, did Odysseus meet, in the adventure just before that of the Cyclops:

> But on the tenth day we landed in the country of the Lotus-Eaters, who live on a flowering food, and there we set foot on the mainland, and fetched water, and my companions soon took their supper there by the fast ships. But after we had tasted of food and drink, then I sent some of my companions ahead, telling them to find out what men, eaters of bread, might live here in this country. . . . My men went on and presently met the Lotus-Eaters, nor did these Lotus-Eaters have any thoughts of

---

*Cannibalism must surely be a bone in the throat of our now fashionable cultural relativism, which will stretch and strain not to pass negative judgment on the sincere ways and beliefs of other cultures. Surely we don't want to say that a sincere, even sincerely spiritual, intention is sufficient to justify every incarnation of it?!

Ritual cannibalism is featured in the famous story about funeral practices, told by Herodotus to illustrate the power of custom and culture: The Greeks burn the bodies of dead ancestors whereas the Indians (a tribe called Callatians) eat them, and neither side can be induced even once to adopt the practice of the other. (*The History* 3.38) But a careful analysis of the story shows that although custom may be king over all, some kings are better than others: We learn that (and also why) the Greek custom is superior, the Indian inferior. (See my "Thinking About the Body," in *Toward a More Natural Science*, especially pp. 280–281 and 295–298).

destroying our companions, but only gave them lotus to taste of. But any of them who ate the honey-sweet fruit of lotus was unwilling to take any message back, or to go away, but they wanted to stay there with the lotus-eating people, feeding on lotus, and forget the way home.[8]

Unlike the Cyclops, the Lotus-Eaters are gentle, peaceful, and hospitable. They gather the flowering food—which they apparently do not plant—and offer it to whoever comes along, without any conversation before or after. They speak not a word, and neither do Odysseus's men, once they have eaten lotus. One use of the mouth drives out the other. Odysseus's men are unwilling to give messages, and Odysseus must forcibly drag them away weeping because they would "forget the way home." The Lotus-Eaters have no civilization or identifiable place; they have their flowers and honey-sweet food, and from this they take their identity and their names. *These* people, it seems, indeed become or are what they eat.

These gentle folk, these flower children and hippies of old, live in a timeless and purposeless hedonic present, free from all troubles and harshness, and blow their minds for pleasure. They take no trouble, face no trouble, and give no trouble. They see no evil, hear no evil, and speak no evil. Yet they *are* an evil, and if unopposed would sweetly disseminate the evils that come from mistaking the pleasant for the good. Their excessive and indiscriminate generosity, in connection with the pleasures of mere life, destroys the conditions for a *good* life and corrupts those who accept their dangerous gift of food. In forgetting about home, Odysseus's men—like their rootless hosts—lose all ties to past and future. They lack all remembrance of mortality and necessity, and therewith lose also the dignity and nobility of living freely and self-consciously *against* them. Their moral defect is matched by an intellectual defect: The distinctions between home and not-home, between kin (or friend) and stranger, between man and animal, between oneself and one's food are all obliterated or undermined. The Lotus-Eaters are tyrants inside-out; they use their freedom and will to annihilate freedom and will—their own and everyone else's. Their excess of apparent humaneness results in dehumanization. Freely giving lotus is a *parody* of human hospitality, for it allows people anonymously and silently to become identified merely with their food—eaters of honey-sweet fruits of lotus.

Subhuman Eating: The Worst and the Lowest

In the case of the Cyclopes and the Lotus-Eaters, we see how two opposite errors regarding the fitting custom of hospitality simultaneously degrade host and guest, in the one case in violence, in the other in mindlessness. Noticing a common outcome from opposed beginnings, we wonder what cannibals and flower children have in common. Is the suggested similarity just an accident, at best a figment of Homer's poetic imagination, at worst only of my own? I doubt it. Consider briefly another pair of (East Indian) tribes, described together by Herodotus, apparently to make a similar point:

> Eastward of these Indians are another tribe, called Padaeans, who are wanderers, and live on raw flesh. This tribe is said to have the following customs: If one of their number be ill, man or woman, they take the sick person, and if he be a man, the men of his acquaintance proceed to put him to death, because, they say, his flesh would be spoilt for them if he pined and wasted away with sickness. The man protests he is not ill in the least; but his friends will not accept his denial—in spite of all he can say, they kill him, and feast themselves on his body. So also if a woman be sick, the women, who are her friends, take her and do with her exactly the same as the men. If one of them reaches to old age, about which there is seldom any question, as commonly before that time they have had some disease or other, and so have been put to death—but if a man, notwithstanding, comes to be old, then they offer him in sacrifice to their gods, and afterwards eat his flesh.
>
> There is another set of Indians whose customs are very different. They kill nothing alive, sow no seed, have no dwelling houses, and eat grass. There is a plant which grows in their country, bearing seed about the size of millet-seed in a calyx: their wont is to gather this seed and having boiled it, calyx and all, to use it for food. If one of them is attacked with sickness, he goes forth in the wilderness, and lies down to die; no one has the least concern either for the sick or the dead.
>
> All the tribes I have mentioned copulate openly like the brute beasts.[9]

The first tribe are nomads; the second have no houses. The former eat raw flesh and kill their own to eat them (the killing is in the service of the eating, to prevent disease from spoiling the meat); the latter eat boiled wild seed and grass and kill nothing ensouled. The first kill the sick early, eat the dead, and sacrifice the old to their gods, afterward eating their flesh; the second neglect the sick and dead and give no burial. Both these extreme carnivores and these extreme herbivores copulate shamelessly in public like the beasts, suggesting—despite their polar differences regarding killing—a common lack of shame, and thus of humanity.

How are these vegetarians like these cannibals? The crucial point is this: Both deny the difference between man and animal, and therewith the importance of form. The Padaeans, pure carnivores, treat even their best friends as good meat: They homogenize men and animals, in mind and deed, on the principle that flesh is flesh no matter what the form. The nameless vegetarians, at first glance preferable because less brutal, turn out also to be homogenizers: Vitality is vitality, no matter what the form. They also assimilate man to the animals: Both are seen as equally inedible because both are equally ensouled. Their implicit insistence on the supremacy of life, health, and sentience denies not only their humanity and the dignity of speech and consciousness. They also fly from necessity and especially mortality, as manifest in their indifference to burial. They close their eyes to the bittersweet truth about life itself—that to be life, life must live with and against necessity. They wish instead for a different world, absolutely free of necessity and harshness—a world of ease, pleasure, and comfort—in which the lion will lie down with the lamb, and all will eat seeds, delicately boiled in their shells, and graze away indefinitely. These men lack even the dignity and nobility of the wild animals; at least in this respect they, too, might be said to number if not among the worst then at least among the lowest of the animals—nameless, godless, spiritless, and living the life fit for cattle.

The Human Food

Not all vegetarians are guilty of the vitalistic failure to distinguish between man and the animals, on the grounds that life is life no matter what the form. In addition to these thoughtless pre- or subhuman forms of fruit picking and seed gathering, there are higher forms of vegetarianism, in which human beings, by acts of thoughtful generosity and self-restraint, curb their appetite for various kinds of meat they enjoy because they sense at least a partial kinship with at least some of the higher animals. To be sure, some of the current arguments for vegetarianism—and especially some arguments for animal *rights*—do in fact proceed by denying the difference of man and by foolishly deriding as "speciesism" all human self-regard and -preference. Against all reason these arguments attack as illegitimate the preferential love of one's own kind and deny the special natural dignity of the human form, which, I claim, we human beings do not invent but merely discover, thanks to the special powers of discovery on which our dignity partly rests. Indeed their argument for the moral equality of man and animals refutes itself: Only such a *uniquely* dignified being can appreciate the splendor of other species and can respond to their needs with moral self-restraint. The tapeworm and the spider, the swordfish and the shark, the frog and the crocodile, the gnatcatcher and the eagle, the hyena and the boar, even the intelligent dolphin and the chimpanzee—none of these knows anything about animal rights or curbs its appetite out of compassion or respect for fellow creatures.

Nevertheless the practice of higher vegetarianism may be more defensible than some of the arguments made on its behalf, especially given our current, often unspeakably cruel, practices of raising and keeping animals for food. And, in any age, a philosophical, not to say superhuman, self-control and magnanimity might be part of a model of human (if not more-than-human) perfection* The gods, after all, eat only ambrosia, an immortal (*a*, privative + *brotós*, mortal) elixir of life, which is, of course, without *brótos*, without running blood or gore. (There is, I am told, even some slight evidence to suggest that Socrates was a vegetarian.)

Yet whatever may be said of gods and such remarkable human beings, one must also face the fact that most human beings are or would be meat eaters; that is, when they can be. Indeed one must face the possibility that animal meat—not fruits or seeds or grasses, any more than human flesh—is *the* human food, the food human beings eat when they first rise to their humanity, the food that marks their self-conscious recognition of their difference from the other animals. According to Genesis—about which we shall have more to say in the last chapter—our earliest ancestors were originally strict frugivores (fruit pickers), but only until they acquired freedom and

---

*We shall explore the biblical treatment of this subject in the last chapter.

self-consciousness; that is, until they became truly humanized; and when God starts the human world a second time with Noah, under its first rules of law and justice, the shedding of human blood is forbidden, but animals are given to men as food.

Rousseau, in his account of human beginnings (in the *Second Discourse*), argues that protoman, when he was but a beast, ate mainly fruit and nuts; but our rise from animality began, according to Rousseau, largely in a dietary shift toward meat (prompted presumably by scarcity), requiring the hunting of wild animals for food. The need to defend ourselves against the predatory beasts somehow led to the discovery of "natural arms"—that is, to the insight that what is for itself, say, a branch of a tree could become, for a human being, a weapon. The making of tools of capture—fishhook, sling, and bow and arrow—stretched the inventive mind; making necessary comparisons with one's prey and predators—say, regarding strength or speed or boldness—stretched the distinguishing mind. The necessary and emotionally charged encounters with the animals eventually awakened human self-consciousness; man's superiority over the animals began rapidly to increase once he became aware of it. Here, according to Rousseau, in the food-seeking encounters with other animals, is the awakening of humanity, which is to say the beginning of human *perfectibility*, that uniquely human power-and-desire for "improvement," always to make life a little better than it now is. In addition hunting rewarded and selected for new virtues: moral virtues such as endurance, patience, tenacity, and boldness; intellectual virtues such as attentiveness, perspicacity, and cunning. New modes of sociality also followed the shift to meat: The need to prepare and apportion the produce of the hunt became the basis of the family meal, hardly a necessity among fruit pickers and nut gatherers, who need not share their directly edible goods. Moreover, it was hunting that first led men from different families to cooperate with one another; their first hunting parties may have been only aggregates of selfishness, but the habits of cooperation thus acquired would eventually lead to more durable and friendly associations. If our protohuman forebears had a nature or lived in a world that required or enabled them to live only on berries and nuts and mother's milk, one wonders—with Rousseau's help—whether or how rapidly humanization would have occurred.

Perhaps the most famous text that suggests the connection between meat eating and humanization is Plato's *Republic*. Early in the
dialogue, while constructing in speech the first or healthy city,
Socrates discusses what the healthy people will eat:

> "For food they will prepare barley meal and wheat flour; they will cook it
> and knead it. Setting out noble loaves of barley and wheat on some
> reeds or clean leaves, they will stretch out on rushes strewn with yew
> and myrtle and feast themselves and their children. Afterwards they will
> drink wine and, crowned with wreathes, sing of the gods."[10]

Glaucon, Socrates' spirited interlocutor, interrupts almost immediately to object that these men are feasting "without relishes": The
Greek word he uses, translated "relish," is *opson*, which means, literally, "something to the bread" and, more specifically, meat. He com-
plains that Socrates is creating a city of pigs—that is, a city without
meat and all that goes with it, a city devoted to mere life and health
and the simple bodily pleasures, not to great human achievements.
From Glaucon's demand for meat—which Socrates does not oppose—begins the humanization of the city-in-speech. Humanization
depends on the addition of the spirited element (*thymos*), which not
only likes meat but gets angry, is ambitious, seeks distinction, defends one's friends and one's honor, competes in athletics, confronts
death, combats harshness, wages war, loves victory, and gets up off
the ground to make a stand in defense of hearth and country. Spiritedness is a dangerous business, as Socrates clearly shows; it introduces a feverishness into human affairs that needs to be tamed and
moderated. Yet he welcomes it nonetheless. For the aspiration to live
better than cows and pigs seems to come along with the appetite to
eat them. To be sure, taming the spirited element in some human
beings may lead them eventually back to a philosophically based (a
perhaps more-than-human) vegetarianism, but meat, according to
Plato (and Genesis), seems to be the food of man as man.

And yet one wonders. Glaucon, after all, asked for relish, for
"something to the bread," something that would make *bread* taste
better. When Odysseus arrives in Lotus Land, he sends his companions to find out "what men, *eaters of bread* [italics added], might live
here in this country." And, in Genesis, when God sends man out
from the fruitful garden to begin his troubled (because humanized)

existence, He predicts that he will be an eater of bread in the sweat of his face. However much human spiritedness loves meat, man as the rational animal, on the threshold of civilization and ethics, is an eater of bread. Bread, even more than meat, is the human food.

There are numerous reasons why this is so. In eating meat, men do pretty much as the carnivores. True, cooking for taste and edibility is a specifically human addition, but we practice it only as a matter of custom. As meat-eaters, men and wolves do not differ according to nature. Our bodies are prepared to digest raw meat, and many cultures actually eat meat or fish without cooking it first. Moreover, the transformations of cooking flesh make relatively few changes in the meat and, more important, require relatively few changes in human psyche or way of life, compared with those connected with making bread. Indeed eating bread involves artfully overcoming the natural incapacity for digesting grain that separates man from, say, the horse. In addition, eating bread both requires and effects massive transformations in the human way of life.

First, remarkable insights are required to lead the mind from wheat to bread: Human beings must discover that certain harvestable and storable but inedible seeds, if ground, will yield flour, which, if moistened, can be kneaded into dough, which, if baked, becomes an edible, relatively nonspoilable product. Not for nothing did the ancients attribute to the gods the gift of the secret of making bread: It boggles the mind to see how any human being could have figured it all out from scratch. Next are the various arts of agriculture, from plowing, fertilizing, and sowing to irrigating, harvesting, and storing—many of which involve other arts, such as metalworking, toolmaking, and animal taming. Next, and vastly more important than these matters of know-how, are the disciplined changes in the human psyche and way of life that the practice of agriculture requires. Men must be willing to settle down and remain attached to a particular place, and an open and exposed place at that. Their natural indolence and their desire for prompt satisfaction of need must be overcome. Men must be able to plan for and anticipate the future, and be willing to defer gratification, in order to accept as a regular way of life laboring today for a goal far in the future—and all for something for which there may be perfectly adequate (and better tasting) substitutes already at hand in nature.

With agriculture a new human relationship to nature and to fellow man emerges: On the one hand there is the nascent idea of ownership, of property in nature, perhaps tied to the admixture of one's own labor, first to the agricultural product and then to the soil; the idea of appropriation eventually makes necessary rules of justice, governing what is mine and thine, and points to new and more complex social arrangements.* On the other hand, because the farmer places all his hopes in his crops and is thus more vulnerable to disaster than if he gathered one meal at a time, bread-eating man turns an anxiously watchful eye toward heaven, and builds towers and plots the motions of the stars the better for to predict—and perhaps control—the behavior of the powers aloft. It is fitting that Cain, the first farmer and hence a man eager for rain, should (without instruction) devise the practice of sacrificing to what is on high. A transformer of nature, a practitioner of art, a restrainer of his own appetites, a settled social creature soon with laws and rules of justice, poised proudly yet apprehensively between the earth and the cosmic powers—man becomes human with the eating of bread.

Many peoples of the earth, of course, do not eat bread; hence bread cannot be literally *the* human food. But much of what has here been said about bread is also applicable to rice, a grain that is the staff of life to half the population of the globe. Its cultivation requires many of the same psychic changes and technical innovations, and produces many of the same social transformations, as does the growth of wheat for bread. As in classical Greece, so in classical China, meat was regarded as relish to the rice: *Fan*, the word for cooked rice in modern China, is synonymous with food in general. (The informal Chinese greeting, "Have you eaten today?"—the social equivalent of our "How are you?"—is, literally, "Have you had rice today?") As in the West, so in the East, this massive reliance on

---

*This new dispensation, though it is the foundation of civilization, is not simply to be celebrated. Rousseau, with his usual hyperbole, vividly presents the problem:

> The first person who, having fenced off a plot of ground, took it into his head to say *this is mine* and found people simple enough to believe him, was the true founder of civil society. What crimes, wars, murders, what miseries and horrors would the human race have been spared by someone who, uprooting the stakes or filling in the ditch, had shouted to his fellow-men: Beware of listening to this impostor; you are lost if you forget that the fruits belong to all and the earth to no one! But it is very likely that by then things had already come to the point where they could no longer remain as they were.[11]

grain transforms man's relation to the earth and greatly alters human society, pushing it toward civilization.[12]

No reader of Rousseau will ever be able to say again that civilization is in every respect an advance: The ideas of technical mastery, property, and the relations of dependency and inequality they establish are even more dangerous than the lust for meat. The rational element, no less than the spirited one, needs further restraint and education. Still the journey toward disciplining *Omnivorosus erectus* is well begun in these delimitations of the proper food: bread (or rice) and something to go with it, but not human flesh.

If bread or rice is the rational animal's calculated food of choice as the staple of life, and if meat satisfies the animal or spirited element of the soul, catering also to taste, a complete account of *the* human food must do justice also to our aesthetic interest, to our concern with taste and flavor. Some of this is, of course, implicit in the desire for meat—*opson*, relish, something to add flavor to the bread. But another leading candidate, ubiquitous in its use, is salt, the first spice of life.

Salt is, of course, not a peculiarly human craving. Herbivorous animals, like the cow or the deer, love salt, whereas carnivorous animals and meat-hunting men apparently find enough salt in the blood of animals to satisfy them. But for human beings salt use is clearly connected with the rise of civilization—specifically agriculture and derivatively metallurgy:

> Australian aborigines and American Indians and Inuit often knew no salt. Early human settlements were apparently not built to be near salt-springs. Human beings, it seems, learn about salt (and become addicted to it) at a very precise moment in their history: when they cease being almost exclusively carnivorous and learn to eat vegetables in quantities available only when they grow them themselves. When people begin not only to eat a lot of vegetables, but to reduce the salt content in their food by boiling it—a cooking method which presupposes the ability to make metal pots that can be set directly over a fire—then salt becomes more desirable still.[13]

Until the last century ordinary salt was a rare and precious commodity. People traded for it, paid taxes with it, and received it as wages (salary, from *sal*, Latin for salt; "he is not worth his salt").

Near the sea, salt was farmed and harvested in artificial tidal ponds; inland it was mined from beneath the earth. Like bread an expression of prudent concern for the future, it was formerly widely used to conserve and preserve foods from spoilage. But it was and is loved for its taste, in amounts above and beyond what is needed physiologically.

By some not-well-understood process, salt in food enables us to taste not only the salt but also the flavor of the dish that is salted. It brings the underlying flavors to life; for those who are addicted to it, without salt all foods taste flat, dull, or not at all. Of course, the tastelessness of saltlessness can be remedied by any of hundreds of other spices, but salt stands first in enhancing the aesthetic experience of a meal, not only in fact but also symbolically: "Its sharp taste suggests sharpness of intellect and liveliness of mind. Salt (bright, dry, titillating, and dynamic) is synonymous in several languages with wit and wisdom."[14] Indeed in some cultures it is salt, not meat, which is treated like the relish for the bread:

> Bread and salt are customarily offered in Russia (where the word for "hospitality" means literally "bread-salt") and in other countries, as a sign of welcome to a guest: bread and salt symbolize the precious stores of the house, the fruits of the host's labour, his patience, his ingenuity, his civilized foresight and preparedness.[15]

In many of these same places, a present of bread and salt is the traditional housewarming gift, for a house thus equipped is thereby a human home, sufficient both for itself and for offering hospitality.

Yet our attempt to match foods to the special features of the human soul will remain incomplete unless we mention the grape, fruit of the vine, and its spiritual essence, wine. Wine at least as much as bread is a peculiarly human "food." Animals eat fruits and vegetables and every conceivable kind of flesh; some animals, as we have noted, lick salt. Only human beings ferment the grape. As with bread, the discovery of fermentation and its psychic properties is a great mystery. Here also the Greeks (and others) claim that it must have been a god who showed man how to make wine—not only because man could not, without divine inspiration, have discovered the process by himself but also because wine inspires elevated and extraordinary states of soul.

In moderate amounts it inspires and encourages. Yielding more than nourishment, it provides partial relief from the hardships of life and the need to sweat for our bread. It gladdens the heart, loosens the tongue, and enlivens the soul. Under its influence we forget our troubles, lose our inhibitions, speak our minds: *In vino veritas*. A psychic midwife, wine delivers us of hidden insights and affections. It can even transport us toward realms apart—in love, in song, in ecstasy, in "madness." Not by accident did Plato make a symposium— a drinking party (*syn-* + *posis*, "together" + "drink")—the setting for the only Socratic dialogue that features a contest between poets and a philosopher and that concerns the nature of a god, the god Eros.

Yet it is with Socrates in mind that some friends of human rationality are disinclined to give wine any such deep human significance. Granting that a certain refinement of discrimination may come from learning to distinguish a good wine from a bad, and granting even that conviviality may be obtained through the measured use of wine, they nevertheless remain doubtful about wine's contribution to the improvement or perfection of either the rational or the moral life. Noting that Socrates, in the *Symposium* and elsewhere, drinks everyone else under the table but does not himself get drunk, they argue that wine may be therapeutic for disharmonious souls but that the fully rational and harmonious human soul has no need of such external stimulants. Perhaps so. Still, one wonders, if this be so, why Socrates—being supremely rational and not in need of wine—chose to drink at all. Must we infer, from the fact that he never got drunk, that he never got high? And leaving the heroically sober Socrates aside, friends of reason on further reflection can make an adequate defense of wine and show its significant contributions to the humanization of life. Indeed Socrates himself seemed to recognize its utility, at least for others.

If human rationality means only or primarily the responsible, calculating, prudent attention to the necessities of life (or the methodical problem-solving conduct of modern science), then wine may be in fact a superfluity. But reason, fully grown and taking cognizance of itself, transcends the limits of such instrumental rationality. As we saw in Chapter 2, reason can discern, behold, and bespeak the forms of things in appreciative awareness. Next, working reflexively, reason becomes aware of its own wondrous powers and of the mystery of life that makes such self-conscious openness to truth possible. And, as we shall see in Chapters 5 and 6, reason through its cultural forms can bring us beyond reason, face to face with the mystery of being altogether. Man's rational capacity, useful of course in meeting necessity, acquires a life of its own and takes man beyond necessity into a realm of freedom, in which heart and mind are liberated for the pleasures of awareness, insight, friendship, song, and spirituality.

Wine represents and encourages this elevated life beyond necessity and calculating rationality. Its very existence depends on surplus; one does not ferment the grapes or grain needed for survival. At a meal, too, it is a sign of freedom and grace, and also their cause. Offered to guests it betokens easy generosity, demonstrating that one clearly has more than the necessities for oneself. Indeed—to reconnect this discussion of the human food more explicitly to the humanizing custom of hospitality—drinking wine with someone goes beyond breaking bread. For wine permits and encourages us to let down our guard, to be at ease and in intimate communion with one another; the offer of wine expresses trust in and desire for such intimacy. For only with certain kinds of people, those who already are or we hope will become our friends, do we let wine dissolve our prudent caution. If basic hospitality, as was said, is an assertion against the dog-eat-dog character of the world, sharing a bottle of wine lifts us to the next step: the assertion of the friend-loves-friend possibility of the world, of human intimacy founded on more than common neediness.*

But wine in excess does not elevate, liberate, or gladden: It makes men wild. Or perhaps one should say that it lets loose powerful animalistic forces latent in the soul; forces that wash out our ability to make distinctions; that work to overthrow our customs and restraints; that conduce to violence; that seek, as it were, to dissolve all form and formality into the primordial watery chaos. These wild and dangerous powers the Greeks attributed to the god Dionysus (Bacchus to the Romans), the god connected with blood and the sap of life and with orgiastic animal sacrifices, the god responsible for bringing wine to mankind. Though the dionysiac is the enemy of civilization, civilized and upright man's failure to recognize and placate

---

*I owe this last insight to Steve Vanderslice, and the discussion of the last two paragraphs to conversation with faculty and students at the University of Dallas. Yet I would also add that real friends do not need wine to attain and enjoy friendship.

the powers of Dionysus could lead to his ruin.[16] Festivals that require ritualized drinking in large amounts—the Bacchanalia of the Greeks, Purim among the Jews—are an attempt to give the dionysiac its due, but only by bringing it under strict regulation.

Wine, like the other human foods we have discussed, thus partakes of the moral ambiguity of the human. Like man himself it can enhance and it can destroy his humanity. Like the temptation to brutality connected with meat eating; like the temptation to domination and pride implicit in the institution of property, linked with bread and agriculture; like the temptation to excessive pursuit of the tasty at the expense of the healthful, implicit in the craving of salt and spices—so too the temptation to violent chaos is present in the gladdening fruit of the vine. Thus merely ruling out the eating of human flesh, though certainly just, is not enough to bring human eating under the aegis of virtue. *How* we eat, more than *what* we eat, will be decisive.

In this chapter I have tried to show how insight into the nature and meaning *of* eating could help us distinguish between better and worse customs *for* eating, in the limited but important case of hospitality and its perversions. In the following chapters we shall consider many more customs and practices, regarding how as well as what one eats; the meaning of cooking; eating at table, together, with implements; the ritualization of the meal; and the refinements of dining and feasting. We shall meet the virtues of graciousness and moderation, governing manner no less than quantity, and best summarized in the maxim, No involuntary participation in another's digestion. Eventually we shall even look at customs that seek to sanctify eating, in recognition of the mysterious source not only of food and living forms but also of mind lodged in living bodies and capable of wonder and self-conscious reflection about food, living forms, and mind in living bodies.

This chapter has laid the foundation. It begins our demonstration of how knowledge and appreciation of form, necessity, and the natural order—knowledge accessible to life only in man—could just possibly contribute to our knowledge of good and bad, so that the most polymorphous animal may avoid becoming the most perverse animal and come to be instead the truly upright animal, as implied and, as it were, advertised in his posture.

4

Enhancing Uprightness
Civilized Eating

Whoever eats in the street or at any public place acts like a dog.
—Talmud
(Kiddushin 40b)

The upright animal's first and most universal custom regarding eating is a taboo against eating the upright animal. Recognizing and (at least tacitly) appreciating the human form, we restrain ourselves from reducing other human beings to mere meat. Recognizing also the common neediness of all human beings—the elevated human form persists only because lowly animal necessity is met—we extend ourselves in acts of hospitality, offering food and drink to the stranger. Through these customs, negative and positive, our peculiarly human self-consciousness both restricts omnivorousness and elevates the meeting of bodily necessity in the direction and support of uprightness. Our humanity thus recognized and acknowledged, we sow the seeds of community in breaking bread together. Company (from *com-*, "together," and *panis*, "bread") comes to accompany the bread.

Precisely because human beings usually eat together, the customs of eating govern not only what human beings eat but also where, when, with whom, and especially how. The manner(s) of eating, even more than what gets eaten, expresses the humanity of the eaters, at least as they have come to understand it. Though the specifics differ markedly from one society to the next, all cultures have explicit or tacit norms governing the "how" of eating—norms that serve to define the group, ease interpersonal relations, and help civilize the human animal.

What exactly do we mean by "civilize"? And how do the customs of civility relate to our underlying nature? Though we will always be attending to these large questions as we proceed, it would be desirable, on the threshold of our discussions of civilized eating, to make these matters briefly thematic.

Civility, originally a political notion referring to the things of the citizen (Latin *civis*, "citizen"), has come to mean the social condition of being civilized. Hard to define concretely, it may be understood as the opposite of being barbarous, rustic, rude, crude, coarse, blunt, violent, bestial, disorderly, undignified, primitive, "natural," or wild. Civility comprises behavior thought to be appropriate to the everyday intercourse of civilized people: regulated bodily posture and carriage and controlled functions of eating, drinking, excretion, sleeping, and sex; ordinary courtesy, propriety, and politeness; and decorous and tactful speech and deed in all usual social relations.

Elaborating the elements of basic civility with respect to eating will be the main business of this chapter.*

Civility, though it sounds like something praiseworthy, especially when seen as the opposite of the barbarous and the bestial, is not without its critics. It has been attacked, in the name of "naturalness" and spontaneity, as being insincere, false, and arbitrary. It has been attacked, in the name of *Kultur*, as being superficial, routine, and mindless. It has been attacked, in the name of morality, as being etiquette not ethics, mere outward appearance rather than deep excellence or right. And it has been attacked, in the name of high wit and amusement, as being too concerned with our embodiment, too serious, and too much enslaved by shame. Though these criticisms are not without their force, it is my contention that they are finally wrong. Civility, while different from high culture, is not at odds with it; one can appreciate Beethoven without being a boor. Etiquette and ethics, rightly understood, are in fact continuous, partly because character is often revealed in outward display; moreover, the principles of self-command and consideration for others shown in "small manners" are of a piece with virtue and justice. Indeed civility may very well be the heart of the ethics of everyday life. Also, as we shall see, the finest wit will not be shameless, and the laughter it seeks and gets is itself a product of our cultivated and communicative embodiment; the coarse rustic is a humorless fellow.

The challenge from the side of nature and naturalness is more complicated, inasmuch as it depends on knowing whether the natural is primarily the native and uninstructed or whether it is the mature and cultivated. Here we again come close to the deepest concerns of this inquiry, the relation between custom and mores and our underlying nature. Do customs of civilized eating suppress our nature? Tame it? Deform it? Transform it? Adorn it? Perfect it? Elevate it? Or transcend it? Even if these cultural forms represent an improve-

---

*My treatment of the basic manners of eating will be guided by the overall argument of the book, and I make no pretense of comprehensiveness. Many fine books exist on this subject, ranging from works on etiquette to scholarly treatises. I would like to single out for special attention a superb recent book, *The Rituals of Dinner: The Origins, Evolution, Eccentricities, and Meaning of Table Manners*, by Margaret Visser, which appeared as my own essay was nearing completion. Every topic of interest is richly covered, and with cross-cultural detail; one can learn something interesting on every page.[1]

ment over our nature uninstructed, do they achieve it by rising above it, by realizing its immanent directions, or by lifting it above what it naturally is or suggests? Or does civility improve us by some combination of restraint and encouragement, suppression and elevation, purgation and purification? We approach the table with these questions in mind.

The Table, Place of the Meal

In most parts of the world people who come together for meals take food at a table. Some tables are round or square; others are elongated, either oval or rectangular. Some are tall, others short; some are . set on an elevated platform ("high table"), others in a slightly sunken hollow, with seating possible on the surrounding floor. Each of these variations has its own import and consequence for what takes place at the table; but because each is nonetheless a table—that is, each shares in this recognizable form—there is also a common theme, with a universal meaning of its own.

The table means the place of the meal. But the meal is already an advanced kind of eating, as Brillat-Savarin observed in his speculations on the origin of the pleasure of the table:

> Meals, in the sense which we attach to the word, began with the second age of man; that is to say, as soon as he ceased to live wholly on fruits [and nuts]. The dressing and apportioning of meat necessarily brought each family together, when the father distributed the produce of his hunting among his children, and later, the children, growing up, performed the same office for their aged parents.
>
> Those gatherings were at first confined to close relations, but gradually came to include friends and neighbours.
>
> Later, when the race of man was spread over the face of the earth, the weary traveller would find a place at those primitive meals, and tell his news of far-off lands: so hospitality was born, with rites held sacred by every nation; for the most savage tribe strictly bound itself to respect the life of him who had eaten of its own bread and salt.
>
> The meal may also be held responsible for the birth of languages, or at least for their elaboration, not only because it was a continually recurring cause of meetings, but also because the leisure which accompanies and succeeds the meal breeds confidence and loquacity.[2]

Having a meal at table is thus more than eating; it gives rise to "the pleasures of the table, which must be carefully distinguished from their necessary antecedent, the pleasure of eating." As Brillat-Savarin put it:

> The pleasure of eating is the actual and direct sensation of a need that is supplied.
>
> The pleasures of the table are reflex sensations, born of the various circumstances of fact, place, things, and persons attendant upon a meal.
>
> The pleasure of eating is common to ourselves and the lower animals, and depends on nothing but hunger and the means to satisfy it.
>
> The pleasures of the table are peculiar to mankind, and depend upon much antecedent care over the preparation of the meal, the choice of the place, and the selection of the guests.
>
> The pleasure of eating requires, if not hunger, at least appetite; the pleasures of the table, more often than not, are independent of the one and the other.[3]*

The civilization of eating, as we shall see, contributes much to enhancing the peculiarly human activities and pleasures of the table. But we proceed step by step, first by unpacking further the meaning of being at table.

To be at table means that one has removed oneself from business and motion and made a commitment to spend some time over one's meal. One commits oneself not only to time but also to an implicit plan of eating: We sit to eat and not just to feed, and to do so both according to a plan and with others. A decision to have a sit-down meal must precede its preparation, and the preparation is in turn guided by the particular plan that is the menu. Further, to be at table means, whether we know it or not, to make a commitment to form and formality. We agree, tacitly to be sure, to a code of conduct that does not apply when we privately raid the refrigerator or eat on the

---

*Brillat-Savarin continues: "Both of the two conditions may be observed at any dinner. Throughout the first course, and at the beginning of the session, each guest eats steadily, speaking not a word and deaf to anything which may be said; whatever his position in society, he frankly forgets all else but the performance of the great work. But when actual need begins to be satisfied, then the intellect awakes, talk becomes general, a new order of things is apparent, and he who hitherto was a mere consumer of food becomes a table companion of more or less charm, according to the qualities bestowed on him by the Master of all things." Though meals need not so sharply separate and sequence the two kinds of pleasures, the pleasures themselves are in their essence distinct. The interesting thing to follow is how regulating the first prepares and informs the second.

run or in our cars, or even when we munch sandwiches in front of the television with our buddies who have gathered to watch the Super Bowl. There we eat (or, more accurately, feed) side by side, as at a trough; in contrast, at table we all face not our food but one another. Thus we silently acknowledge our mutual commitment to share not only some food but also commensurate forms of commensal behavior. To be sure, the forms will vary depending on the occasion; the dinner table at home with family, the dinner table at home with guests, a banquet table at a testimonial dinner, and a picnic table in the park have different degrees and (in part) different kinds of formality, as do also the family breakfast and the family dinner. But in all cases there are forms that operate, regulate, and inform our behavior and that signify our peculiarly human way of meeting necessity.

A table, all by itself, silently conveys the beginning of this meaning. Unlike animals, most of whom feed directly off the ground, we take our food higher up. The table everywhere rises above the ground; even in Asia, where people eat lower than we do, the table is still separated from and higher than the floor.* The table's elevation is even the implicit idea in the ancient Greek word for "table," *trapeza*, thought to be derived from *tetra* + *peza*, "four-footed."

But though it is elevated, we who join it are not. We sit down to eat. The table goes with sitting (or kneeling), as opposed to both reclining and standing. In sitting down the upright creature abandons his mobility and his struggles against the larger world; he settles in, at least for awhile, to attend directly to his most basic needs. He adopts an intermediate, semiupright posture, a mean between life and lifelessness, between full wakefulness and sleep, between man and beast. Although submitting to what is necessary, the seated eater does not abandon his human attitude; even while resting himself in part from the effort to stand erect, he persists in the effort to keep his spine straight. Indeed, our aspiration to uprightness is even supported by the relatively uncomfortable character of dining room chairs (compared with "easy" living room chairs). With their help we straighten our backs, holding our upper half erect. Our lower half we both yield to nature and hide beneath the table. Only what is hu-

---

*Even at a picnic, which is the deliberate return to a more naturalistic, rustic, and informal mode of having a meal, a blanket (or other cloth) is spread on the ground as the symbolic equivalent of the raised table, the food is spread across the blanket, and all sit around its edges.

manly most significant do we keep in view, precisely as we meet the most elementary of animal necessities. The satyr's nether parts are kept out of sight and, we hope, out of mind. The opposite of upright conduct is conducted "under the table," the place where indiscretions tend to occur, the place where the philanderers play footsie or allow their hands to roam, the place where dogs hang out but where even small children are not supposed to go crawling around.

The Latin root of "table," *tabula*, a "board or slate," emphasizes not its legged-elevation but the hard and flat features of its surface. Any large board, horizontally placed, can become a *tabula*. Indeed in earlier times and in closer quarters a removable board (sometimes the same one used for sleeping) was set up and taken down before and after each meal (one board for both bed and board); not only the food but also the table was specially created for each dining occasion. The one large common board around which everybody sits is a symbol of the in-commonness of the activity. In fact, the table itself constitutes the individuals as a commensal (*com-*, together, + *mensa*, table) group, those who eat at table together. Those who take their food sitting or standing apart, even in the same room, are outsiders.

The table as such forms the group, but the shape of the table can both *in*form the group and express its order. Rectangular tables have two heads; fully round tables are headless. In the typical family meal, at a rectangular table, the father and mother occupy the head places; at a dinner party the host and hostess usually do, though occasionally pride of place is given to an honored guest. In both these less and more formal orderings, where one sits reveals one's relation to the order. The round table is more "egalitarian" and communal, and at least in principle more conducive to fostering a single conversation. In China, for these reasons, people formerly ate at circular tables, all sharing food from common dishes placed in the center. But this arrangement may not in fact always be the most commensal; a round table need not be very big before speech across it becomes impossible and each person's company gets reduced to two, one on either side, neither face-to-face. Curiously the more "hierarchical" rectangular table is often more compatible with greater intimacy.

The table is not only an instrument of ease and a cause of community. It is also an embodiment of human rationality, with its remarkable capacity to distinguish, to recognize, and especially to measure. The Sanskrit root *ma*, meaning "measure," is the likely source of the Latin word *mensa*, "table," as well as of the Greek word *metron*, "measure," which in turn is related also to the Latin verb *metior, metiri, mensus sum*, "to measure" (and with the dative, "to measure out," to distribute). Table is the place where food is apportioned, measured out, and distributed. In principle, it is not only doled out, it is meted out, in a *fitting* manner. Food is not just shared, it is shared justly: As the Homeric formula puts it, "And no man's hunger was denied a fair portion."* Justice in distribution of food, unlike justice in distribution of honors, must pay primary attention to need rather than to rank or merit. And because need need not be equal, neither must the portions: "Suppose that to eat ten mina is much, and two mina is little; it does not follow that the trainer will prescribe six mina; for perhaps even this will be large or small to the recipient. For Milo [a famous wrestler] this is little; for a beginner in gymnastic it is much." [4] Measured distribution, commensurate (*com-*, "with" + *mensus*, "measure") especially with need, is implicit in taking food together at table—that is, com-*mensa*-lly.

The table at which we sit is usually set. A single cloth covers the entire surface; individual place settings locate each person as a discrete participant in the shared meal, with each plate a promise of a personal portion to be received. The table itself may have other uses between meals. Its surface may be used for folding laundry, doing homework, paying bills, playing games. As mealtime approaches, however, the table is cleared of all matter unrelated to the ceremony of eating together; mail, newspapers, and scissors are removed, and the table gets set. The cloth separates eating from all other possible uses of the same table. A mark of distinction as well as of refinement, it demarcates and honors the common meal.

The principles of distinction and specialization inform also the settings of place. Multiple utensils—plates, glasses, cutlery—announce, even to the uninitiated, a more-than-one-course meal, and promise a temporal sequence. The use of utensils as such is of course mainly in the service of cleaner, neater, and more aesthetic eating—a matter to which we shall soon return. But the sanitizing

---

*In Homer the just king is he who knows the proper portion or share that one man gives another, the portion or share which the gods allot. The just king is therefore identical to the excellent host.

actual distance created and bridged by the utensils (the fork between hand and plate, the spoon between mouth and bowl, the knife between teeth and meat) is matched by greater psychic distance, and with it the possibilities for discriminating awareness. Indeed the plurality of tools—even if only a single knife, fork, and spoon—with their plurality of functions directly teaches also the need for attention and discrimination. The use of the various implements, our most visible activity at table, distracts both feeder and viewer from the homogenizing activity of feeding itself. More complicated than biting, chewing, and swallowing, the human and humanizing use of tools partially disguises the underlying animal necessity. For if human eating is more than feeding, and if the ordered meal encourages the discrimination of different tastes and courses, it makes sense to highlight these distinctions through the use of separate and specialized implements. Moreover, the formalized common rules governing their usage—which fork for the salad, which glass for the water—reinforce the sense of community, distinguishing those who are inside from those who are not.

The set table in the home is in fact an embodiment of the community that is the family. On special occasions, when the good china and the embroidered tablecloth are used, the family heirlooms reappear and, with them, memories of generous ancestors responsible for their existence in our midst. Even at the ordinary family dinner, the very existence of the set table, with something to be served on it, reminds everyone—especially the young—of our indebtedness to those who come before, those who are the provisioners. Being together at table thus encapsulates the meaning of being at home, where bonds born of biological necessity are celebrated and elevated by our (albeit tacit) recognition of the meaning of time and kinship and our expression of generous love and sustenance.

Basic Table Manners

Whether at home or away, whether as host or guest, being at table and eating with others obliges proper conduct. Table manners are learned first around the family table, as young children are taught by direct instruction and by example the dos and don'ts of dinner. We who are by now well habituated—and even the less mannerly among us—are almost certainly unaware of the countless rules that we unconsciously practice, each of which had to be learned. We are probably equally unaware of just how long it took the human race to articulate and institute these manners of civility.[5] A quick corrective for our ignorance on these points is available in early books on manners, whose reading show us both how much we have taken instruction and how much we needed it.

Perhaps the most famous and influential of these books was written by the great humanist Erasmus of Rotterdam in 1530, near the end of his life. Entitled *De civilitate morum puerilium* (*On Good Manners for Boys*), it is a founding text for the very notion of "civility." The book is addressed to the youthful reader,[6] providing him with instruction on a wide range of topics, all of them involving "outward bodily propriety": the care and carriage of his body, dress, behavior in church, manners at table, meeting people, play, and the bedroom.[7] Fully one-third of the text concerns table manners.

To a modern reader some of what Erasmus has to say may seem obvious, in part because the conduct he seeks to restrain is crude beyond our experience. Still it reminds us that such instruction was once not only necessary but also against the then-prevailing habits. And what now seems obvious to us has become so thanks in no small part to Erasmus and his descendants. We shall consider his instructions in some detail.

There are basic rules about our physical appearance at table, first aimed at cleanliness and neatness:

> Sit not down until thou have washed but let thy [finger]nails be pared before, so that no filth stick in them, lest thou be called a sloven and a great niggard [literally "dirty knuckled"]. Remember the common saying, "Before make water," and if need require ease thy belly; and if thou be gird too strait [that is, if your belt is too tight] it is wise to unloose thy girdle [beforehand], which to do at the table is shame[ful]. . . . When thou sittest with greater men, see thy head be kemmed [combed]; lay thy cap aside, except the manner of some devotion cause thee otherwise or else some man of authority command the contrary, whom to disobey is against manners.[8]

Other rules regarding appearance concern our posture and bodily attitude, which are to be kept erect and steady, resisting the temptations to yield altogether to the downward pull of necessity:

It is permissible for the elderly and convalescent to lean one or both elbows on the table; but this, as practiced by some affected courtiers who consider their every action elegant, is something to be avoided, not imitated. . . . Fidgeting in one's seat, shifting from side to side, gives the appearance of repeatedly breaking wind or of trying to do so. The body should, therefore, be upright and equally balanced [that is, on both buttocks].

The placement of the hands also requires instruction:

When sitting down have both hands on the table, not clasped together, nor on the plate. It is bad manners to have one or both hands on one's belly as some do.

And again:

Some people eat and drink without stopping not because they are hungry or thirsty but because they cannot otherwise moderate their gestures, unless they scratch their head, or pick their teeth, or gesticulate with their hands, or play with their dinner knife, or cough, or clear their throat, or spit. Such habits, even if originating in a sort of rustic shyness, have the appearance of insanity about them.

These instructions, governing the body, hardly exhaust the subject. But with even a moment's reflection they remind us of the enormous array of appearances, postures, and other movements and uses of the body that are banished from the table. The multiple possible uses of hands—like those of the body generally—are circumscribed, restricted, and rendered harmonious with the work of eating undertaken in a communal setting.

In addition to controlling our external appearance, manners seek also to control our internal appetites or, at least, their influence on our overt conduct. These customs quite directly address the matter of human voracity, especially by teaching the boy to be the master of his belly.

Some people have scarcely seated themselves comfortably before they thrust their hands into the dishes. That is the behavior of wolves or of those who, as the proverb puts it, devour meat from the pot before the sacrifices are made. Do not be the first to touch food set on the table, not only because that convicts you of greed, but because it does, on occasion, involve danger, since someone who takes a mouthful of burning hot food without first testing it is forced either to spit it out, or, if he swallows it, to scald his gullet—in either event appearing both foolish and pitiful. Some degree of delay is necessary so that a boy becomes accustomed to controlling his appetite. With such an end in view, Socrates never let himself drink from the first wine bowl of the evening even when he was an old man. If seated with his elders, a boy should be the last to reach for his plate—and only when he has been invited to do so. It is boorish to plunge your hands into sauced dishes.

The boy must learn not only to control the demands of his belly, he must also not be enslaved to the delights of his palate:

> Nor shall you select from the entire dish as epicures do but should take whatever portion is in front of you. . . . Just as it is, therefore, a sign of intemperance to thrust your hand into every part of the dish, so it is equally impolite to turn the dish so that the choicer morsels come to you.

Erasmus also provides, as one might expect, instruction on a variety of other topics, including the proper use of utensils, the correct placement of one's cup and knife, how to receive and refuse various servings, how to carve, and how to execute various other aspects of the process of eating. Understandably much attention is paid to the workings of hands, mouth, and eyes. These customs are of special interest to us because they govern the most important bodily aspects of the upright posture. Here especially we can see how fitting customs can validate and enhance the natural promise of the upright human form.

Regulating Hands, Mouth, and Eyes

Human beings, we remind ourselves, do not bring their mouths down to their food. They lift their food to their mouths, using their hands. In Erasmus's time, well before the fork was in common use, men used their hands quite directly. ("What cannot be taken with the fingers should be taken on your plate." "If seated with his elders, a boy should not put his hands to the dish until he has been invited to do so.") But even so, suggestions were made both to make the practice less crude ("What is offered should be taken in three fingers" [rather than with the whole hand]; "It is ridiculous to pick an eggshell clean with finger-nails or thumb. . . . the polite way is to use a small knife") and to remove the greasy results in ways unknown to animals ("To lick thy fingers greasy or to dry them upon thy clothes be both unmannerly; that must rather be done upon the board-cloth[!] or thy napkin"[W]). The natural human form, having liberated the human mouth from the need to apprehend and grasp its fodder, is now enhanced by customs that moderate and partly disguise the need even for human hands to dirty themselves with the low business of serving ingestion. Human hands are not just stuffers for the mouth; thus they must themselves not become mixed up with or clothed by the food.

This desideratum is achieved by means of the implements of eating; in the West, mainly knife, fork, and spoon; in the East, often chopsticks. The fascinating history of these utensils encapsulates the gradual progression of the civilizing process, itself tied to changes in what and where people eat and to evolving standards of feeling and disgust.[9] Cultural differences in the nature and use of implements are legion, reflecting and incorporating different sensibilities and judgments. For example, in the English manner, the fork, held in the left hand, enters the mouth with tines down, the food balanced—not impaled or "spooned"—on their rounded backs; this compels the taking of small mouthfuls, for very little can be lifted at one time, and prevents pushing the fork far into the mouth—both points of refinement. The American manner of shifting the fork to the right hand after cutting makes lifting to mouth easier, but being more cumbersome, slows down the process; moreover, it means that only one hand (the right) does any work and that the knife cannot be brandished while food is being put into the mouth—likewise points of refinement. Yet these differences are small variations atop some larger underlying generalities.

Utensils are, in the first place, useful, as the name implies. Solid food needs to be cut, grasped during cutting, and then lifted to the mouth; before personal forks came into common use, lifting was done with the knife (or fingers). Lifting liquids requires a small-cupped container with a handle, the spoon. But the main benefit of the implements is that they get food to mouth neatly and cleanly, without dirtying or greasing the fingers (and face). The concern here is more aesthetic than hygienic; it was clearly expressed as early as the sixteenth and seventeenth centuries, before the appearance of the personal fork:

> It is *very impolite* to touch anything greasy, a sauce or syrup, etc., with your fingers, apart from the fact that it obliges you to commit two or three more *improper* acts. One is to wipe your hand frequently on your serviette and to soil it like a kitchen cloth, so that those who see you wipe your mouth with it feel nauseated. Another is to wipe your fingers on your bread, which again is very *improper*. And the third is to lick them, which is the height of *impropriety*.[10]

In the West it was the spread of the personal fork that solved the distasteful problem of dirty fingers. The Italians and Spaniards in the seventeenth century began furnishing each diner with his own small fork; the English ridiculed the practice for years before grudgingly accepting it.

> The fork revolution did not . . . present the world with an utterly strange new instrument; what did constitute an important change in the West was the spread of the use of forks, their eventual adoption by all the diners, and their use not only to hold food still while it was cut, but to carry it into people's mouths.[11]

In the use of the knife, correlative changes over recent centuries have been governed mainly by considerations other than utility, neatness, and a concern to avoid ugly or disgusting appearance. The instrument of violence, used both in killing and severing, it has undergone changes in shape and sharpness that render it less dangerous. First the double-edged knife was reduced to single-edged, the point was rounded off, and finally even the cutting edge of the table knife was deliberately dulled: Margaret Visser reports that "according to Tallement des Réaux, Richelieu was responsible for the rounding-off of the points on table-knife blades in France in 1669, apparently to prevent their use as toothpicks, but probably also to discourage assassinations at meals. It became illegal for cutlers to make pointed dinner knives or for innkeepers to lay them on their tables."[12]

More important, the use of the knife came increasingly under the rule of strong taboos. These taboos further reduce the already small risk of actual bodily harm, but they function mainly symbolically, to hide altogether the violent possibilities of the knife. Whereas in the Middle Ages the sharp dagger-knife was lifted to mouth, today one must never put even the dull table knife to mouth. Norbert Elias gives a plausible explanation:

> The caution required in using a knife results not only from the rational consideration that one might cut or harm oneself, but above all from the emotion aroused by the sight or the idea of a knife pointed at one's own face. . . . [I]t is the general memory of and association with death and danger, it is the *symbolic* meaning of the instrument that leads, with the advancing internal pacification of society, to the preponderance of feelings of displeasure at the sight of it, and to the limitation and final exclusion of its use in society. The mere sight of a knife pointed at the face arouses fear: "Bear not your knife toward your face, for therein lies much dread." This is the emotional basis of the powerful taboo of a later phase, which forbids the lifting of the knife to the mouth.[13]

Margaret Visser adds that the horror we feel when we see people pointing a knife at themselves is less a fear of actual danger, and more the worry that people will relax the relatively new rule against using knives to deliver food to mouth, the silent fear that knife lifting will make a comeback.[14]

Other taboos reinforce the retreat of the knife: One does not use it on fish; one may not cut a potato, boiled egg, or other round objects; one must not keep it in one's hand when it is not in use; where possible, one should cut with the side of the fork. In none of these is the purpose health, cleanliness, or the reduction of danger. Rather it is to continue to augment, through symbolic deeds, the psychic distance between human eating and the violent destruction that all eating—especially meat eating—necessarily entails.

The retreat of the knife parallels major shifts in the manner in which meat is served at table. Again from Elias:

> In the upper class of medieval society, the dead animal or large parts of it are often brought whole to the table. Not only whole fish and whole birds (sometimes with their feathers) but also whole rabbits, lambs, and quarters of veal appear on the table, not to mention the larger venison or the pigs and oxen roasted on the spit. The animal is carved on the table.[15]

As manners begin to soften during the succeeding centuries, whole animals are no longer brought to or carved at the table (save at rare "olde style" dinners on holidays like Thanksgiving). Carving is done behind the scenes. The animal form is so altered in preparation of the meat dish that one cannot recognize when it is served what its animal origin was—or sometimes even that it *had* an animal origin. Our tastes keep us carnivorous, but our practice shows that we are not proud of the fact. Many cultures have sought, in the civilizing process, "to suppress in themselves every characteristic that they feel to be 'animal.' They likewise suppress such characteristics in their food."[16]

The Chinese and Japanese have advanced this process farther than the West. The knife has for centuries been utterly banished from the table. All foods, including meat, are precut into bite-size pieces. Chopsticks make for—and celebrate—small mouthfuls. The distance from the violent knife and the grasping hands couldn't be greater. To many Chinese even refined Western habits appear uncivilized: "Europeans are barbarians: they eat with swords." Yet the principles of distance and delicacy fulfilled by the Chinese and Japanese customs are the same ones that have been slowly at work in the West, at least since the Renaissance.

As might be expected, the regulation of eating itself is carried mainly by rules concerning the mouth. Returning now to Erasmus, we find that graphic unflattering comparisons—with animals or thieves or choking men—bear the rhetorical burden of persuasion. Here are some choice examples (with my italics added):

- To gnaw bones is *for a dog;* good manners require them to be picked with a small knife.
- To lick a plate or dish to which some sugar or sweet substance has adhered *is for cats,* not for people.
- Some devour rather than eat their food, just like those who, as the saying goes, are shortly to be marched off to prison. Such gorging should be left *to brigands.*
- Some stuff so much at one time into their mouth that their cheeks swell like a *pair of bellows.*
- Some in eating slubber up their meat like *swine.* (W)
- Some snuff and snort in the nose for greediness, as though *they were choked.* (W)

These various rules proscribe improper use of the teeth (gnawing), tongue (licking), and cheeks (stuffing), as well as improper modes of swallowing (without chewing), chewing noisily (slubbering), and breathing while eating (snuffing and snorting). Taken together they made a singular teaching: Eat inconspicuously and like a human being. We are urged to eat self-consciously, affirming in our manner of eating that we are—and know that we are—different from animals and different also from those deformed human beings who cannot or will not live in human society.

Even in eating, we remember that the organ of eating has a more peculiarly human function: speaking. An act of speaking should not be "contaminated" with food: "It is neither polite nor safe to drink or speak with one's mouth full." Those to whom we speak should not be showered with particles of food; neither should they be compelled to witness our half-chewed food. Yet, at the same time, because eating itself is private, human eating together requires speech: "Continuous eating should be interrupted now and again with stories." Without conversation the belly rules the mouth, and the table becomes no different from a trough.

It is shared speech, even more than the shared food, that makes a community of diners. Bread can be shared only partially: Each person's share is not shared with others, and any portion eaten by me diminishes what is left for you. True, that each person will get his share creates a shared atmosphere of comfort and ease: Because each one's need can be satisfied without fear of attack, guards are lowered and intimacy becomes more possible. But it is really only speech that can be shared in full. Indeed, each person's portion of the conversation is enriched by others' taking part. In the course of privately restoring the (necessarily private) body with food, the soul keeps its head erect, taking and giving nourishment in conversation. This deep insight into who and what we are informs these elementary rules about eating and speaking. As we shall see in the next chapter, they invite the question of whether the common meal is not finally better understood—to overstate the point—as an "excuse" for conversation.

Yet the rational animal, when at table, does not forget his animality. Though filled with conversation, the meal is not a philosophical seminar or a scientific investigation. Because the participants eat as well as speak, the attitude of the speakers cannot be one of detached beholding, and certainly not toward one another. For these reasons humanized eating means also regulating the use of our eyes. Our eyes, windows through which we can gaze on the world with wonder and curiosity, cannot be indulged at table. Shame dictates the main rule: Do not watch others eat. Again Erasmus:

> It is bad manners to let your eyes roam around observing what each person is eating, and it is impolite to stare intently at one of the guests. It is even worse to look shiftily out of the corner of your eye at those on the same side of the table; and it is the worst possible form to turn your head right around to see what is happening at another table.

Because eating, even when conducted in public, remains in essence a private or intimate matter, it is governed by "protective shame," which enables us to meet our needs and to manifest our incompleteness without corrosive self-consciousness. Paradoxically, eating with others enables us to draw attention away from our neediness and from the power that hunger exercises over us. Having company in meeting necessity permits selective inattention to the brute fact of necessity. But when we see others staring at our food—or at our biting and chewing—we cannot hide from ourselves both that we are feeding ourselves and also what it means—including our enslavement to appetite and our submission to the largely involuntary acts of biting, chewing, and swallowing.

But the rules against staring are meant not only to hide ugly or embarrassing conduct. They are meant to protect the immediacy of our *social* activity against objectification. As Erwin Straus has noted: "All looking and being looked at is a lapse from immediate communication. This is demonstrated in everyday life by our annoyance and irritation at being observed."[17] Here again manners come to the aid of protective shame, that mysterious power of the soul that stands guard over immediate and open participation in life:

> The secret that shame protects is not, however, as prudery makes the mistake of believing, one that is already in existence and only needs to be hidden from outsiders, for those who are in becoming are also hidden from themselves. Their existence is first made explicit in their shared immediate becoming.[18]

Commensal friends, in a way not unlike lovers, seek the half light of mannerly eating and silence about its merely physiological side, in order to be able to commune intimately—immediately, unselfconsciously, directly—over the sharing of food. The curtain of invisibility shame drops between ourselves as detached beholders and ourselves as engaged participants is destroyed when we are stared at. We are then compelled to look at ourselves, and at ourselves *eating*.

What we would not have done to us we ought not do to others. Gazing and staring at other eaters objectifies their conduct. We cease to regard them as fellow companions; we come to see them as isolated *Fresser*. In gazing and staring we remove ourselves psychically from the community of human animals humanly meeting animal necessity and adopt the vantage point of voyeur,* or, at best, of disinterested observer, from which we look down on these lesser creatures caught in the act of stuffing their mouths. To do so furtively, say, while hiding behind one's drinking glass, is one of the worst violations of propriety: "To look aside when thou drinkest is a rude manner and like as storks to wry the neck backward. (W)" The shameless viewing of Olympian detachment, like the shameful *fressen* of subhuman animals, is absolutely out of place at table.

Just as detached looking is out of place at table, so eating is out of place in public, except at those public occasions explicitly convened to include it (like public festivals) or in those public places set aside for eating (like restaurants or picnic areas). A man eating as he walks down the street eats in the face of all passersby, who must then either avert their gaze or observe him objectifiedly in the act. Worst of all from this point of view are those more uncivilized forms of eating, like licking an ice-cream cone—a catlike activity that has been made acceptable in informal America but that still offends those who know why eating in public is offensive.

I fear that I may by this remark lose the sympathy of many readers, people who will condescendingly regard as quaint or even priggish the (not-only-Talmudic) view that eating in the street is for

---

*"The behavior of the voyeur is not an inherently meaningful surrender to fate, like that of lovers [and, I would add, of eaters]. . . . The voyeur reveals, in his objectifying attitude and in his furtive entry into the Other's most intimate experience, the antithesis of two modes of being—the public mode and that of immediate being."[19]

dogs. Modern America's rising tide of informality has already washed out many long-standing customs—their reasons long before forgotten—that served well to regulate the boundary between public and private; and in many quarters complete shamelessness is treated as proof of genuine liberation from the allegedly arbitrary constraints of manners. To cite one small but telling example: yawning with uncovered mouth. Not just the uneducated rustic but children of the cultural elite are now regularly seen yawning openly in public (not so much brazenly or forgetfully as indifferently and "naturally"), unaware that it is an embarrassment to human self-command to be caught in the grip of involuntary bodily movements (like sneezing, belching, and hiccuping and even the involuntary bodily display of embarrassment itself, blushing). But eating on the street—even when undertaken, say, because one is between appointments and has no other time to eat—displays in fact precisely such lack of self-control: It betokens enslavement to the belly. Hunger must be sated now; it cannot wait. Though the walking street eater still moves in the direction of his vision, he shows himself as a being led by his appetites. Lacking utensils for cutting and lifting to mouth, he will often be seen using his teeth for tearing off chewable portions, just like any animal. Eating on the run does not even allow the human way of enjoying one's food, for it is more like simple fueling; it is hard to savor or even to know what one is eating when the main point is to hurriedly fill the belly, now running on empty. This doglike feeding, if one must engage in it, ought to be kept from public view, where, even if *we* feel no shame, others are compelled to witness our shameful behavior.

To a lesser extent the same problem sometimes arises even with civilized dining in designated public places, say at sidewalk cafés or even for those eating at a window table in a restaurant—a truth recognizable when we consider our discomfort when a passerby presses his face to the window to see who's there or what they are eating. Beyond our annoyance at the uninvited intrusion into "our space," we are uneasy lifting food to mouth when we are stared at. The gaze of any stranger makes us self-conscious; putting our eating before his eyes makes him self-conscious. Uninvited to share our food, he is forced into one-way, voyeuristic "participation," in which he sees not human eating but animal feeding. At best we share nothing but embarrassment at this involuntary meeting over intimate things.*

"Let Mirth Be with Thee"

Also out of place at table is the display of emotions or conduct that would interfere with the enjoyment of the meal. Erasmus's very first rule regarding manners at table concerns the matter of mood and its display: "At table let mirth be with thee, let ribaldry be exiled. . . . When thou wipest thy hands put forth of thy mind all grief, for at table it becometh not to be sad nor to make others sad. (W)" Similarly, one ought to govern one's tongue: "Nothing should be blurted out at table that might diminish mirth. It is wrong to defame the character of those not present; nor should one's personal sorrow be unburdened to another on such an occasion." It is also antisocial to retreat into oneself, for whatever reason:

> It is impolite to sit at table rapt in thought. You may, however, observe some people so withdrawn into their private thoughts that they neither hear what others are saying nor are aware that they are eating, and if you call them by name they give the appearance of being roused from sleep—so completely absorbed are they in the dishes.

Any conduct that arouses fear or worry, sadness or pity, anger or disgrace, or even any conduct that conspicuously draws attention to itself, "diminishes mirth" and threatens the merriment of the meal.

Yet precisely because there is oft merriment at table, especially when men's tongues are loosened with drink, there is need for forbearance and discretion: "It is bad taste for anyone, but much

---

*Even seemingly innocent public eating and drinking can violate tacit social relations, if they are out of joint with time, place, or the spirit of the occasion. I was brought to self-consciousness in these matters some twenty years ago by the late Simon Kaplan, a much-beloved, kind, gentle, witty, and deeply wise Russian-born-and-bred tutor at St. John's College. As I was taking a cookie and cup of coffee from the brief reception into the Conversation Room for the question period that followed the weekly Friday-night formal lecture (many students and tutors did so), Mr. Kaplan stopped me and asked: "Mister Kass, do you think it right, when a man who comes to us from out of town to present a lecture based upon many years of study, that we should sit in front of

more so for a boy, to gossip about an indiscretion of word or deed someone has committed when in his cups." The intimacy of the meal and the shame that protects exposure extend not only to the activity of feeding but to everything that arises around it. Because the occasion is free and open, because guards are down, because speech is tentative and playful, because what is said is tied to the occasion and to those present, the entire meal is like a sacred rite, wrapped in mystery and guarded in secrecy: "It is a reproach, as Horace said, to blow abroad what someone lets slip at dinner, without thinking. Whatsoever be done or said there should be lapped up in the cloth. (W)" What is said at table stays at table.

Though one should be most exacting regarding one's own conduct, one must be tolerant and liberal regarding the faults of others: "Finally, if someone through inexperience commit some *faux pas*, it should be politely passed over rather than mocked [other translation: "It should be dissimulated rather than had in derision" (W)]. One should feel at ease during a party." It is more unmannerly than unmannerly eating to shame a fellow eater.

The Why of Table Manners

The basic civilizing manners propounded by Erasmus more than 450 years ago are, needless to say, hardly the last word in table manners—though few if any of his teachings have been rendered passé. Indeed the additional refinements added over the centuries are by and large further elaborations of the basic goals and principles that inform the rules we have so far surveyed.

True, part of the purpose of at least some of the rules is good health. One might choke if one speaks or drinks while chewing food. One can scald one's esophagus by hastily gulping hot food. But we should distinguish, as Erasmus does, between what is unwholesome and what is unmannerly, between what is healthy and what is seemly

---

him and eat and drink in his face?" I stopped the practice on the spot. On similar grounds I do not allow eating or drinking in my classes (all roundtable discussion seminars), save for reasons of medical necessity or when, on a rare occasion, students want to celebrate the end of a class by distributing cookies or brownies to the entire class. Why should those who come to the sanctuary of the classroom, a place governed by shared speech in search of truth, be compelled to participate in their colleagues' ingestions and chewings? (The reader may now discover for himself why as youngsters we were admonished not to chew gum in class.)

and proper.* What, then, is the point and purpose of the seemly and the mannerly?

To begin with, good table manners show consideration for the comfort and pleasure of one's fellow diners. Slovenly and noisy eating are annoying; greasy chins and filthy hands are painful to see; belching and spitting are revolting; obscene speech and raucous laughter are disturbing; most generally, all forms of animal-like *fressen* inspire disgust. Dis*gust*ing speech or behavior, quite literally, causes others to lose their taste (Latin *gustus*) for food; in the extreme case it causes them even to feel nausea at the sight of food. Table manners, in the first instance, function to prevent disgust in others, to avoid every occurrence that could interfere with their delight in the meal. This goal can be simply formulated: to repeat, No involuntary participation in someone else's digestion.

Manners not only prevent disgust. Along with the other customs of the table—including what is eaten, where, when, and with whom—manners also promote community. In shared rituals of eating, as in all its other customs, the community defines itself and sets forth its own peculiar way. Because the taking of meals is the most common and regular social occasion, the manners of eating, though observed quietly and without fanfare, are among the most powerful communal forms. Tacitly but deeply, subtly but surely, they mark us and make us feel at home among our own, producing also the considerable pleasures of familiarity and repetition. Though superficial in fact, they are deep in meaning. As symbols, they carry our group's sensibilities and attitudes—about life, necessity, violence, dignity, and our human place in the world. Amending slightly Brillat-Savarin's famous aphorism, "Tell me what [*and how*] you eat: I will tell you what [*and who*] you are."[20]

Table manners also serve the individual diners. To begin with they facilitate eating, despite the demands they make upon our actions and appetites. They render habitual the entire process of taking food, thus routinizing what would otherwise be a matter for repeated conscious yet unguided decision. Should we find ourselves at table in a strange land, with vastly different customs, our enjoyment

---

*Here is one clear instance of such a distinction: "To begin a meal with drinking is the hallmark of a drunkard who drinks not from need but from habit. Such a practice is not only *morally degrading* but also *injurious to bodily health*." (italics added).

of the meal will be compromised because we do not know how to behave, because we must consciously attend to matters that, at home, have become second nature. Yet even at home there can be embarrassments when the reliable forms fail: Consider, for example, the dilemma we face when our food cannot be cut because we lack a sharp-enough knife. The removal of the need for decision making regarding the process permits each diner the freedom to enjoy both his food and his companions. His mind, freed from self-attention and the business of getting food properly to mouth, can be given over to savoring tastes, swapping stories, and enjoying the occasion.

Table manners, like civility in general, far from constraining the immediacy and intimacy of life, help make them possible. For the human meal is an intimate gathering. Though we sit at table face to face and are, in a sense, on view to others, we neither feel nor act the way we do in public. In the public sphere, we perform a specified role and display ourselves accordingly, always (at least tacitly) with a view to how we will be regarded. But our intimate person remains concealed by our public figure, and others participate in our lives only as observers or fellow performers—nonmutually, noncommittally, nonimmediately. Only in nonpublic being together do we get a respite from public performance, an opportunity to become who we are on our way to becoming, a chance to open and reveal ourselves to others because they too seek mutual and immediate participation. The family meal especially is such an intimate gathering, but so generally are meals shared with friends. On these occasions mannerly eating, though it constitutes "good behavior," is in fact a shield against corrosive self-attention and objectification. Manners, having become second nature, keep both us and our companions from becoming so self-conscious about our behavior that we objectify ourselves (or them) and our surroundings. If we eat unobtrusively, and our partners do too, no one will even notice that food is being cut, lifted to mouth, chewed, or swallowed. No one will notice that he or she is in the midst of a conversation. No one will notice that he or she is immediately and directly enjoying a genuine experience of real life and the world. Such open and participatory relations with the world and with others depend absolutely on a kind of self-forgetting that civility, including mannerly eating, makes possible.

Yet manners are not only useful for life, they are also ennobling. Despite differences from one culture to the next, table manners everywhere effect a certain beautification of the eater, as he displays himself to be above enslavement to his appetites. An activity that is inherently ugly is beautified by graceful deed and tactful speech. An activity that is violent and destructive is tamed by gentle manner that keeps its destructive character mostly out of sight. An activity that deforms and dissolves living forms is given a form-ality of its own by the work of the human intellect. Given psychic distance from animal *fressen* by the work of manners, intellect and aesthetic imagination are free to play. Ever mindful of discrete and different forms, human reason flourishes especially in the making and the appreciating of distinctions. The pleasures that accompany observing and discriminating—of flavors, spices, aromas, textures, appearances, implements, courses, gestures, speeches, stories, and manners—are themselves no small part of the higher pleasures of the table. Both aesthetically and intellectually satisfying, mannerly eating—like the habit of hospitality—is our peculiarly human way of dignifying and gracing necessity, and also ourselves. These civilizing customs are tailor made to fit and reveal the human form and to nourish the hungry soul.

The Virtue of Eating

The foregoing remarks suggest that mannerly eating is not only socially useful, say, in expressing communal norms and promoting group identity or in protecting the immediacy of communal experience. It can also be an expression of our personal humanity, indeed, of excellence or virtue. As in other matters the social setting becomes a stage on which individuals display their characters, virtuous or not. The common meal is such a stage, and the relevant virtues and vices are well known, even if little discussed these days. The first and cardinal virtue of the table is temperance or moderation.

In Benjamin Franklin's list of virtues, a list he prepared for his "bold and arduous Project of arriving at moral Perfection," the first virtue mentioned altogether is temperance. Franklin's precept for temperance: "Eat not to dullness, drink not to elevation." Temperance tempers appetites mainly by limiting quantity. Counseling against excess, Franklin urges moderation in food and drink, but not, it seems, as an end in itself. Excess eating makes the mind dull, whereas too much to drink lifts one altogether out of one's right mind. As he does with all the moral virtues, Franklin gives temperance a purely utilitarian defense. Temperance stands first among the virtues because "it tends to procure that Coolness and Clearness of Head, which is so necessary where constant Vigilance was to be kept up, and Guard maintained, against the unremitting Attraction of ancient Habits, and the Force of perpetual Temptations."[21] Temperance helps keep the mind sharp while the body is being tended. Though of primary importance, it is not desirable or attractive in itself.*

If we look, however, to premodern thinkers, the virtue regarding eating and drinking is seen not only as useful but also as good in itself. For example, in Aristotle's *Ethics*, it is part of moderation (*sophrosyne*)—the keynote, as it were, of all of Aristotle's ethical teaching; for Aristotle everywhere treats moral virtue as a mean between two vices and regards virtue as the habit of finding and taking the mean or the fitting, the just right thing to do here and now. The virtue of moderation, according to Aristotle, is displayed most prominently with respect to certain bodily pleasures, namely those tactile pleasures man shares with the animals, the pleasures of eating, drinking, and sex.

> Moderation, then, and profligacy [or "self-indulgence"; *akolasia*, literally, "unrestrainedness," "unchastenedness"] are about such pleasures in which also the other animals share, whence they [the pleasures] seem slavish and bestial, and these are touch and taste. But they seem to involve taste slightly or not at all; for judging flavors is the concern of taste, which the wine-tasters do and those who prepare savoury foods. But they do not rejoice exactly in these things [flavors], or at least not the self-indulgent ones, but in the enjoyment of the object, all of which comes from touch, both in food and drink and in the things called aphrodisiac. Wherefore someone, who was a gourmand, prayed for his throat to be longer than a crane's, as taking pleasure in touch. . . . To rejoice in such things and to love them most of all is beast-like.[22]

---

*The utility of temperance is made even clearer by the sequel: "This [that is, temperance] being acquir'd and establish'd, *Silence* would be more easy, and my Desire being to gain Knowledge at the same time that I improv'd in Virtue, and considering that in Conversation it was obtain'd rather by the use of the Ears than of the Tongue, and therefore wishing to break a Habit I was getting into of Prattling, Punning, and Joking, which only made me acceptable to trifling Company, I gave *Silence* the second Place."

As necessitous animals human beings share in the urgent animal needs and desires and enjoy the pleasures that accompany their satisfaction. But as human beings our excellence and its opposite turn on the question: Will the human being rule or be ruled by his basic animal desires?

The desire for nourishment is natural (both inborn and fitting), necessary, and, universal; the desire for this or that particular food is usually acquired, gratuitous, and particular—in some cases, even idiosyncratic. It is a rare fellow who puts chocolate sauce on his vegetables or ketchup in his cereal. Regarding the common, natural desire for nourishment, Aristotle observes, the usual error is toward excess in quantity: "For to eat whatever happens to be around or to drink until one is overfull is to exceed the natural in amount; for natural desire is for filling-up the need [or "lack"]. Therefore these are called 'greedy-bellies' [gluttons], since they fill it beyond what is right [or "necessary"]. The overly slavish become like these." But regarding the peculiar pleasures and desires, "Many err and in many ways; for when people are called lovers-of-such-and-such, it is either for delighting in what one ought not, or by rejoicing more than or as the many do, or not as one ought." The self-indulgent man is led by his bodily desires, preferring these to all other pleasures, and experiencing pain when he does not promptly get what he desires.

Opposite to the self-indulgent man would be the man who takes no pleasure in his food. But, as Aristotle observes, such a type barely occurs, "for such insensibility (*anaisthesia*) is not human. . . . [I]f for someone there is nothing pleasant, and one thing does not differ from another, he would be far from being a human being."

The moderate or virtuous man is, as the name implies, neither profligate nor ascetic, neither self-indulgent nor self-denying. The necessary pleasures he enjoys measuredly and as one ought, and the nonnecessary ones similarly, if they are not unhealthy, ignoble, or extravagant:

> Insofar as there are pleasures that conduce toward health and fitness, these he reaches for moderately and as one ought; and he reaches for the other pleasures if they do not impede health and fitness or *are not contrary to the noble* or beyond his means. . . . For he loves such pleasures not more than their worth and as right reason would say.[23]

Aristotle's moderate man is concerned with health and fitness, and also with his purse, both threatened by self-indulgence. But he is, unlike Benjamin Franklin or the merely calculating man, centrally concerned with *nobility*: "Thus, it is necessary in the moderate man for the desiring-power to harmonize (*symphonein*) with reason (*logos*). For the *target of both is the noble*; and the moderate man desires what one ought and as one ought and when, and thus also as *logos* directs."[24] Unlike the calculatingly measured man, who curbs his appetites only to stay trim or to save money, the virtuously moderate man will not be a boor at table. He will avoid forcing his digestive processes on others and will not display a lack of self-control over his appetites. Understanding the difference between eating and feeding, he desires and displays in manner the human way of meeting bodily necessity. He eats and drinks at the proper place and time—for example, not at the theater or in the law courts or in the classroom, or, for that matter, walking down the street. These things he will do or avoid not only or mainly in order to avoid giving offense to others; rather he is moved by a desire to attain or share in "the noble" for himself.

The word translated "noble" is, in Greek, *kalon*—beautiful, fine, splendid, noble—in German, *schön*. It is, to begin with, an aesthetic notion; as captured for ethics it implies a beautiful outward display in deed of a beautiful or well ordered soul within. This display is no mere appearance; neither is the conduct merely *in external conformity* with what is seemly. As with any manifestation of genuine excellence, it is done willingly and knowingly, not gritting one's teeth but with pleasure, and precisely in order to do what is beautiful because one loves it. Connoisseurs of nobility can tell the real thing when they see it.

An example may convince the skeptic. Have you ever watched a gracious and tactful hostess with a handicapped guest? It is relatively easy to describe the principle that should guide her conduct: Be helpful without causing embarrassment. But it is extraordinarily difficult to put the principle into beautiful practice. Yet if you have seen it done, you immediately recognize both the beauty of the deed and, at the same time, the grace, tact, sensitivity, perspicacity, and love of the gracious in the doer herself. Without the last, the deed itself could not be flawlessly done.

What, then, would it mean to attain and manifest nobility in the rather lowly matter of eating?

Possible answers have already been given: Negatively, eat so as to display that you are not a slave to your appetites; positively, eat like a human being, not like an animal. Freedom and distance seem centrally involved. An animal in the grip of hunger is entirely focused on the object promising satisfaction. It is incapable of taking other relations into account. With the important exception of parents feeding the young, there is no animal analogue of civility regarding eating: It is, so to speak, every "man" (dog) for himself, or, better, every desire for itself. Only after hunger is satisfied are certain social rituals (for example, grooming) restored, only after eating is the social order reestablished. Human beings, in contrast, because they are self-conscious of the power and meaning of hunger, do not—except in extreme circumstances—simply yield to it. While eating we maintain some at least partial distance between our desire and its objects, enough so that we do not become solely absorbed in them. We remain open to fellow feeders, to conversation, to a larger horizon. We maintain our sense of community through habits of civility; our conduct reveals that we remain simultaneously aware of ourselves as intellectual and social, not merely physical, beings. Moderation keeps us free from enslavement to desire and free for receptivity and responsiveness.

It is tempting to suggest that nobility consists in "rising above" or "transcending" our animality, through acts of what one might call "self-levitation." Like the ballerina who "defies" gravity, so the graceful eater "defies" neediness and eats as if he were not compelled to do so. But the ballerina does not so much defy as exploit gravity. Similarly, also, the moderate and graceful human eater exploits animal necessity. He shapes a virtue out of necessity. The animal need to eat and the animal processes of eating become material for the display and enhancement of the human form.

Everything that is ours due to our animality is nevertheless different in us (than in animals) precisely because we are not merely or simply animals, incapable of understanding animal necessity, incapable of departing however slightly from fixed instinct. Our peculiarly human form of animality thus always provides an arena in which we can display our difference. "Nobility" is not so much a transcendence of animality as it is the turning of animality into its peculiarly human and regulated form. "Beautiful" eating shows off the human difference: Violence done to the food is banished or suppressed; bodily attitude is regulated; appetite is controlled and in harmony with what is reasonable; tastes are savored; eyes and mind are not wholly submerged in putting food into mouth and remain open to the world around us; order and form preside at table; consideration for others is strictly observed; and, at best, a certain grace adorns all our movements. We show off the human difference—we manifest what it means to be upright.

However, while a perfection of our nature, mannerly eating is not, in another sense, natural to us. That is, it is neither inborn nor automatically acquired. On the contrary, it must be taught, by precept and example, and it must be learned through habituation. Moreover, the shaping of the appetites for food and drink requires instruction that often seems to go against the grain—unlike, say, teaching children to speak or young birds to fly. Many a reprimand—for example, "Chew with your mouth closed," "Use your napkin," "Don't reach," or "Don't stare"—is needed before the little human animals are fit company at the dinner table:

> For little children also [that is, in addition to the self-indulgent ones] live according to desire and especially large in them is the appetite for pleasure. If, then, it will not be obedient and beneath the ruler, it will grow great. For the appetite for the pleasant is insatiable and indiscriminate in a mindless being, and the *activity* of desire increases the inborn tendency. If the desires grow great and strong, they can even knock out the power of reasoning.[25]

However, being in themselves indiscriminate and unformed, the desires take direction. If given proper direction—*no* direction being, of course, also a direction, namely, toward self-indulgence—the desires can become focused, pruned, reasonable, and even amenable to seeking satisfaction in a gracious manner, and all without great turbulence in the soul: "Therefore it is necessary for them [the appetites] to be measured and few, and never opposed to *logos*—for such we call obedient and restrained—and, just as the child should live according to the command of his tutor, so all the desiring-power should live according to *logos*."[26] Though chastisement and restraint are necessary adjuncts in the habituation of appetite and the cultivation of manners, the image of tutor educating child strongly suggests that violence is not being done to human nature. On the contrary, as growing up means movement from childishness to maturity, from (relative) mindlessness to (greater) reasonableness, so our infantile and childish desires grow up, under tutelage and through habituation, to bear the form of what is reasonable. In the best case, reason and desire will sound with one voice, and the conduct displayed—even in eating—will partake of harmony and grace.

Such beauty need not require the eye of a beholder. The gentleman or lady who is fully self-conscious takes aesthetic pleasure in enacting and appreciating his or her own nobility. Even when dining alone, and—let me push the point—even were he or she the last human being on earth eating the last meal, the virtuous human being would cover and set the table, use the implements properly, and would chew noiselessly with mouth closed. He or she would announce, by such self-presentation, that nobility, though it had to be acquired, is nonetheless the natural garb of the truly upright animal.

5

Freedom, Friendship, and Philosophy

From Eating to Dining

Beasts feed: man eats: the man of intellect alone knows how to eat.

—*Brillat-Savarin*

Man does not live by bread alone. Neither does he like to take it alone—all by himself. While the mannerly eater eats gracefully even when forced to eat without company, company manners are meant especially for eating with companions. Human beings, like the animals, must be fed. Human beings, unlike the animals, not only feed but usually eat. But civilized human beings, at least on special occasions, not only eat, but even dine, and sometimes feast. Having attended to the customs that lay the floor beneath human eating, we turn now toward those that elevate it festively toward the ceiling. If our hunches are correct, we will discover in these "higher" customs a continuation and refinement of the principles evident in the foundation—principles, we have argued, that are tied to a true account of animal nature, our human nature, and our place in the world.

There are, of course, a variety of principles (already known to us from previous chapters and all connected with the human form and its powers) that invite our attention and that bid fair to command the direction of human improvement brought about by custom. One could speak about freedom—the ever-increasing emancipation from the bonds of instinct and appetite and the progressive cultivation of self-command. One could speak about beautification—the adornment of self and surroundings, the grace of gesture and movement, the delight in taste and tastefulness. One could speak of friendship and love, beginning with the companionable sharing of bread and moving, through the appreciative sharing of speech, to the meeting and cherishing of souls. One could speak about the cultivation of the mind, beginning in speech liberated by the satisfaction of necessity and moving through playful conversation and wit in the direction of the pursuit of wisdom. And one can speak also about piety and reverence, and the human impulse toward transcendence, beginning in awe and fear and, sometimes encouraged by wine, moving through feelings of gratitude and songs of praise in the direction of encountering the divine. This last, the sanctification of eating, we shall consider by itself, in the last chapter. The other principles, somewhat intertwined, will be treated here, as they are manifested in that ennoblement of eating we call dining.

Dining is, all by itself, a vast subject. Customs and practices vary not only from one society to another but also, within any one society, from one type of occasion to the next. Dining for the same individual will differ, sometimes greatly, depending on whether he is at a state dinner at the White House, a class reunion banquet at his alma mater, his daughter's wedding, a fiftieth wedding anniversary celebration for his parents, a holiday meal at his church or synagogue, a retirement dinner held in a private dining room of a family restaurant, or an intimate dinner party given at the home of a friend. The mood and meaning of dining will vary also depending on what kind of food and drink is being served and on who is present—for example, only immediate family, also close friends, grandparents and children, distinguished guests, visitors from abroad, business associates, business rivals, ardent suitors, prospective in-laws, fine storytellers, notorious wits, and so on. It would be a daunting task to attempt a comprehensive treatment of the myriad forms and intricacies.

The Dinner Party

Fortunately our purpose here is different. We are following a line of argument for which such comprehensive treatment is not necessary. A suitably rich and revealing instance should suffice to illustrate the general principles, principles that, one suspects, sound a common theme throughout all the other variations. We take as our example the "ordinary" dinner party, given at home and on no special occasion, for a gathering comprising friends and acquaintances rather than family members. Several reasons recommend this selection. First, most readers will be familiar with such occasions, however modest or elegant; nearly all of us have been dinner guests at someone's home or have had friends over to dine with us. Second, it is the most generalizable and least specialized kind of dining, apart from the family meal—which cannot be, because of hierarchic family relations, a gathering of simply equal dinner partners. Finally, and most important, the dinner party displays all the elements and principles of the "higher" eating. The social forms of dining should reveal—just as they promote—the more elevated manifestations of the upright onmivore.

Any dinner party is a special occasion, to be regarded not just as one event among many—though one may attend many such parties—but as a unique and unrepeatable occasion. (In this respect every dinner party could be said to partake of the meaning of the Last Supper, though it is part of the spirit of the party to keep this aspect of the occasion out of sight.) A dinner party does not happen by itself; it requires advance planning, preparation, and care, especially by the host and/or hostess. First is the matter of selecting the guests, putting together a convivial group of people who already do—or who probably would—like each other, who would mix and match well together, who at the very least would enjoy one another's company at least for the evening. Next comes the inviting, in high society still done by written invitation—a practice that permits the invited parties to accept or decline free from the awkward presence and subtle pressure of the voice on the telephone that has just surprised them by requesting their company. Invitation, whether by speech or in writing, flatters with attention, bids welcome in advance, and sets the occasion apart, permitting all to imagine, to anticipate, and to look forward to future companionship—a very high and self-conscious instance of the forward-looking, outward-reaching aspects of world-relation in eating already adumbrated in our account of animal life (Chapter 1). Then there are the preparations: selecting the menu, cleaning and adorning the setting, arranging and setting the table, and the well-timed, sequential preparing of the food and drink, with advance attention also to the manner and means of its conveyance to and service at the table. Special needs, preferences, and aversions of the guests will, if known, be taken into account in the planning of the meal.

Guests, too, find themselves preparing for the party. They respond to the invitation, not only literally but also psychically, in anticipation; they mark it on the calendar, where it helps configure the passage of time. They prepare by dressing *up* for the occasion: to distinguish this dinner party from ordinary eating, to show respect for the host and hostess and for other guests, and to express pleasure at the invitation and desire for the festivity of the occasion. (The aristocracy and those who imitate them would nightly dress for dinner, separating the evening meal from the humdrum events of the working day and dignifying it frequently with invited company.) Guests also "equip themselves" to enjoy the dinner: They are careful not to eat before leaving for the party, lest they spoil their appetite. Some will even take a nap to ensure their lively attention. (Tolstoy's old

Prince Bolkonski did this daily: "A nap after dinner was silver, before dinner, golden."[1]) And guests will arrive promptly, among other reasons, to show their eagerness for the party and their pleasure at having been invited.

On the arrival of the guests they are welcomed to the house by host and hostess, ushered into the living room, and introduced to the other guests. As a preface to the meal, the guests will usually be served drinks while they share in opening conversations. The delay in entering the dining room and in serving the meal makes clear that all have set aside the entire evening, that they have not come just to eat, that they have come to a party built around a meal, not just to the meal itself. Though it is understood that guests will go hungry to a feast, all hold their hunger in abeyance while drink and light talk allow the pretense that everyone can wait for dinner—a pretense made more bearable by the presence of hors d'oeuvres to accompany the drinks, delicate concessions to take the edge off hunger and, simultaneously, to whet the appetite for dinner.* At the just-right time dinner is served.

As to the food served at such a dinner, we shall have little to say. Usually several, often many, and always varying courses are served, offering the diners a well-orchestrated sequence of contrasting tastes and textures, each to be savored and appreciated. Ordered and flavorful variety, not mere satisfaction of hunger, is the point of the menu. Though the party is more than the meal, the quality of the food—how well it is prepared and presented and above all how it tastes—makes a huge difference to the common mood, as do the quality and fittingness of the accompanying wine. Though fancy gourmet cooking is today quite the rage, we are pikers compared to our ancestors in this regard. At an old-fashioned formal dinner party, so Miss Manners reports, there were, typically, fourteen courses:

1. Oysters or clams on the half shell. Fruit or caviar may be served instead.
2. Soup, giving each guest a choice of clear or thick.
3. Radishes, celery, olives, and salted almonds.

---

*This practice has a sound physiological foundation: The tidbits increase the flow of gastric juices, both directly in the stomach and indirectly through psychic stimulation.

4. Fish, served with fancifully shaped potatoes and cucumbers with oil and vinegar.
5. Sweetbreads or mushrooms.
6. Artichokes, asparagus, or spinach in pastry.
7. A roast or joint, as we say, with a green vegetable.
8. Frozen Roman punch, to clear the palate and stimulate you to go on.
9. Game, such as wild duck or little birdies, served with salad.
10. Heavy pudding or another creamed sweet.
11. A frozen sweet. It is a nice touch to have tiny crisp cakes with this.
12. Cheeses, with biscuits and butter. Or you may serve a hot savory of cheese, which is more filling.
13. Fresh, crystallized, and stuffed dried fruits, served with bonbons.
14. Coffee, liqueurs, and sparkling waters.

Each course requires its own plate and flatware, and as only three knives and forks are permitted on the table at the start, the others must be brought in with their courses.

Miss Manners offers this only as a basic list; you needn't consider yourself limited to it.[2]

Brillat-Savarin and others of equally discriminating palate would have found at such dinner parties a compendious encyclopedia of gustatory delights.

We no longer eat fourteen-course meals, but our dinners also come in staged courses. The order of courses for the festive dinner (as for the less elaborate daily family meal) varies from one culture to the next and seems to be somewhat arbitrary. In the United States one common simple pattern begins with soup or some other appetizer, rises to crescendo in the main course comprising an entrée of meat, fish, or fowl in the company of a starch and/or a vegetable, and descends first to salad, then to sweet dessert accompanied by coffee or tea. In Japan the meal proper consists of first rice and then soup; preceding these are all the elegantly prepared and beautifully presented Japanese delicacies that are in fact understood to be the necessary accompaniments to the drinking of sake. The hostess is obliged to continue serving these dishes until *all* the guests have indicated that they have had enough to drink; only then are rice and soup served to conclude the dinner. The order and structure of the festive meal are very likely to have a special meaning, relative to and decipherable for each culture;[3] but the existence of such a meaningful and perhaps decipherable order is universal, as are some of the elements of that order—hot and cold, moist and dry, light and heavy, sweet and savory, raw and cooked, boiled and roasted, and so on—along with the guiding principles of variation, contrast, and balance. The order—like the entire party—adorns the bread and salt, meat and wine, and expresses the refined humanity of the host.

The variety of the fare is reinforced by the variety of the accoutrements. Not only does each course receive its own fitting plate and flatware—and, at more elegant tables, its own fitting wine—but the sequence of courses, tastes, utensils, and maneuvres forms, as it were, a well-choreographed ballet or orchestrated symphony, with alternating gustatory themes and variations, each enjoyable both for itself and as part of the larger whole. A festive and colorful table, with candles and flowers, provides also a feast for the eyes, as will the attractive presentation of the feast itself, whether on serving platters or individual dishes. Taken together, sights, smells, textures, movements, and tastes blend into a rich, harmonious aesthetic experience, whose pleasures ride high above the hard necessity that requires us to eat in order to live.

It will be observed that the list of aesthetic pleasures of dining was silent on the subject of sound. This was not an error of omission. Noiseless eating is music to the diners' ears. They are attuned not to ingestive or digestive sounds but rather to the voices of their dinner companions. We approach the subject of dinner conversation by taking up first the question of seating.

What is the point of arranged seating? Why, since we are, in dining, demonstrating our freedom from the grip of necessity, should we not also sit wherever, and next to whomever, we wish? A thoughtful host and hostess will, no doubt, anticipate our possible or likely preferences, but they have an entire party to orchestrate, and it cannot be harmonious if one or two players alone get preferential treatment. Besides, because their knowledge of all the guests is likely to exceed that of any particular invitee, they may even be able to arrange the seating more to our own pleasure than we could on our own, choosing largely in ignorance. In any case, before we can judge the success of the means, we need to get clear about the end.

Several possible purposes could be served in arranged seating: honor, ease, appearance, and conversation. Recognition and preservation of rank and hierarchy are often considerations, if, indeed, there are distinguished and honored guests present. The host and hostess, as the patrons and directors of the party, are themselves persons of honor, even though they are honored because of their deferential concern for their guests. Other things being equal, they preside over the table from either end (or, in larger gatherings, sometimes from the middle on opposite sides), recognizing special guests by placing them at their side. (At official dinner parties there is much more elaborate and highly specific protocol regarding seating honors, but this need not concern us here.) But honor and distinction, however important to be respected and acknowledged, are in tension with the principle of equality that makes for convivial dining. Should the purpose of the dinner be to honor one of the guests, the occasion takes on an entirely different tone and meaning. And should the guest of honor tower above his dinner companions, mandatory deference rather than easy intercourse will (and should) prevail.

The ease and comfort of diners with special needs sometimes influence where they should be seated. A handicapped guest needing assistance would be placed next to someone—frequently the host or hostess, sometimes an able guest—who knows how to provide assistance without causing embarrassment. Very left-handed people are best accommodated at the left ends of tables, where their cutting will be neither hindered nor hindering. But these special needs account only for modifications, not for the basic plan of seating.

The alteration of men and women around the table was once considered *de rigueur*. Its rationale seems to have been mainly aesthetic, "as important and decorative as the pairing of candlesticks and saltcellars on the table."[4] The regular pattern of alternating appearances colorful and sedate, feminine and masculine, produced a symmetrical and matched human border to the already adorned table. However, another part of the function of gender-alternate seating was to promote a certain kind of conversation. Its contribution to the dinner's speech and companionship was even more important than its contribution to the dinner's look.

In former times, when men and women worked in different "spheres," and when the public and private aspects of life were more clearly separated, the dinner party was that special semiprivate, social-but-not-public gathering in which men and women came together as peers. By preventing gendered clustering, alternate seating prevented "shoptalk," both men's and women's. Though men and women no doubt brought different outlooks and sensibilities to the table, conversation was forced to seek and play on common ground—in tacit affirmation of both the common necessity that brings all to the table and the common humanity that humanizes and ennobles necessity by transforming it into dining. Dinner partners, at a minimum, must be conversationally compatible. At best they are conversationally convivial, each enlivening and delighting the others. The chief consideration governing the arrangement of seating at dinner is conversation.

Table Talk

What kind of conversation is fit (or unfit) for the table, and, more specifically, for the dinner party? And how is it related to the meal? Conversation, loosely understood, means any back-and-forth exchange involving two or more people. But not all such mutual speaking and listening go with dinner. Conversation, in the more precise sense, is something more restricted and, indeed, refined. In spirit and manner, if not also in content, it can be distinguished from communication, recital, argument, boasting, advertisement, announcement, gossip, inquiry, small talk, shoptalk, exchange of opinion, edification, and even discussion.

In communication (from *communis*, Latin for "common"), we seek to make known what we think and, these days, especially how we feel. We disclose, and hence make public or common, what was previously hidden and private, indeed, for the purpose of just such disclosure and spread.* "Good communicators" are able to "express" themselves effectively, to force out (*ex* + *press*) in understandable speech their own feelings and opinions, welcome or not:

> In communication, people express their true feelings and tell everything about themselves with complete honesty, holding back nothing except their last names. "Hi," a good communicator will open, "I'm Josh!" Or

---

*The verb "to communicate" also means "to transmit a disease" to others.

"I'm Heather!" And by the end of the soup course, you will know how this person feels about our environment, the role of women, an ex-spouse and/or recent ex-lover, joggers, Humphrey Bogart, people who are not afraid to show their feelings, people who are not afraid to be vulnerable, the materialistic society, the media, what people would eat if they knew what was good, and the rewards of working with people.

A true communicator will take the trouble to find out your name and to insert it into his recital often, the way creators of form letters are now able to do through the wonders of technology. A form question will appear now and again also, inviting the communicatee to fill in his or her taste preferences, but only if they conform to those stated.[5]

This is hardly conversation. Neither are recitals and reportage.

Reports of the day's events have become regular parts of the family dinner, when we catch each other up on the adventures in school, office, or playground. But these recitals hold attention mainly because we care about the lives of the reporters, not because we find the content of the reports intrinsically engaging. True, an anecdote drawn from a recent happening may spark a conversation, but to engage in mutual recitals of experiences and adventures is not yet to converse, not even when there is follow-up questioning and answers given in response.

Though conversation permits disagreements, it is in spirit different from argument. Argument is earnest and seriously bent on victory or conversion. It is therefore incompatible with mirth and conviviality. So too are boasting, advertisement, and other forms of self-promotion, designed to enhance one's status or to promote one's career. Gossip about people who are absent, or even about oneself, is likewise different from conversation. Gossip need not be malicious and can be entertaining; it can even be instructive, especially insofar as it reveals something general about the variety of human types. Indeed it is sometimes difficult to distinguish a personal anecdote that illustrates a general point from idle gossip. But a true conversation is recognizably different from the mutual exchange of gossip. The mutual exchange of ideas comes closer, but even this formulation, as we shall soon see, misses the mark: Conversation is not a species of trade or exchange, in which each trader is seeking to swap for or to receive what belongs to another.

Inquiry, discussion, and edification are all high forms of human speech, carried on in pursuit of truth, clarification, or instruction. The family dinner is often put into the service of such instruction—though chastisement and criticism violate the table's spirit of mirth and are probably bad for digestion. Benjamin Franklin reports, with an approval that one suspects to be ironical, on his father's educational use of the dinner table:

> At his Table he lik'd to have as often as he could, some sensible Friend or Neighbour, to converse with, and always took care to start some ingenious or useful Topic for Discourse, which might tend to improve the Minds of his Children. By this means he turn'd our Attention to what was good, just, and prudent in the Conduct of Life; and little or no Notice was ever taken of what related to the Victuals on the Table, whether it was well or ill drest, in or out of season, of good or bad flavour, preferable or inferior to this or that other thing of the kind; so that I was bro't up in such a perfect Inattention to those Matters as to be quite Indifferent to what kind of Food was set before me; and so unobservant of it, that to this Day, if I am ask'd I can scarce tell, a few Hours after Dinner, what I din'd upon. This has been a Convenience to me in travelling, where my Companions have been sometimes very unhappy for want of a suitable Gratification of their more delicate because better instructed Tastes and Appetites.[6]

Such indifference to food is hardly conducive to dining. Moreover, however useful and edifying the instruction, dinner—or rather dining—is not simply a seminar with food.

What, then, is conversation and why is it the fitting form of dining discourse? The word *conversation* goes back to the Old French *converser*, meaning, first, to pass one's life or to live or dwell with someone and, later, to exchange words. The primary Latin source, *conversari*, literally and originally means "to turn oneself about" and "to move to and fro." This self-turning and moving to and fro presumably became the image that conveyed the later meanings of passing one's life and keeping company with others, toward whom one turns and with whom one moves, sometimes this way, sometimes that. This more comprehensive sense of conversing as "living with" gradually was transformed and narrowed to conversing as "talking with." Yet, even so, the connotations of leisure and passing time, of unhurriedness and spontaneity, of exploration and invention, of being well turned and well rounded, and, above all, of openness and responsiveness are still attached to the idea of conversation.

A conversation has no script or plan. It is a construction built by the free play of the mind, out of information, stories, experiences, and opinions contributed by the participants, each of whom is open both to the already contributed speeches, and to the souls, of the contributing speakers. Conducted on topics of general and common interest, and therefore *not* highly personal or private, conversation turns where it will, often moving far afield as the participants respond to what is put before them. Though wit is welcome, indeed prized, in such conversation, it is not a contest of wit but a "game" in which there are no losers. For all (in principle) share in the common construction and in each of the several contributions as it is offered. One person's speech turns another's mind around. The topic, too, is turned round and round, looked at and appreciated from all sides and idly—which is to say for its own sake. And, as the listeners and speakers take turns turning toward one another, round and round, each speech provides another glimpse of the speaker's soul.

Spontaneous conversation, curiously, imitates the artfully prepared dinner. There is frequent change of course and topic. Each course in the meal is carefully prepared to look beautiful and to taste good, yet to be different from the rest. Conversation, too, will reflect that variety, yet each "course" will please the palate of the mind. Because our interest is in both the speakers and the speeches, conversation enables us to taste, indeed to savor, the souls of our fellow diners—not their intimate private depths or their polished public personae, but that wonderful side of the soul at play, when it is unself-consciously and immediately being its open, companionable, and responsive self. The openness and responsiveness of the diners is, on the occasion, not unrelated to the meal; stimulation of the palate stimulates the mind. Conversation at dinner, though not *about* the food, can often be inspired *by* the food. Good talk and good food go naturally together.

Conversation is a special, playful perfection of speaking, as dining is of eating, in which we delight in finely turned speech and speaker as well as in the finely turned roast. The goal is neither mainly understanding nor nourishment but tasteful appreciation. We come to ideas in the same way as we come to flavors, spices, textures: to be able to discern their being and their variety, and to appreciate them exactly for what they are worth—which is, in a way, not very much. The high play of thought and ideas, built around a meal, is a human ballet, in which both our appetites and our rationality are transformed and integrated into a very exquisite and specifically human form—graceful, lively, tasteful, delightful, free.

The Virtues of Dining

Grace, good taste, and freedom are indeed the keynotes of dining. Indeed they are the virtues of refined eating and, even more, of refined hospitality. In ordinary hospitality, as we saw in Chapter 3, we recognize and serve the stranger's needs for food and drink. We act from self-conscious recognition of our common humanity and our mutual neediness. But in arranging and hosting a dinner party we go beyond what is necessary. We entertain not strangers but friends (or at least acquaintances), and we do so gladly and with an open hand. In the best case we display the virtue of liberality, the virtue par excellence—as the name implies—of *free* human beings.

When Aristotle, in his *Nicomachean Ethics*, turns to the moral virtues displayed in ordinary social or civic life, he places liberality at their head.* The Greek word *eleutheriotēs*, translated "liberality," means, to begin with, the character becoming a free man as opposed to a slave. Aristotle narrows it to the virtue pertaining to giving and spending wealth, perhaps because enslavement to wealth is the most common temptation for the free man, or perhaps because the exercise of generosity is the virtue most accessible to all free men. Not everyone has the opportunity to display courage in battle or to show greatness of soul in holding office; but everyone not owned by an-

---

*The discussion of liberality is preceded by the treatment of courage and moderation, virtues dealing with what Aristotle calls the nonrational aspects of the soul, fear of death and bodily harm and love of bodily pleasure. But liberality stands first in the "gentlemanly" virtues, the virtues of nobility in civic life. These have to do with money, honor, anger, and social intercourse. Wittiness, a virtue to which we shall return, concludes the virtues of this group, after which Aristotle treats justice and practical wisdom, which—along with courage and moderation—comprise the so-called cardinal virtues. In short, the noble virtues (all presented in book 4), from liberality to wit, are the special feature of the moral life as presented by Aristotle. I would argue that they remain among the most admirable virtues of social life even today.

other is free to give. Everyone with a home can freely invite others to enjoy his hospitality.

Though, because they are useful to others, liberal people are, of all virtuous people, perhaps the most beloved, Aristotle argues that their excellence rests mainly not on grounds of utility but rather on those of nobility. For the truly liberal man gives, rightly and gladly, for the sake of the noble. He gives precisely in order to display an inner freedom from enslavement to money, for he understands that money is a mere means, not an end. To exaggerate—but only slight-ly—money, because it is merely useful, is most properly used when it is freely spent or given away. The free disposition regarding money is best displayed not when money is to be spent on necessities but when it is spent gratuitously—that is, in gracious giving beyond what is needed or owed. Because he is inwardly free *from* attachment to money, the liberal man is outwardly free *to* give and to give cheerful-ly and well. He gives what is fitting, to those whom it fits, at appro-priate times and in the gracious manner.

Generally speaking the liberal man gives for the sake of giving. Thus, for example, the liberal man or woman hosts a dinner party simply for the pleasure of doing so—and of doing so well. Throwing a party is perhaps the most characteristic activity of liberality, for one hosts a feast or a party, just as one presents gifts of all sorts, not for the needy but for those who are near and dear; liberality is different from charity. It is distinguished also from justice, for liberal giving has nothing to do with what one *owes* to another. Though it is, of course, mannerly to return invitations, there is something constrain-ing—that is, illiberal—in entertaining others mainly in return for their having entertained you. To give what is owed, though surely praiseworthy, is not a fully free act, especially insofar as it is given *be-cause* it is owed rather than from the nobility and beauty of giving rightly and finely.

In light of these general comments about liberality, we see more clearly how excellence as a host is a manifestation of liberality. Though expenditure is made for food—that is, for the necessities— the generous host and hostess are no slaves to necessity and show it by providing and doing all kinds of unnecessary—that is, free and gratuitous—things. They are open handed, not tight fisted, neither calculating nor penny pinching. But neither are they wasteful nor ostentatious; generosity that is confident of itself as generosity has no need to go overboard in excessive abundance or vulgar display. Though one cannot be liberal without some surplus, generosity is *not* a function of the amount of money spent on dinner.

Some moralists argue that it is more liberal to give not out of surplus but out of sacrifice. They point to the great praise reserved for those who give when they have next to nothing, who will deprive themselves to feed a stranger, who despite being poor act as if they were rich. We all know stories, both actual and fictitious, of people who have little or nothing but who nonetheless manifest extraordinary generosity (see, for example, the classic tale of Baucis and Philemon, told in Ovid's *Metamorphoses*). Rather than forget about necessity, these necessitous benefactors transform necessity while remembering and feeling—through acts of self-sacrifice—its necessary character. There is no question that these are acts of virtue. But there is a difficulty in this attempt to make the greater generosity one of self-sacrifice, a difficulty that undercuts the claim: The host must deny or hide the fact that his gifts are difficult to offer, for otherwise the guests will be unable to enjoy the meal. Especially at a dinner party, both host and guest must look upon the host not as needy but as "rich"—not in any absolute sense, but in the sense of having more than enough, more than is necessary. True, many who are literally wealthy will be stingy and many who are not will be generous, and liberality is not a matter of how much you have but what you do with it. Nevertheless the freest acts require some surplus, for they must be absolutely untainted with what is owed or what is needed. As a general matter the habitual practice of liberality depends on a certain degree of emancipation from necessity; one needs freedom from numbing toil and grinding poverty to be able to look upon life through the lens of liberality and nobility, of giving and living for the sheer pleasure of doing so.*

Because the expenditures of liberality are relative both to one's means and to the occasion, an excellent host and hostess show their generosity much more in the spirit and manner of their hospitality.

---

*The relation of nobility and sacrifice, however, should be kept in mind. Later we shall see how such noble generosity might relate to sacrifice in the sense of making something sacred or of doing the sacred thing—of sanctification.

They set the table with their best cloth and dishes, they take special pains over the menu and its preparation and service, they create a welcoming mood by receiving guests graciously and by tactfully attending to their several needs and pleasures, and they see to it that there is mirth and conviviality at the table. Above all they make clear by their demeanor and conduct that their guest's enjoyment is their own greatest pleasure. They adhere to the aphorism of Brillat-Savarin: "To entertain a guest is to be answerable for his happiness so long as he is beneath your roof." Yet they aim to do so effortlessly, in a manner that hides any hint of duty or difficulty; guests cannot enjoy themselves if they feel their presence is a strain or a burden. When all goes as it should, the virtuous freedom of the hosts becomes contagious, emancipating and enlivening all the assembled diners and promoting the spirit of companionable good fellowship around the well-furnished table.

The generous intention of the hosts' liberality has its outward manifestation in tact and grace; by these evident marks the connoisseur can often distinguish truly liberal acts from certain counterfeits—for example, when the right deeds are done but done against the doer's grain. Tact (from the Latin *tactus*, past participle of *tangere*, "to touch"), that virtually indescribable exquisitely keen feel and touch for the nuances of every situation, enables the just-right-word to be spoken and the just-right-gesture to be made, at just the right time. A well-timed question brings a silent guest into the conversation, a host's arm delicately offered en route to the table prevents an unsteady elderly guest from corrosive self-attention. Tactful speech and deed make it possible for guests not only to feel welcome but also to accept easily and without any obtrusive burden of gratitude the gifts of hospitality extended toward them. There may be a guest at dinner who will be unable to reciprocate equally, in kind and in degree, but it is terribly important to his enjoyment of the evening that such inequalities never cross his mind. Tact is the means for obscuring any odious distinctions and for smoothing over other possibly abrasive surfaces in the social to and fro.

If tact attends deftly to the details of social intercourse, grace (from the Latin *gratia*, "favor," "charm," "thanks"; from *gratus*, "pleasing" or "grateful") gives light and warmth to the party as a whole. The host and hostess display their own gratitude for the company of their guests, in a manner both courteous and charming. An attractive appearance, a pleasingly easy air and bearing, a ready and cheerful responsiveness, and supple and harmonious movements all charm the guests and beautify the entire occasion. The desire to please gives no trace of unctiousness, obsequiousness, or servility: All kindness seems effortless, all solicitude seems easy, all service seems free. Like the prima ballerina and her partner, hostess and host move everyone around them into a delicate and uplifting dance. The Greeks would see on such occasions the mysterious presence of the three sister goddesses, the Graces, givers of charm and beauty.*

If liberality, expressed with grace and tact, is the supreme virtue of the host, what is the correlative virtue of the guest? At first glance it might seem to be gratitude. Gratitude is certainly a fitting response to generosity received, and expressions of thanks, properly tendered, are surely in order—not only at the end of an evening when saying goodnight, but soon thereafter by a handwritten note. Gratitude is usually felt and certainly expressed mainly if not exclusively after the event. While fitting, however, it is not the complementary virtue of the dining guest during the meal itself: That virtue is wittiness.

Wit is the toast of a perfect dinner party. The witty guest, master of arts in conversation, makes the table sparkle with splendid talk: a sharp observation here, a charming anecdote there, now an engaging question, later a touching reminiscence—always adeptly and aptly inserted into the conversation. Thanks to the witty guest, speech flows freely, cheerfully, and energetically wherever the conversation naturally leads.

The anecdote or story is the stock in trade of the witty guest, who tacitly knows what is tacitly expected of him when dining out. A collector of stories, he does not come empty headed to the table. Writes Joseph Epstein of one such master raconteur:

> Shortly thereafter . . . my friend died, and not long after that I met another friend of his, and we condoled with each other about how we

---

*From here it is but a short step—as we shall soon see—to the biblical notion of grace, that unmerited divine assistance that regenerates and sanctifies ordinary human life, and, in recognition of this possibility, to the saying of grace before a meal, by means of which diners give thanks for (unmerited) food and companionship or ask for a bestowal of grace upon the present dinner and their fellow diners.

should miss him. "He was a great storyteller," this man averred. "You must know that story of his about there being so many witnesses on the street." He then told me other of our now-deceased friend's stories, and I had to allow that I knew them, too, including one that involved a splendid imitation of Sir Isaiah Berlin. Plainly we were talking about an established repertoire of successful anecdotes that a bachelor, as our dead friend was, used to help pay his social way when dining out. (Hence the meaning of the phrase, which I did not understand when many years ago I first heard it, "dining out on a story.") My dear friend's performance was superior; his bill was marked paid in full in our home and, my guess is, in every other where he was a guest.[7]

Epstein, of course, exaggerates when speaking of wit as payment for dinner. Were it understood in this way, it would hardly be the spontaneous and gratuitous thing it is. True, many of us must work hard to be amusing or entertaining, but for the witty man or woman the power of sparkling speech is, as it were, second nature.

Wittiness, the sort that is a human excellence and the toast of dining, needs to be distinguished from other sorts of amusing speech and conduct. Not everything funny belongs at table. Neither is every funny man excellently funny. The witty person is certainly different from the clown or buffoon, a title originally given to the man who literally peddled laughs for his supper.

A buffoon in classical Greece is a *bomolochos*, from *bomos*, "altar," and *lochos*, "one who lies in wait." The *bomolochos* was, in its original meaning, a fellow who lurks about the altar, the place of sacrifices to the gods, looking for the scraps of food one can get there—that is, a beggar. Metaphorically the term was applied also to that fellow who would do any dirty work or say any outrageous thing to get a meal—a lickspittle, a low jester, a clown, a buffoon. Though such men live by their wits, they are in their speeches and deeds usually ribald rather than witty, coarse rather than fine, bumptious rather than deft. For these confident demythologizers, a bone is a bone and a meal a meal, containing no possibility of anything high—neither mental nor sacred. Indeed for them a meal is not even a meal—an integral unit—but merely an aggregate of scraps, a heap rather than a whole (analogous to the view of the anatomized human body that is often the butt of their coarse humor). Irreverent, crude, and derisive, they expose everything to ridicule. Of course they can be very funny, but their humor is not the stuff of either virtue or dining.

Opposite to the *bomolochos,* and opposed also to the witty man, is the humorless oaf, in Greek, *agroikos,* literally, "the man of the fields." He is all work and no play. Because he toils for his food, he takes it with deadly seriousness. A man of necessity, he is not truly free. Such a man can have many virtues: He is likely to be sober, dependable, hardworking, enduring, even patriotic and courageous. He could well be the model yeoman-citizen-soldier of classical republics, much esteemed in the United States by the anti-Federalists and (recently) by communitarians,* but he would hardly be an enjoyable and lively dinner partner, nor would he himself delight in finding himself seated next to one.

The virtuously witty man stands between the buffoon and the rustic. His speech is characterized by tact and dexterity. He can deftly insert a good anecdote or turn back a clever riposte. But he does so with delicacy. He will say and allow to be said to him—especially at table—only the sort of things that are suitable to a free and decent man. His is the jesting of a gentleman (or lady), not of someone servile. In his every remark he respects and speaks *up* to the intelligence of his companions. He avoids giving pain to the object of his railleries; he avoids causing embarrassment by a tactless remark. And he stays away from certain subjects—for example, obscenity—which, though they might draw a laugh and at nobody's expense, are beneath the dignity of civilized conversation, certainly while dining.

Wittiness, like liberality embracing both grace and tact, is a virtue of character. At its core it is a disposition toward social speech, and even more, toward one's social partners—to lighten and cheer without giving offense. Though the virtuously witty person is more than clever, wittiness more than most of the other moral virtues requires a dexterous and lively mind.

Wit, like humor in general, depends on mental distance. We must detach ourselves from the object under view in order to behold and scrutinize it. And we must at least partially detach ourselves affec-

*When Rousseau blasted progress in the arts and sciences and other refinements of civilized life, he did so in the name of these civic virtues. Though himself a great wit, he saw the tension between refinement and republicanism. See his *Discourse on the Arts and Sciences.*

tively in order to see humor; strong identification with the subject precludes our finding it amusing, let alone ridiculous. (True, we can laugh at ourselves, but we do so only because and when we are capable of relaxing our mental and emotional self-attachment; we adopt toward ourselves the view of wry Olympian detachment.) In this respect wittiness is perhaps the most philosophical of the social virtues. It draws us away from our bodily concerns and our self-preoccupations. It deflates our vanity, stimulates our mind, encourages leisurely and unencumbered noticing. Its levity levitates the soul, yet never so enjoyably as during a splendid meal.

One might think that wit, being lighthearted, is the enemy of moderation, the heart of sobriety. But this is to mistake wit for ribaldry and moderation for asceticism. Civility in table manners and urbanity in speech and humor are entirely compatible. Both aim at something graceful, noble, refined. To be sure, the primal table manners (Chapter 4) were connected with shame, and the need to suppress the ugly features of eating—noisy slubbering, and so on. But the more developed and gracious manners of table, as we see, not only hide the ugly but cultivate the beautiful. Bodily need is not dressed down but dressed up.

In contrast to wit, ribaldry—ever mindful of our underlying animality—refuses to allow it to be dressed up or suppressed. In truth a nervous attempt to prevent a falling into the ugly, ribald humor often makes ugliness its theme, pretending thereby to put at least laughing distance between the mind and the body, the latter being treated as obscenity. Or, in other cases, where an ascetic cultural norm deprecates the body, ribald humor overcompensates by laughing down all suggestions of human loftiness and by glorying in the body made grotesque.* But a dinner party, properly conducted, is itself a refutation of all such misanthropic views: it already celebrates embodied life; it has found the fitting way to integrate and nourish both soul and body, the activity of speaking with the activity of eating (and tasting). Analogously refined humor or wit understands that embod-

---

*See, for example, Rabelais' tales of Gargantua and Pantagruel, which contain such episodes as "How Gargantua Ate Six Pilgrims in a Salad" and "How Pantagruel with His Tongue Covered an Entire Army, and What the Author Saw in His Mouth." These enjoyable stories in their time provided a necessary corrective for Medieval undervaluing of earthly embodied life. But one would not want them recited at dinner.

iment is not, finally, laughable or ridiculous. Our bodily and psychic needs bring us together for shared meals and shared speech. And the aesthetic pleasures in tastes and stories are perfections of our mindfully embodied being. Grace is impossible both for disembodied minds and for mindless bodies.

So too is friendship, whose beginnings are made possible by dinner. The shared meal itself grounds our being together. Amiability and friendliness are required and shared around the table. But it is the community of stories and conversation that is the true communion. Fellow diners get to know each other's minds and hearts, even though no one explicitly is baring his soul or trafficking in personal matters. We are drawn to those whose tastes and tales we find admirable and charming. We arrange to dine with them again on another occasion. Unlike the specifically philosophical friendship, with minds joined in the shared pursuit of wisdom, the aesthetic friendship of good taste celebrates the complete psychosomatic grown-to-getherness that is the human being. At the same time the enlivened mind is free to reflect, often well after dinner is over, on the deeper meaning of a well-told tale or even on the splendid variety of human types that one has "tasted" while at the dining table. The generous and philanthropic hospitality of the gracious host and the nimble wit of the charming guest, all warmly remembered, enlarge our hearts and minds and beckon us toward friendship.

It might be said here, and fairly, that the friendship of the dining table may not be the highest or fullest kind of friendship. Just as pointing is out of place at table, so too is the philosophical friendship to which it points. Precisely the avoidance of serious discussion and philosophical inquiry, necessary for maintaining the light and convivial mood of dinner, precludes the deepest meeting of minds.* Amiable enjoyment of what we know differs from determined pursuit of what we do not know. Fine as it is, dining is not the highest peak of human life, nor is witty conversation the supreme expression of our rational humanity. Upright posture has still-higher possibilities.

---

*I freely admit that I would rather be a silent guest at the banquet described in Plato's *Symposium*, listening to Socrates and Aristophanes discourse on *eros*, than a sparkling participant in the wittiest of dinner parties.

Yet, that said, we are not wrong in esteeming the humanity displayed in dinner conversation, which, I would argue, still represents a peak activity for the *hungry* thoughtful animal. Far from being an escape from the serious demands of life, witty and convivial dining—a species of high play—pays tribute to the meaningfulness of human life and its possibilities for community, freedom, and nobility—all in the act of sustaining life through nourishment. Further, the detachment needed for wit and laughter is akin to that needed for seeking truth, and the free play of the mind in conversation often provides food for deeper thought. Philosophy, it used to be said, begins in wonder, and (as I have tried to show) there is much that is wonder-ful in the things seen and heard around the dinner table. Dining is both excellent in itself and a token of something more: Its amiability anticipates friendship, its free speech anticipates pursuit of truth or philosophy, its beauty (or nobility) promises and beckons to the good.

The Culinary Artist and the Moment of Truth

In concentrating to this point on the virtues of host and guest, we have managed to overlook the one person without whom a dinner party would be just a party—the cook, preparer of the meal. The host may be supremely generous and gracious, the guests may be ever so witty and charming, but it is the virtuosity of the chef that makes for especially festive dining. The virtues of the master chef are preeminently artistic, comprising order, balance, harmony, and—above all, especially in the present matter—good taste.

Any work of art is, in a sense, the artist at work. As the poet lives in his poem, and the painter in his painting, so too the cook as cook lives in his cooking. The good taste of the chef is manifest in the good tastes of the ordered meal. Moreover, when appreciated by the discerning tastes of the diners, the virtues of the meal itself transform and elevate the souls of the diners. The aesthetic experience mysteriously provides both bodily and spiritual satisfaction.

Nowhere is this phenomenon more beautifully presented than in a short story by Isak Dinesen, "Babette's Feast," which has been made into an excellent film (of the same name). The experience described, which can only be captured in the imagination, deserves an artistic treatment; allow me then a modest attempt at retelling, with help from the author in the form of frequent excerpts from the original.

The story is set in the late nineteenth century in a tiny Norwegian fishing village, where the weather is severe and life is hard. The inhabitants of the village are devoted followers of a forceful minister and prophet who had founded his own very pious Lutheran sect and whose legacy is faithfully preserved by his two maiden daughters, Martine (named for Martin Luther) and Philippa (for Luther's friend Philip Melanchthon). The two sisters, reared to deny all earthly pleasures, cheerfully spend their lives performing good works for the needy and lonely inhabitants of the village, celebrating their father's teachings in meetings of prayer and singing of hymns, and preparing for the New Jerusalem hereafter. Babette, a French-woman fleeing Paris and its civil wars of 1871, comes to the village seeking refuge and is given shelter by the sisters, for whom she becomes a maid of all work.

Suspicious of French luxury (and papism), the sisters promptly initiate Babette into their ascetic (and Lutheran) ways and show her how to prepare a split cod and an ale-and-bread soup:

> They . . . explained to her that they were poor and that to them luxurious fare was sinful. Their own food must be as plain as possible; it was the soup-pails and the baskets for their poor that signified. Babette nodded her head; as a girl, she informed her ladies, she had been cook to an old priest who was a saint. Upon this the sisters resolved to surpass the French priest in asceticism. And they soon found that from the day when Babette took over the house-keeping its cost was miraculously reduced, and the soup-pails and baskets acquired a new, mysterious power to stimulate and strengthen their poor and sick.[8]

Babette has been in the sisters' service for twelve years when the sisters decide to celebrate the hundredth anniversary of their father's birth, "as if their dead father were still among his disciples." They are, however, saddened by the growing discord and dissension among the members of his flock, now smaller in number and advanced in years. In the absence of their spiritual leader, fifty-year-old grievances and antagonisms resurface; ancient guilts and recriminations fester. In the midst of the sisters' apprehensions, Babette learns that she has won ten thousand francs in the French lottery. Soon thereafter she begs the sisters to let her cook a celebration dinner on the dean's birthday, a real French dinner, and to let her pay for the French dinner with her newly gained money. The sisters (who had not intended to have a dinner at all) resist but finally yield to Babette's pleading:

> Ladies, you who say your prayers every day, can you imagine what it means to a human heart to have no prayer to make? What would Babette have had to pray for? Nothing! Tonight she had a prayer to make, from the bottom of her heart. Do you not then feel tonight, my ladies, that it becomes you to grant it her, with such joy as that with which the good God has granted you your own?[9]

Recognizing that this was Babette's first request in those twelve years, and that "their cook was now better off than they, and a dinner could make no difference to a person who owned ten thousand francs," the sisters relent and accept Babette's proposal.

Babette, transformed by the sisters' consent, sets about planning and preparing the feast. But when the goods ordered from France arrive in the village the sisters are horrified. First of all there is a wheelbarrow full of wine:

> "What is there in this bottle, Babette?" she [Martine] asked in a low voice. "Not wine?" "Wine, Madame!" Babette answered. "No, Madame. It is a Clos Vougeot 1846!" After a moment she added: "From Philippe, in Rue Montorgueil!" Martine had never suspected that wines could have names to them, and was put to silence.[10]

But, even worse, Babette has imported a huge, live tortoise, the sight of which horrifies Martine. That night Martine dreams that she and her sister were lending their father's house to a witches' Sabbath, with the diabolical Babette "poisoning the old Brothers and Sisters, Philippa and herself." In the morning she visits each of the faithful and warns them that she cannot vouch for what they will be served to eat at the celebratory dinner. The old people "promised one another that for their little sisters' sake they would, on the great day, be silent upon all matters of food and drink. Nothing that might be set before them, be it even frogs or snails, should wring a word from their lips." Said one white-bearded Brother: "On the day of our master we will cleanse our tongues of all taste and purify them of all delight or disgust of the senses, keeping and preserving them for the higher things of praise and thanksgiving."[11] Shaking hands on this vow, the community of the pious steels itself against the dangerous culinary corruption of voluptuous France.

An unexpected visitor to these parts, a nephew of one of the dean's first supporters, who still lives on an estate in the surrounding countryside, is invited with his aunt as the twelfth guest at dinner— where, it turns out, he will play the crucial part. General Lorens Loewenhielm had thirty years earlier visited his aunt, having been commanded to do so by his father, who hoped this retreat would lead his dissolute young officer son to mend his ways. Young Loewenhielm had then fallen in love at first sight with the beautiful Martine, who inspired in him a "mighty vision of a higher and purer life, with no creditors, dunning letters or parental lectures, with no secret, unpleasant pangs of conscience and with a gentle, golden-haired angel to guide and reward him."[12] But forced to see her only in the company of her father and his disciples, in prayer meetings, he found himself tongue-tied and more and more insignificant, and incapable of reconciling his hope for a purer life with his very earthy erotic desire for Martine. Believing himself ill-fated in this pursuit, he left, vowing never to return. Instead, to forget his sorrow over impossible love, he threw himself wholly into career and society. By the time of Babette's feast, he has become a highly decorated general, well-married and prominent in royal circles. Yet, though both successful and morally upright, the now-elderly Lorens Loewenhielm is strangely unhappy, "worrying about his immortal soul." As he prepares for the celebratory dinner, the general resolves that night to settle accounts with his younger self—"who had felt himself to be a shy and sorry figure in the house of the Dean, and who in the end had shaken its dust off his riding boots. He would let the youth prove to him, once and for all, that thirty-one years ago he had made the right choice."[13]

As the general and his aunt are traveling to the village in their sledge, the disciples gather in the home of the sisters and begin singing hymns composed by their master. The words reassure the sisters about the impending event: *"Take not thought for food or raiment careful one, so anxiously"* and *"Wouldst thou give a stone, a reptile to thy pleading child for food?"* Just at this point the Loewenhielms arrive. General Loewenhielm, "tall, broad and ruddy, in his bright uniform, his breast covered with decorations, strutted and shone like an ornamental bird, a golden pheasant or a peacock, in this sedate party of black crows and jackdaws." [14] The story is set for its climax, Babette's feast.

When the guests were seated at the candlelit and well-set table, all elegantly furnished from abroad by Babette,

> the eldest member of the congregation said grace in the Dean's own words:
>
> > *"May my food my body maintain,*
> > *may my body my soul sustain,*
> > *may my soul in deed and word*
> > *give thanks for all things to the Lord."*
>
> At the word of "food" the guests, with their old heads bent over their folded hands, remembered how they had vowed not to utter a word about the subject, and in their hearts they reinforced the vow: they would not even give it a thought! [15]

But as the first glass of wine is solemnly lifted, the general, startled by its taste and bouquet, remarks to himself, "Amontillado! This is the finest Amontillado that I have ever tasted." To test his senses, he tries the soup, with the same result: "'This is exceedingly strange!' he said to himself. 'For surely I am eating turtle-soup—and what turtle-soup!' He was seized by a queer kind of panic and emptied his glass." [16]

Although the people of Berlevaag do not usually speak much during meals, "somehow this evening tongues had been loosened." People tell stories of how they first met the dean or about the wondrous happenings that took place under his pastorship. The general dominates the conversation, but he, too, speaks in reverent tones. But as each new dish or wine is served, he is dumbstruck, not only by pleasures of taste and recognition—"Incredible! . . . It is Blinis Demidoff," or "But surely this is a Veuve Cliquot 1860?"—but also by the silent indifference of his companions, who are "quietly eating their Blinis Demidoff without any sign of either surprise or approval, as if they had been doing so every day for thirty years." [17]

The company "grew lighter in weight and lighter of heart the more they ate and drank." When the main course is served the general sits transfixed. He remembers a dinner that had been given in his honor, at which the same "incredibly recherché and palatable dish" had been served. His host, a certain Colonel Galliffet, had told him that it was named "Cailles en Sarcophage" (quail in sarcophagus) and that

> the dish had been invented by the chef of the very café in which they were dining, a person known all over Paris as the greatest culinary genius of the age, and—most surprisingly—a woman! "And indeed," said Colonel Galliffet, "this woman is now turning a dinner at the Café Anglais into a kind of love affair—into a love affair of the noble and romantic category in which one no longer distinguishes between bodily and spiritual appetite or satiety! I have, before now, fought a duel for the sake of a fair lady. For no woman in all Paris, my young friend, would I more willingly shed my blood!" [18]

Remembering the colonel's remarks, and now filled with awe, General Loewenhielm turns to his neighbor and says, "But this is Cailles en Sarcophage!" His neighbor, looking at him absentmindedly and then, nodding his head, answers, "Yes, Yes, certainly. What else would it be?"

The conversation moved from the master's miracles to the kindly acts of his daughters. Warmth and goodwill abounded. No longer wondering at anything, the general, at meal's end, "felt that the time had come to make a speech. He rose and stood up very straight. . . . The old people lifted their eyes to the face above them in high, happy expectation. They were used to seeing sailors and vagabonds dead drunk with the crass gin of the country, but they did not recognize in a warrior and courtier the intoxication brought about by the noblest wine in the world." [19]

The general, though a trained speaker, spoke as he had never spoken before, as if he were "but a mouthpiece for a message which meant to be brought forth."

> "Man, my friends," said General Loewenhielm, "is frail and foolish. We have all of us been told that grace is to be found in the universe. But in our human foolishness and short-sightedness we imagine divine grace to be finite. For this reason we tremble . . ." Never till now had the General

stated that he trembled; he was genuinely surprised and even shocked at hearing his own voice proclaim the fact. "We tremble before making our choice in life, and after having made it again tremble in fear of having chosen wrong. But the moment comes when our eyes are opened, and we see and realize that grace is infinite. Grace, my friends, demands nothing from us but that we shall await it with confidence and acknowledge it in gratitude. Grace, brothers, makes no conditions and singles out none of us in particular; grace takes us all to its bosom and proclaims general amnesty. See! that which we have chosen is given us, and that which we have refused is, also and at the same time, granted us. Ay, that which we have rejected is poured on us abundantly. For mercy and truth have met together, and righteousness and bliss have kissed one another!"[20]

The assembled, though they only partly understood the general's words, were deeply moved by his inspired countenance and his use of familiar and cherished words. Yet what followed was more remarkable still:

> Of what happened later in the evening nothing definite can here be stated. None of the guests later on had any clear remembrance of it. They only knew that the rooms had been filled with a heavenly light, as if a number of small halos had blended into one glorious radiance. Taciturn old people received the gift of tongues; ears that for years had been almost deaf were opened to it. Time itself had merged into eternity. Long after midnight the windows of the house shone like gold, and golden song flowed out into the winter air.[21]

Grace and redemption arrived on the wings of Babette's feast, and each of the twelve companions at the table experienced a share in the eternal.

The story ends with a conversation in the kitchen, after the guests leave, between the sisters and Babette, to whom the sisters express their gratitude. Now, for the first time, Babette reveals that she was once the cook at the Café Anglais in Paris. She also informs the sisters that she will not be returning to Paris, as they had feared she would. For one thing all the grandees for whom she cooked (but against whom she fought in the civil wars) are dead. For another, she has no money, having spent her entire lottery fortune on the feast. (" 'What will you, Mesdames,' said Babette with great dignity. 'A dinner for twelve at the Café Anglais would cost ten thousand francs.' ")

When Philippa protests that Babette ought not to have given away all she had for their sake, "Babette gave her mistress a deep glance, a strange glance. Was there not pity, even scorn, at the bottom of it?"

"For your sake?" she replied. "No. For my own."

She rose from the chopping block and stood up before the two sisters.

"I am a great artist!" she said.

She waited a moment and then repeated: "I am a great artist, Mesdames."

Again for a long time there was deep silence in the kitchen.

Then Martine said: "So you will be poor now all your life, Babette?"

"Poor?" said Babette. She smiled as if to herself. "No, I shall never be poor. I told you that I am a great artist. A great artist, Mesdames, is never poor. We have something, Mesdames, of which other people know nothing." [22]

Babette then reveals her sadness at the loss of her Parisian clientele, who, although many of them were cruel and evil, had been bred to appreciate her great artistry. The great artist needs those of comparable taste. The great artist wants to be applauded only for doing her utmost, not for doing second best.

Philippa, trembling from head to foot, embraces Babette:

For a while she could not speak. Then she whispered:

"Yet this is not the end! I feel, Babette, that this is not the end. In Paradise you will be the great artist that God meant you to be! Ah!" she added, the tears streaming down her cheeks. "Ah, how you will enchant the angels!" [23] *

What are we to make of this story, and especially of its heroine, Babette? The economically minded will see that she has squandered her fortune, and hence sacrificed her entire future, for one dinner, while those who esteem self-sacrifice will praise her precisely on these grounds. The spiritually minded will say that she seeks to create a holy occasion in order to teach the community of self-denying

---

*Thus ends the story, with Philippa repeating to Babette words spoken to her thirty years earlier by a French suitor, a famous opera singer who fell in love with her angelic voice. It was he who later would give Babette a letter of introduction to the sisters when she fled France for Norway.

Lutherans that God's grace manifests itself from the bottom up and does not require the denial of our bodies, or, alternatively, to give these crabbed do-gooders a foretaste of the heavenly New Jerusalem—food, drink, light, love, and reconciliation—which their piety has merited. But according to Babette herself she is a great artist and is moved by a deep desire to practice her art. Great genius of all sorts declines to stay hidden; great virtuosity drives itself forward, endeavors to show itself, seeks to be known. Babette, the greatest culinary genius in France but long deprived of the opportunity for its activity, jumps at the chance once more to be-at-work-what-she-is, even though she surely believes that none of the guests could properly appreciate her feast. She practices to her utmost the art of high cookery utterly alone, for her sake and for its sake—which is to say for the sake of the noble.

But though the noble performance of her art is Babette's own goal, her deed acquires an unforeseen significance, thanks in part to the accidental but grace-ful presence of the general. This connoisseur of fine dining is able to inform the other guests (and the reader), beyond their knowledge, of why this is such a singular meal. And he is himself moved, beyond his own knowledge, to speak of spiritual and transcendent matters; thanks to the delights of the palate, mysterious powers are awakened within him and work part of their magic upon his tongue. But he gives voice to what the others are also silently experiencing. These more humble (but in one respect, perhaps, even better) guests, who graciously agreed to endure the feast in order not to embarrass their hostesses, also play a vital role and reap the reward of their generosity. Though they did not want it, the food and wine—the dreaded Dionysus—work on them to reknit the community in an expression of piety.

Thanks to genius and taste, thanks to the extreme generosity and openness of both host and guest, the visage of the eternal shows itself in the midst of the most temporal, as superb food and wine nourish also the spiritual hungers of the assembled. It is a transcendent moment of grace: Souls and bodies nourished, people are reconciled, united as one, imbued with the old spirit, awake to the presence of the divine. It seems that there are possibilities embedded in the noble that those who pursue and supply the noble may not see.

Isak Dinesen's story—and the film based upon it—magically convey the mysterious possibilities for spiritual elevation available at dinner through the genius of the culinary art. To those who open themselves to its possibilities, festive dining can indeed become a kind of love affair, which simultaneously fulfills the appetites of body and soul. Though the experience may be rare, gracious dining can be graced by the arrival of powerful insight and overflowing humanity. As General Loewenhielm remarks: "Grace, my friends, demands nothing from us but that we shall await it with confidence and acknowledge it in gratitude."

6

Sanctified Eating:

A Memorial of Creation

*If there is no meal there is no Torah, if there is no
Torah there is no meal.*

—*Pirke Aboth (Sayings of the Fathers)*

3:21

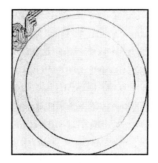

In the last three chapters we have reviewed a variety of customs that restrain human appetite and refine human eating. We began with rules of justice that exclude fellow human beings from the domain of the edible. We moved through manners of civility that seek to distinguish human eating from animal feeding. And we looked into the more refined habits and virtues of dining that further ennoble and beautify human eating, aspiring toward a community of upright, well-turned, and generous human beings, mindful and appreciative of both distinctive tastes and distinctive souls and open to the graceful mysteries of being. We have in large measure succeeded in our effort to show how customs can and do work to improve the human animal, in the directions implicit in his upright posture.

But we are not finished. The upright being may stand tall above the animals, but he remains dwarfed by the larger whole of which he is a part, albeit a special part. As he gazes, thanks to upright posture, on the distant horizon and on the lofty heavens, as he comes to know the many-splendored forms that share with him the earth and help him to survive, and as he comes to reflect on both his neediness and his capacities, he is moved to recognize his dependence on powers and possibilities not of his own making. He is moved by awe, fear, wonder, and gratitude to try to understand his place and meaning in the larger whole. He is moved to discover just how it stands between human beings and the divine. Such concerns and outlooks, too, are incorporated into the customs of eating, in innumerable religious practices and mores throughout the world. Thus the meaning of eating not only reflects human self-understanding, it also embodies the intimations we have regarding our relation to divinity.

I make no attempt here to survey past or present religious practices regarding eating or to attempt, empirically, to gather up their common and divergent strands. Rather, I propose to consider as illustrative a particular set of religious dietary laws that show how the activity of eating can be not only ennobled but even sanctified. For if the argument of this book is sound, one would expect to find exemplary culminating customs regarding eating that manifest a more or less true understanding of the world, including the place of man within the whole. Such an understanding, I submit, is embodied in the dietary laws of the Israelites, first established in biblical times and still practiced by religiously observant Jews down to the present day.

The laws of interest are enunciated primarily in the eleventh chapter of the Book of Leviticus, which sums up its contents as follows: "This is the Law (*torah*) of the beast and of the fowl and of every living creature that moves in the waters and of every creature that swarms upon the earth; to make a difference (*lehavdil*) between the unclean and the clean, and between the living thing that may be eaten and the living thing that may not be eaten" (vv. 46–47). The distinctions elaborated in this chapter define the central dietary laws of the Children of Israel, just as these dietary laws are themselves central to defining Israel as a separate people. But they intend not just a separate people but a *holy* people. God concludes his speech to Moses and Aaron, detailing these laws about eating (and touching),* by connecting their observance with holiness. For the first time in the entire Torah, God enjoins the pursuit of holiness in imitation of His own holiness: The exhortation, "Be ye holy, for I am

---

*This discussion will not treat the laws regarding touching. The text connects but also distinguishes between becoming defiled through contact with *unclean* (*tame*) things and becoming detestable through eating *detestable* (*sheqets*) things. The former pollution, harder to avoid but less serious, lasts only until the evening, whereas the duration of the latter, though not stated, is presumably permanent. The eater becomes akin to what he eats, because it comes to be part of him. The defilement of touching is more superficial; the boundary between the toucher and the outside is

holy," occurs *twice* at the end of the eleventh chapter (vv. 44–45), and offers the apparent purpose for the preceding dietary laws.

Why *these* dietary laws? What have they to do with holiness? These are questions I consider in this chapter. They are not new questions—they have been raised, by friend and foe alike, for centuries[1]—and the many answers that have been proposed indicate how unlikely we are either to say anything new or to say anything definitively true. Moreover, from the point of view of the tradition whose laws these are, it is a questionable practice to raise questions about the why of the dietary laws. The first and also the last thing to be said about them is that they are laws, to be obeyed; that they are commanded by God is the sole and sufficient reason for obeying them. Like law in general, the dietary laws are to be kept, not interrogated. To inquire about the reason or meaning of the law—any law—threatens to weaken its force, given that its binding power lies mainly in its *being* law, rather than in the reasonableness of its content—all the more so in this case, its being a divine commandment. True, if the content of the law, on examination, turns out also to seem reasonable or if it points clearly to the source or principle of law—in this case, to the holy—obedience will not become irksome or less acceptable for this discovery; on the contrary, it might even prove psychically helpful to obedience if the laws, once thought about, can be shown to be not utterly unintelligible and founded not only on the lawgiver's arbitrary will. True, Joshua was commanded to meditate on the Torah day and night (Joshua 1:8), admittedly as a preparation for obedience, but to meditate nonetheless, and the First Psalm calls blessed the man whose delight is in the law of the Lord and who meditates in it day and night. Still, one risks misunderstanding, not to mention disrespect, by treating the dietary laws as a subject of philosophical inquiry, even when the approach is sympathetic.

Nevertheless, I am willing to run these risks, for two reasons. The lesser reason is for cultural self-understanding. Everyone acknowledges that the West is what it is largely because of biblical religion; Jerusalem is one of the sources of our civilization. A central document of Western civilization, the Torah, or Pentateuch, has at its center a set

---

soiled but not penetrated. Though one can show in this way the resemblance between eating and touching—with eating producing, one might say, a "permanent contact"—it is possible that the prohibitions of certain touchings function (also? rather?) as a fence around the law regarding eating; what cannot even be touched is much less likely to get eaten. (See, in this connection, Genesis 3:3, where the woman enlarges the divine prohibition to include not *touching* the tree of knowledge of good and bad.)

of dietary regulations. Though these now strike even many believers as quaint, and though the tradition (especially among Christians) now regards them as much less important than the so-called ethical teachings of the Bible (for example, the Decalogue), the Bible itself makes no such distinction. At the very least we risk ignorance of our own Judeo-Christian tradition if we do not try to understand even these seemingly irrational rules of eating and their place in the way of life set forth by the Bible. To gain such understanding, there is no alternative but to scrutinize the text. One must therefore put aside both one's fear that such scrutiny constitutes an act of impiety and one's suspicion that only the religiously observant have access to the text's meaning. There is even biblical warrant for this venture: According to Deuteronomy 4:6, the law is Israel's wisdom and understanding *in the eyes of the nations*. Thus, even though the law had to be revealed, once revealed anyone ought to be able to recognize it as wise.

The search for wisdom is, in fact, the second and more important reason, and clearly the one most pertinent to the present volume, which is one long philosophical (that is, wisdom-seeking) inquiry and argument about the nature and conduct of eating. Previous chapters have explored customs of eating in relation to notions of the just and the noble; the account would be incomplete without an exploration of customs of eating related to notions of the sacred and divine. In this way the end of the inquiry returns to the beginning, as custom returns to seek contact with that which lies beneath custom and beyond convention—the natural order, the cosmic whole. For, as this chapter will suggest, the Jewish dietary laws reflect—and mirror—a comprehensive anthropological and cosmological teaching, one that can still command assent. They embody and reflect a more-or-less true understanding, first, of the problematic character of eating, but, more significantly, of the nature of nature and of the place of man within the whole. They (a) implicitly pay homage to the articulated order of the world and the dignity of life and living form; (b) incorporate into the act of eating an acknowledgment of the problematic character of eating as a threat to order, life, and form; and (c) celebrate, in gratitude and reverence, the mysterious source of the articulated world and its generous hospitality in providing food, both for life and for thought. These remarkable customs not only restrain and thwart the bad, they also commemorate the true and beckon to the good. As I shall now try to show, the dietary laws of Leviticus commemorate the Creation and the Creator and beckon us toward holiness.

Genesis 1: The Created Order

Perhaps the preferable way to proceed would be inductively—that is, to begin with the dietary laws themselves and to try to elicit from them certain intimations of the Creation. But in the interests of brevity I shall speak first and directly about the Creation itself. If the dietary laws are to remind us of the Creation, we need first to learn or remember some things about it so that we can then be reminded of them. By "the Creation" I mean the "world" as presented in the first chapter of Genesis; this account gives us a complete cosmology, a full articulation of all the parts of the whole and of their relation to one another.*

It seems reasonable to suggest that the two most important assertions or claims of the so-called first creation story are, first, that the heaven and earth and everything therein are creatures (that is, creations) and creations of God—that is, they are not themselves eternal or divine; the sun and the stars are not gods; second, that the whole as created was seen and proclaimed by its maker to be very good—and, it seems, also very good for man—man, who stands divinelike at the peak of the creatures, at home in the world, addressed and cared for by God, blessed with fruitfulness and dominion, and well provided with food.† There are, needless to say, deep mysteries in the account—most especially about the very beginning (the first two verses) and also about the meaning of "the image of God." But for the most part—and for my purposes this is most important—we are presented an articulation of the created world as we know it and as human beings have always known it, free of mythical beasts and imaginary generations of gods and goddesses. We are given, through a sequential unfolding, *our* world, hierarchically arranged, in an account that, carefully read, can be made to reveal also the *rational* principles embodied in the articulated world. God is mysterious, but not entirely so. Much in the text is accessible to human reason and, I think, still affirmable by human reason, even today.

Such a claim will, no doubt, surprise many a modern reader who thinks that modern science, especially in its discoveries of evolution or

---

*In offering comment on the beginning, I lean heavily on U. Cassuto, *A Commentary on the Book of Genesis*[2] and especially on a remarkable essay, posthumously published, by Leo Strauss, "On the Interpretation of Genesis."[3]

†The text tacitly implies that the evils in the world that afflict human beings are mainly of human origins—a thesis explicitly, even loudly, proclaimed by the Garden of Eden story related in Genesis 2–3.

of multiple solar systems and in its current theories of the origin of the universe, has rendered simply "unbelievable" the entire account of Genesis 1. But if we take care to separate questions about either the origin and coming-into-being of the universe (cosmogony) or of the ultimate cause(s) or source(s) of this process from questions about the character or nature of that universe *once it is present* (cosmology), we can see that certain things long ago thought true about our world might remain true, even in the face of changing explanations of how they got to be that way. As we argued in Chapter 1, a science of how things work and of where they came from has only limited power (and, often, less interest) to understand *what* things are and how they might be relatively ranked, either in power or dignity. Or, to put it another way, scientific (or historical) evidence and argument can refute (or confirm) only that which is itself presented as science or history; and it is my contention that Genesis 1 is neither. Certainly the categories "science" and "history" (and also "religion," "politics," and "philosophy") are foreign to the text. Since we do not know from the text what kind of text we have, we have no better choice than to try to read it without categorical or disciplinary prejudice, and see if what it says is intelligible and reasonable.*

Let us first remember the order of creation (see table 1): day one, light and the separation of light and dark; day two, heaven, a dividing vault that separates the waters above from the waters below, opening up room before heaven, beneath which life can move; day three, *first*, the gathering of the waters to reveal the dry land—that is, the separation of earth and seas; and *second*, the earth's putting forth of vegetation, after its kind. The second three days bring creatures that all have locomotion, beginning with the creation of the heavenly lights on day four; day five brings the fish and fowl, each after their kind; day six, *first*, the land animals, after their kind; *second*, man, created in the image of God. Table 1 shows at a glance how the second three days closely parallel the first, bringing (respectively) motion, life, and the possibility of freedom and creativity to the realm of light, to sea and sky, and finally to the earth (twice the focus of a day that brought two creative acts). The creatures of the second three days each depend upon and exploit the corresponding creatures of the first three days, as, for example, the land animals and man depend upon the earth and its fruitful vegetation.

---

*For an extensive discussion of the ability of the biblical cosmology to withstand the challenge of modern science, see my essay, "Evolution and the Bible: Genesis 1 Revisited," *Commentary*, November 1988, pp. 29–39. This article offers a more complete exegesis of Genesis 1 than is possible here.

TABLE 1
The "Creatures," Day by Day

1. Light	4. Lights (heavenly)
2. Heaven* (waters and sky)	5. Fish and fowl
3. a. Earth (dry land)	6. a. Land animals
b. including plants (makers of fruits)	b. including man*

*Not said to be "Good."

We must not forget that there is, either completing or transcending the creation, a seventh day on which God desisted from creating. We also note that three blessings were given: the fish and fowl for fecundity ("Be fruitful and multiply"; 1:22); man for fecundity and rule over other living things ("Have dominion"; 1:28); and the seventh day, not only blessed but separated, hallowed—that is, made holy (2:3).* Three blessings: for life, for rule, and for holiness, or as we scholars might say, the natural, the political, the sacred—an ascending order that, as we shall see, is imitated in the Torah's unfolding account of human life.†

The main principles at work in the creation are *place, separation, motion,* and *life,* but especially *separation* and *motion*; places are necessary regions for the placement of separated kinds and backgrounds for the detection of their motion, while life may be looked at—at least at a first glance, which I must later correct—as a higher and more independent kind of motion.‡ Further, if one then treats locomotion as a more advanced kind of separation, in which a distinct being already

---

*The blessing of the fish and fowl is directly quoted (v. 22); the blessings of the man and woman are not only directly quoted, but God's speech is explicitly said to be addressed *to them* (v. 28). In contrast, we have only the narrator's *report* of the blessing of the seventh day, not the actual words. The seventh day and its holiness are, to begin with, beyond the human realm altogether. A major concern of the subsequent biblical teaching is to bring the human into relation with the holy. This is accomplished, as I will argue, largely through the sanctification of everyday life, beginning with eating.

†This ascending order is imitated also in the movement of this book—from nature, to human nature, to laws and customs (of justice and nobility), to holiness.

‡Actually the correction has already been given in Chapter 1, where we saw that life entails not only local motion but also self-forming and other-transforming motions (or activities), and (especially) desire and awareness. The heavenly movers lack appetite, awareness, and receptivity.

separated from others also separates itself from place, we could say that *the* fundamental principle through which the world is created is *separation*. Creation is the bringing of order out of chaos largely through acts of separation, division, distinction. This view is encouraged by the language of the text: the word "divide" or "separate" (*badal*) occurs explicitly five times in the first chapter, and the idea is implicitly present ten more times in the expression "after its kind," which implies the separation of plants and animals into distinct and separable kinds.*

We cannot here attempt a thorough line-by-line analysis of the chapter, but here is how Leo Strauss summarizes the sequence of creation in the first chapter, showing the principle of separation at work:

> From the principle of separation, light [which allows discernment and distinction]; via something which separates, heaven; to something which is separated, earth and sea; to things which are productive of separated things, trees, for example; then things which can separate themselves from their places, heavenly bodies; then things which can separate themselves from their courses, brutes; and finally a being which can separate itself from its way, the right way. . . . The clue to the first chapter seems to be the fact that the account of creation consists of two main parts [days 1–3, days 4–6]. This implies that the created world is conceived to be characterized by a fundamental dualism: things which are different from each other without having the capacity of local motion and things which in addition to being different from each other do have the capacity of local motion. This means the first chapter seems to be based on the assumption that the fundamental dualism is that of distinctness, otherness, as Plato would say, and of local motion. . . . The dualism chosen by the Bible, the dualism as distinguished from the dualism of male and female, is not sensual but intellectual, noetic, and this may help to explain the paradox that plants precede the sun.[4]

---

*If one considers further that the separations actually made were all make*able*, one might even come to think that the creatures—or at least the broadly possible *kinds* of creatures—were present *potentially* in the world, well before they were called forth into being (that is, "created"). With this addition, one begins to see how one might attempt a doctrine of *evolving* or unfolding creation or, in other words, how even certain evolutionary accounts of the emergence of living forms are compatible with the Bible's presentation of a graded and sequential unfolding of the cosmos through progressive acts of separating out implicit or latent possibilities. "Creation" and "evolution" might be perfectly compatible, at least in principle; everything depends on what is meant by each notion. Such speculations, however, are beside the present point, which is the primacy of separation in both the activity of creating and the "world" created: Creation is creation by separation.

The creation of the world, in accordance with these intelligible principles, proceeds through acts of intelligible speech. Creation through speech fits creation by separation, for speech implies the making and recognition of distinctions. To name something is to see it distinctly, both as the same with itself and as other than everything else. To predicate or combine words in speech is to put together what mind has first seen as separate. Separation, otherness, distinction— or, if you prefer, the principle of contradiction, that A is other than not-A—is the very foundation of the possibility both of speech and of an articulated world. With this in mind, we look again at the order of creation, as it is called into being through acts of speech. I again quote Strauss (see figure 1):

FIGURE 1
Creation by Division

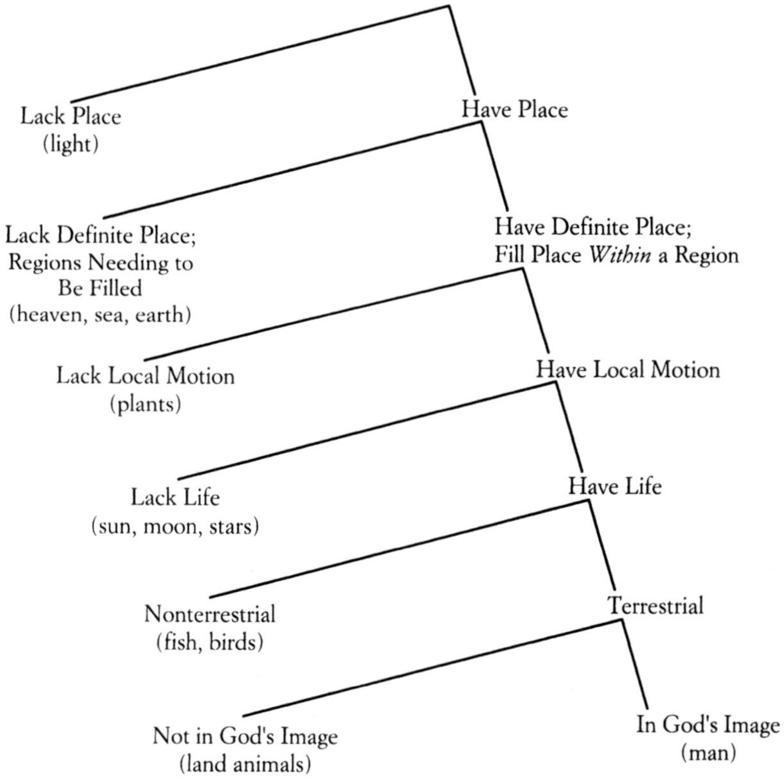

The first thing created is light, something which does not have a place. All later creatures have a place. The things which have a place either do not consist of heterogeneous parts—heaven, earth, seas; or they do consist of heterogeneous parts, namely, of species or individuals. Or as we might prefer to say, the things which have a place either do not have a definite place but rather fill a whole region, or [are] something to be filled—heaven, earth, seas; or else . . . they do not fill a whole region but [fill] a place within a region, within the sea, within heaven, on earth. The things which fill a place within a region either lack local motion—the plants; or they possess local motion. Those which possess local motion either lack life, the heavenly bodies; or they possess life. The living beings are either non-terrestrial, water animals and birds, or they are terrestrial. The terrestrial living beings are either not created in the image of God, brutes; or in the image of God—man. In brief, the first chapter of Genesis is based on a division by two, or what Plato calls *diaresis* (division by two).[5]

It has not escaped our notice that this account of the world, though presented in a religious text, is in substantial agreement with the world as we experience it and as we reflect on it. Our world is indeed an articulated world, with distinctly different kinds of beings occupying different kinds of places, and moving with varying degrees of freedom—some in fixed courses, some in fixed ways, and, with human beings, in ways partly of their own devising. A formed world is necessarily a world of distinction, a world of forms ordered along intelligible lines. In our world and in the world according to Genesis, the most interesting and lively forms are the various forms of animal life.

The work of creation is completed by living things, created on days five and six. Living things are higher than the heavenly bodies, by virtue of having greater freedom of motion, man most of all. They are characterized also (1) by having a *proper place*—in the waters, above the earth before the firmament, or on the earth; (2) by being *formed* according to their *kinds*; (3) by having *motion appropriate* to their *place* (freer on land); and (4) by reproducing themselves, according to their *kinds*. Unlike the heavenly lights, they also have (5) powers of awareness—especially hearing—which are implied in the receipt of God's blessing; they can recognize the distinctions that are manifest in the world, and ultimately, at least one of them—

man—can understand those conveyed in speech. Finally they are characterized also (6) by neediness and vulnerability, which may be what makes them in need of God's blessing.*

Though brought into being in company with the land animals (both on the sixth day), man also stands clearly at the peak of the creatures. Blessed with dominion or rule over the other animals, man is the most godlike or godly of the animals: Man alone is said to be in the image of God. Understanding what this means is no small task, but it is probably safest to begin with the term *image* itself and to consider its meaning in the local context provided by the text.

The Hebrew word translated "image" is *tselem*, from a root meaning "to cut off," "to chisel"; *tselem*, something cut or chiseled out—in the first instance a statue—becomes, derivatively, any image or likeness or resemblance, something which both *is* and *is not* what it resembles. Although being merely a likeness, an image not only resembles but also points to, and is dependent for its very being on, that of which it is an image.

To see how man is godlike, we look at the text to see what God is like. In the course of recounting His creation, Genesis 1 introduces us to God's activities and powers: (1) God speaks, commands, names, blesses, and hallows; (2) God makes and makes freely; (3) God looks at and beholds the world; (4) God is concerned with the goodness or perfection of things; (5) God addresses solicitously other living creatures. In short: God exercises speech and reason, freedom in doing and making, and the powers of contemplation, judgment, and care.

Doubters may wonder whether this is truly the case about God—after all, it is only on biblical authority that we regard God as possessing these powers and activities. But it is certain that we human beings have them, and that—as we argued on quite independent grounds in Chapter 2—they lift us above the plane of a merely animal existence. Human beings, alone among the creatures, speak, plan, create, contemplate, and judge. Human beings, alone among the creatures, can articulate a future goal and use that articulation to guide them in bringing it into being by their own purposive conduct.

---

*This biblical account of living things squares perfectly with the account I have given in Chapter 1. Notice the intimations of the three great powers—action, awareness, and appetite—based on neediness.

Human beings, alone among the creatures, can think about the whole, marvel at its many splendored forms and articulated order, wonder about its beginning, and feel awe in beholding its grandeur and in pondering the mystery of its source.

These demonstrable truths do *not* rest on biblical authority. Rather, our reading of the text, addressable only to us, and our responses to it, possible only for us, provide all the proof we need to confirm the text's assertion of our special being. *Reading* Genesis 1 demonstrates the truth of its claims about the superior ontological standing of the human. This is not anthropocentric prejudice but cosmological truth. And nothing we shall ever learn about *how* we came to be this way will ever make it false.

But the text does not exaggerate our standing. Man may have powers that resemble divinity, but he is also at most merely an image; man, who, quite on his own, is prone to think of himself as a god on earth (*Omnivorosus erectus*, the potential tyrant) and to lord it over the animals, is reminded by the biblical text that he is, like the other creatures, not divine. He, like the animals, shares in the precariousness and neediness of life.

The vulnerability and neediness of life, not a prominent theme, is in fact not forgotten. The very last subject of the first chapter, before God's pronouncement that everything was very good, is the matter of food. After blessing man to be fruitful and multiply (as He also did the fish and fowl) and to have dominion over all life, God teaches man that dominion over the animals does not mean appropriation or exploitation, at least not as food:

> And God said: "Behold I have provided you with all seed-bearing plants which are on the face of all the earth, and every tree which has seed-bearing fruit; to you I have given it as food. And to every living being of the earth and to everything that creepeth upon the earth which has a living soul in it, I have given every green herb as food"; and it was so. (vv. 29–30)

The only instruction given to man, the ruler, created in the image of God, is about necessity, about food—his and that of his subjects. Though they are to eat different things—seeds and fruit for man; green herbs for all other animals (yes, including the lion and the tiger)—they are all to be what we call vegetarian. Keeping to this diet would disturb almost not at all the order of creation: Eating seeds and fruits does not harm the parent plants; eating fruit and discarding the seeds does not even interfere with the next generation. And the green herbs to be eaten by the animals are constantly produced by the earth, almost as a head produces hair. (The plants, from the Bible's point of view, are not alive: They lack sentience and motion—that is, liveliness; they more or less belong to the earth in which they are rooted and from which they originate. Indeed, in the "command" to the earth to produce vegetation, God uses the cognate accusative construction—"Let the earth grass grass"—as if grass were (to be) the surface display of the earth's native activity.*) The disruptions caused by meeting necessity through eating would, in the idealized case, be negligible.

We must, however, imagine that man and the animals as created *were capable* of eating meat. True, they were encouraged not to do so, especially as the fruits of the earth were said to be bountiful. But that they needed to be told what to eat is perhaps a sign that, left to their own devices, their appetites might have extended to incorporate one another. In this very subtle way the text hints that the harmonious and ordered whole contains within it a principle—life, or if you will, appetite, and eventually omnivorousness and freedom—that threatens its preservation as an ordered whole. Once again the biblical account speaks truly: Life is destabilizing and threatens itself; man does so in spades. Despite (because of?) being created in the image of God, man alone among the creatures—except for heaven—is not said to be good.[†] The sequel indicates that life's destructive power is not an idle concern, especially regarding man but even also with the animals. Perhaps this is even the reason that the animals are in need of a ruler.

---

*Curiously, the earth in "complying" is said to "put forth" grass, not to "grass" it. The desired harmony or unity of activity and product sought in speech was not attained (not possible?) in deed. This observation has led some to suggest that the earth was first in disobedience. (For these observations I am indebted to Robert Sacks's remarkable commentary on Genesis.[6])

[†]On what understanding of "good" might it be simply true that man, as created, cannot yet be said to be good?

"Good" as used throughout Genesis 1 cannot mean *morally* good; when "God saw the light that it was good," He could not have seen that the light was honest or just or law abiding. The meaning of "good" seems rather to embrace notions such as the following: (1) fit to the intention; (2) fit to itself and its work—that is, able to function for itself and in relation to the unfolding whole; and, especially, (3) complete, perfect, fully formed, clear and distinct and fully what it is. A being is good insofar as it is fully formed and fully fit to do its proper work.

As we showed in Chapter 2, man as he comes into the world is not yet good. Precisely because he is the free being, he is also the incomplete or indeterminate being. More pointedly, precisely in the sense that man is in the image of God, man is not good—not determinate, finished, complete,

Biblical Anthropology: The Problem of Eating

We leave behind the majestic first chapter, with its timeless presentation of the hierarchic order of creation, and move to the account of human life. In this account, beginning in the Garden of Eden, the problem of eating and its regulation—barely hinted at in Genesis 1—receives prominent attention. The Bible seems to agree with Aristotle that the *first* reason for dietary laws is the need to restrain, moderate, and define the naturally unrestrained, immoderate, and boundless appetites of human beings—appetites that are by no means restricted to the desires for food but for which the problem of eating is somehow emblematic. The need for dietary laws is, to begin with, identical to the need for law in general, and the acquisition of laws to regulate conduct is very often heralded by or presented in terms of regulations of eating. Indeed the Torah presents us with a series of stages in the development of the human race—leading up to the formation of the people of Israel—each of which is marked by a change in the diet, usually involving restriction. For example, at the beginning, in the bountiful Garden of Eden, the man was a fruit eater, allowed to eat of every tree of the garden save one. Though the tree of knowledge of good and bad is only metaphorically a tree—knowledge does not grow on trees—the image suggests an explicit connection between human autonomy and human omnivorousness, by representing the limit on the former in the form of a limit on the latter.

Though we learn from the sequel that he was even in his origins a being potentially possessed of reason, and hence of open appetite and choice, man was, to begin with, guided by nature, instinctively seeking only the things needful for life, which—his needs (food, water, and rest) being simple—nature adequately provided. A prescient and benevolent God, solicitous of the man's well-being,

---

or perfect. It remains to be seen whether man will *become* good, whether he will be able to complete himself (or to be completed).

Man's lack of obvious goodness, metaphysically identical with his freedom, is, of course, the basis of man's moral ambiguity. As the being with the greatest freedom of motion, able to change not only his path but also his way, man is capable of deviating widely from the way for which he is most suited or through which he—and the world around him—will most flourish. The rest of the biblical narrative elaborates man's moral ambiguity and God's efforts to address it, in the service of making man "good" — complete, whole, holy.

sought to preserve him in this condition; He sought to keep him from trying to guide his life by his own lights, exercised on the things of his experience, from which he would form for himself autonomous—that is, self-prescribed, freely chosen—knowledge of good and bad, which is to say, knowledge of how to live. Or, to put the same point in terms of appetite, God sought to protect man from the expansion of his desires beyond the naturally necessary, or from the replacement of desire given by nature with desires given by his own mind and imagination. These tempting but dangerous prospects—of autonomy, choice, independence, and the aspiration to full self-command, and of emancipated and open-ended desire—lay always at the center of human life; for to reason is to choose, and to choose for oneself (even to choose to obey) is not-to-obey, neither God nor instinct nor anything else. The rational animal is, in principle, the autonomous and hence disobedient animal.

When the voice of reason awoke, and simple obedience was questioned (and hence no longer possible), the desires of the man began to grow. Though he did not know what he meant exactly, he imagined that his eyes would be opened and he would be as a god—that is, self-sufficing, autonomous, independent, knowing, perhaps immortal, and free at last. Such did the serpent promise—the smooth voice that asked the world's first question and so disturbed its peace of mind forever: "Ye shall *not* surely die; for God doth know that in the day ye eat thereof, then your eyes shall be opened, and *ye shall be as gods* [or God] knowing good and bad" (3:5; italics added). The human imagination is liberated by the rational assertion of opposites, of negation, of the possibility of "not": Things may not be what they seem; even better, things need not be as they are. With alternatives now freely before her, the woman's desire grows on its own, partly enticed by the promise of godlike wisdom, mostly fueled by her newly empowered imagination.

The biblical narrator connects this imagining of godliness with new imaginings about the forbidden food: "And when the woman *saw* that the tree *was good for food*, and that it *was a delight to the eyes*, and that the tree *was to be desired to make one wise*, she took of the fruit thereof and did eat; and she gave also unto her husband with her, and he did eat" (3:6; italics added). The tree was looked upon with fresh eyes—perhaps, in fact, *really* looked at here for the very

first time—under the sway of new desires tied to new imaginings.*
We have here the momentous and transforming act of free choice,
based on new judgment about what is good (and bad).† The result,
as we know, is the beginning of concerned self-consciousness—
shame and vanity, modesty and love, and all higher human aspirations: in short, the first stages of humanization.

---

*However mistaken the woman may have been in these imaginings about the tree, their an-
nounced sequence shows a progressive, ever-more-humanizing direction: first, "good for food,"
second, "delight to the eyes," third, desire for wisdom. First comes animal necessity; second, aesthetic pleasure; third, intellectual enlightenment and/or prudent insight and judgment. The hungry
human soul, quite on its own, aspires to climb a ladder of human ascent, roughly similar to the one
imitated in the structure of this book. (I owe this observation to Michael Fishbane.)

†Compare the marvelous discussion of these biblical passages given by Kant in his "Conjectural
Beginning of Human History":

So long as inexperienced man obeyed this call of nature all was well with him. But soon reason began
to stir. A sense different from that to which instinct was tied—the sense, say, of sight—presented
other food than that normally consumed as similar to it; and reason, instituting a comparison, sought
to enlarge its knowledge of foodstuffs beyond the bounds of instinctual knowledge (3:6). This experiment might, with good luck, have ended well, even though instinct did not advise it, so long as it was
at least not contrary to instinct. But reason has this peculiarity that, aided by the imagination, it can
create artificial desires which are not only unsupported by natural instinct but actually contrary to it.
These desires, in the beginning called concupiscence, gradually generate a whole host of unnecessary
and indeed unnatural inclinations called luxuriousness. The original occasion for deserting natural instinct may have been trifling. But this was man's first attempt to become conscious of his reason as a
power which can extend itself beyond the limits to which all animals are confined. As such its effect
was very important and indeed decisive for his future way of life. Thus the occasion may have been
merely the external appearance of a fruit which tempted because of its similarity to tasty fruits of
which man had already partaken. In addition there may have been the example of an animal which
consumed it because, for it, it was naturally fit for consumption, while on the contrary, being harmful
for man, it was consequently resisted by man's instinct. Even so, this was a sufficient occasion for reason to do violence to the voice of nature (3:1) and, its protest notwithstanding, to make the first attempt at a free choice; an attempt which, being the first, probably did not have the expected result.
But however insignificant the damage done, it sufficed to open man's eyes (3:7). He discovered in
himself a power of choosing for himself a way of life, of not being bound without alternative to a single way, like the animals. Perhaps the discovery of this advantage created a moment of delight. But of
necessity, anxiety and alarm as to how he was to deal with this newly discovered power quickly followed; for man was a being who did not yet know either the secret properties or the remote effects of
anything. He stood, as it were, at the brink of an abyss. Until that moment instinct had directed him
toward specific objects of desire. But from these there now opened up an infinity of such objects, and
he did not yet know how to choose between them. On the other hand, it was impossible for him to
return to the state of servitude (i.e., subjection to instinct) from the state of freedom, once he had
tasted the latter.⁷

One further remark about eating and autonomy. To have reached for the tree already implied
possession of the knowledge that, allegedly, was to be acquired only by eating, autonomous knowledge of good and bad; in fact, eating merely ratified (or symbolized) the autonomous (that is,
nonobedient and, hence, disobedient) act of *choosing* to eat, which was based on the self-generated belief that the eating would be *good*. Only a being who already distinguishes good and bad and
who has opinions about which is which can make such a choice.

The expulsion from the garden is coupled with a shift from fruit to bread,* *the* distinctly human food, and marks the next major step toward humanization through civilization. Men turn from gathering naturally available food (fruits) to toilsome cultivation of grain, itself in need of artful transformation before it becomes edible as bread. Cain, the first man born of woman and the first man who never knew the garden (that is, *the* human prototype), is a tiller of the ground and presumably, therefore, an eater of bread. He is also the founder of the first city (4:17) and his descendants are the originators of the arts (4:20–22). But civilization here proceeds in the absence of law. Men are left to their own devices and, beginning with the fratricide of Cain, the whole earth soon becomes corrupt and violent—including also the animals (6:12), by which we may understand that they have become carnivorous. By the tenth generation men are disordering and dissolving the created order, with no respect for life and limb. The return through the flood to the watery chaos of the beginning completes the dissolution into chaos that life itself has wrought.

The next and crucial stage, just after the flood, is marked by the first law for all mankind and the first covenant between God and man, through Noah. To use nonbiblical language, man here emerges from what Rousseau would later call the state of nature and becomes civilized or political, in "the moment when, right taking the place of violence, nature was subjected to law." [8] The first law of the first law sanctions for the first time man's eating of all animal flesh,† but, at the same time, prohibits the eating of blood, which is the life.

Why does this move to law come about? An answer is suggested by the episode that immediately precedes the covenant. Noah, im-

---

*Genesis 3:19 announces the shift prospectively. The first explicit mention of agriculture comes with Cain, after the expulsion from the garden.

†The institution of law, which permanently distinguishes man from all other animals, has as its first instance this permanent separation of man from all other animals—viz., the permission to eat (use) them. The Bible, despite its clear misgivings about this step (see below), hints in this way that meat eating (but with restrictions: not raw) is, in some sense, *the* specifically human way of nourishing. To this extent, then, the Bible shares the view of Plato's *Republic* (discussed in Chapter 3) in which the full humanization of the city built in speech occurs with the eruption of the spirited element in the human soul, made evident when Glaucon faults the first or healthy (vegetarian) city, declaring it a "city of pigs," and insists on his desire for meat. As in the *Republic*, the biblical account seeks to tame the spirited element and, as we shall see, leads the Israelites back toward a thoughtful or pious (a more-than-human?) vegetarianism, but meat would seem to be the food of man as man.

mediately on leaving the ark, builds an altar and (presumably in an act of thanksgiving, but without command or instruction) sacrifices some of the animals God had him rescue from the antediluvian world of violence and bloodshed. God, in reaction to Noah's sacrifice, remarks, one imagines sadly, "The imagination of man's heart is evil from his youth" (8:21).* Even Noah, righteous and simple Noah, is not pure at heart and has a taste for blood. God decides against blotting out and starting over; it would not do any good to begin again. Instead God chooses the way of law. The covenant with Noah makes a concession to man's violence and carnivorousness,† but only by bringing it somewhat under law. In becoming a creature under law, quasi "political," man is decisively separated from his animal friends and relations, in the interests of elementary decency and justice in human life. For the Noachic law also for the first time prohibits murder and compels human beings to execute its punishment. We surmise that God was willing to tolerate meat-eating in the hope that man's ferocity would thereby be sated, that murder might become less likely if human bloodlust could be satisfied by meat.

We skip lightly over the transition to the next stage, in which man becomes fully political—that is, divided into *separate* nations. The Noachic covenant had separated mankind, homogeneously considered, from *all* other animals, homogeneously considered (as nonhuman),‡ but as yet there were no separate polities. Of the division of mankind (as with the Creation), two accounts are given, the second

---

*Noah's sacrifice is certainly ambiguous. The narrator's opening remark, "And the Lord smelled the sweet savour" (8:21), is generally taken to be evidence that God was pleased with the sacrifice. But in view of the negative judgment later in the same verse, one might interpret the beginning to mean that God discerned that the smell of roast meat was sweet *to Noah*. Noah, not having been told how to express thanksgiving, gave God a gift on the assumption that God would like what he, Noah, liked. To give of what one treasures most is praiseworthy; to kill the animals (his former roommates on the ark) and to relish their flesh is not. Neither is the presumptuous assumption that "God likes what I like"—that is, that "I am like God." (I was first made aware of the ambiguity of Noah's sacrifice by Robert Sacks, St. John's College, Santa Fe, New Mexico. See his *Commentary on the Book of Genesis*, cited earlier in this chapter.)

†That it is a concession to something fundamentally questionable is indicated by the fact that the eating of blood is prohibited. Bloodlust may have to be tolerated, but it is not simply approved.

‡This abstraction from the distinctions among the animals, i.e., from the principle of "kinds" and "forms," reflects the form-homogenizing tendency of eating as such, qualified here only in excluding human beings from the realm of the edible (or killable and usable). Attention to distinctive forms returns with the dietary laws of Leviticus (see below).

connected with the audacious project toward self-sufficiency that is the city and tower of Babel, the first connected with the descendants of the sons of Noah. Once again men show themselves prone to chaos and the effacing of distinctions: Noah, drunk on wine, lies prostrate and undignified in his tent; Ham ratifies his father's unfathering of himself by looking on him naked; and (in the other account) the builders of Babel defy God's order to disperse by seeking to close the gap between the human and the divine.[9] The remedy for these distinction-denying tendencies is, in both accounts, the emergence of distinctions among nations: politics (and war) come into being, and presumably also distinct customs, including distinctive dietary practices.

Laws governing diet do more than restrain human omnivorousness and ferocity. Well before Leviticus, Genesis already hints that dietary laws are not merely ethical or, in the broad sense, political, designed to moderate human appetites so that men may live more justly with one another. It shows us that dietary laws are also meant to help distinguish one people from another. Peoples are distinguished from one another most decisively by what it is they look up to and revere—by their gods. And their view of the divine and their experience of the divine is often reflected or embedded in their customs and laws. As practiced, the laws bind a people to a particular and distinctive way. But as objects also of reflection, they may serve as symbols and reminders—in the highest instance, of the divine and our relation to it. Genesis gives us a dietary model.

The specifically Jewish dietary laws are anticipated in the story of Jacob's wrestling with the mysterious being that later traditions call an angel (Genesis 32:25–33). As a result of this striving with God, Jacob acquires the name that becomes the name of his people, Israel, but he is also marked with a limp in his thigh. The text interrupts its story of the wrestling to announce the first specifically Jewish dietary law: "Therefore the children of Israel—[this, by the way, is the Torah's first mention of the name of the future people "children of Israel"; they get their name in the same verse that announces their first dietary law]—eat not the sinew of the thigh which is upon the hollow of the thigh, unto this day:

because He touched the hollow of Jacob's thigh, even in the sinew of the thigh." (v. 33) The children of Israel *remember* by a dietary practice that ambiguous and mysterious encounter of their father Jacob with the divine. They are restrained in eating, as was Jacob by the limp; but they are touched in this denial with a memorial of a divine encounter. They remember, negatively, that Jacob was injured in the process of struggling against God; positively, that God was close enough to be encountered and struggled with.

The basic anthropological sequence, as taught in Genesis, is this:

1. A prehuman condition (Garden of Eden)	Men eat fruit
2. A prepolitical condition, before law (Cain to the Flood)	Men eat bread, but they lapse naturally also into eating meat
3. A political condition, (a) beginning with elementary justice (Noah)	(a) Men eat meat, but under law, respecting the blood as life
(b) continuing to the formation of separate peoples (Descendants of Noah; after Babel)	(b) (Presumably) Different peoples have different dietary practices, based on differing conventions
4. A more-than-political condition, in which one people is brought beyond the just into some relation with the holy, finally to to aspire to holiness itself	Further restrictions of diet, connected with purity and holiness, eventually to be built on the distinction between clean and unclean

After this much-too-hasty review of the pre-Levitical dietary restrictions,* we are ready to approach Leviticus 11 and ask about

---

*There are additional dietary regulations between Genesis and Leviticus 11. Some clearly serve as memorials of the deliverance from Egypt; that is, those instituting and governing the feast of unleavened bread (Exodus 21:14–20). Also in Exodus (23:19) is the prohibition against seething a kid in his mother's milk, the textual basis for the Jewish refusal to mix meat and dairy products in the same meal; explanations for this proscription vary but include the suggestion that the death-

the particular laws governing the eating of other living things. The thesis is that these particular and parochial laws build into the fabric of the daily life of the people of Israel a reminder of the nonparochial and universal beginning and source of all form and life.

The Dietary Laws of Leviticus: Metaphysical Seasoning

Why *these* dietary laws? Many people now seek to explain or rationalize the dietary laws of Leviticus in terms of concrete practical benefits that observance would yield to the Israelites, say, for example, in improved health. But attempts to explain the laws in terms of hygiene and public health cannot be supported by the text. Only a benighted Enlightenment reason, which holds cleanliness to be more important than godliness, could confidently imagine God as the forerunner of Louis Pasteur, threatening to cut men off from their people in order to keep them from trichinosis. In fact the law does not say that the pig or the eagle is unclean simply; it says it is unclean *to you*—though we shall see in a moment in what sense the pig is in fact itself a defiler. Perhaps more plausible is the thesis that the laws intend to provide a discipline good for the soul, partly by the mere acts of self-denial, but mainly by the need to attend scrupulously to details of diet. But this explanation (or any other that alleges a different concrete benefit) cannot suffice, for it fails to account for the *particularities* of the prohibitions: Why rule out the camel, the lobster, or the raven? Why permit the locust but not the ant?

There is much to be said for the view (favored by Maimonides and others) that the laws are meant solely to separate the children of Israel from other peoples, most especially from the Egyptians behind and the Canaanites before, peoples whose practices (especially in sexual matters) and pagan beliefs are from God's point of view abominable: Whatever the Egyptians eat, let that be unclean to you—lest you stray easily into their ways. But left at this point, this

---

dealing activity of cooking ought not to be mixed with life-giving milk, or, similarly, that the cruel necessity of eating meat not be compounded by the cruelty of slaughtering the animal in the presence of its mother or with the participation of her life-giing juices. In addition, early in Leviticus (3:17, 7:22–27), a new prohibition against the eating of fat is added to the Noachic prohibition of blood. The reason for this prohibition is not given.

explanation does not go far enough. For, as I have argued, the ways of the Egyptians and the Canaanites—indeed, the practices of any people—embody their beliefs about the world and especially about the divine, in this case a belief in nature gods. The avoidance of the abominable turns out to be the start of the turn toward holiness. The true concern of the dietary laws is holiness.*

The context in which the dietary laws of Leviticus are given demonstrates that the concern is with purity and sanctity. Most of the laws governing the moral or political relations between man and man had already been given in Exodus. These were followed by laws addressing the religious passions, laws for the building of the Tabernacle, and laws regarding sacrifices.† In fact, the immediate an-

---

*Accordingly, we expect that considerations having to do with holiness—with the being and ways of God—will help to explain the particularities and peculiarities of the dietary regulations.

†The institution of animal sacrifice, not only divinely commanded but conducted in the holy sanctuary, raises a difficulty for part of the explanation I shall offer below for the designated "uncleanness" of some animals, namely, their carnivorousness. If life is to be respected, why animal sacrifices, and on such a large scale? But what if the crucial fact about the law of sacrifices is not that God desires or enjoys sacrifice but that He restricts and regulates the ambiguous human impulse to sacrifice under the strictest laws and confines it to a single and special place? The passions for sacrificing have been present almost from the beginning, and the moral ambiguity of the practice—like that of eating—has been subtly indicated throughout, beginning with the sacrifices made by Cain (the initiator of sacrifices) and Noah. Because we simply assume that the human disposition to sacrifice is good, we fail to see its questionable character: Sacrificing rests on certain assumptions one has no right to make, at least not before the divine reveals itself and makes its wishes known. Uninstructed sacrifice is always a manifestation of pride in the guise of submission. To bring animal sacrifice uninstructed, one would presumptuously have to assume at least the following: (1) God would like to hear from me; (2) God is the kind of god that likes presents; (3) God, being an eating god, likes presents of food—just like me—and especially animal flesh: God is a carnivore. The biblical account does not support these assumptions, and there is no evidence that God *for His part* wants sacrifices. On the contrary, the one sacrifice He requests—Isaac, from Abraham—He makes clear He does not want; it is as if He were trying to purge Abraham of such bloody notions about the divine. What God wants, rather, is man's wholehearted devotion to uprightness and man's acknowledgment of his dependence on God.

When animal sacrifice is finally commanded, the context suggests the rationale. The laws regarding the Tabernacle and the institution of sacrifices were given in the immediate aftermath of two disquieting episodes, reported at the end of Exodus 24: (1) a rather wild animal sacrifice, initiated by Moses without God's instruction, with much strewing and sprinkling of blood; and (2) the encounter of the elders with the divine, which they experienced only sensually and in whose presence they did eat and drink. The impulses to animal sacrifice, the desire for sensual religious experience, and other enthusiasms and forms of zealousness cannot, it seems, be eliminated from the human soul; they can only be delimited, by bringing them under law. Indeed it is the giving of regulations for these ineradicable Dionysiac passions that the Torah presents to be coincident with Moses' forty days and forty nights on the mountain; these same passions erupted in Moses' absence, in the episode of the golden calf. Animal sacrifice, like meat eating, would seem to be a concession to human weakness or wildness.

tecedent to the giving of the laws about the clean and unclean beasts is the problematic sacrifice of Nadab and Abihu, who "offered strange fire before the Lord, which He had not commanded them" (Leviticus 10:1), just as the immediate antecedent to the Noachic law was the problematic, uninstructed massive sacrifice of animals by Noah, immediately on taking them from the ark. It is in the sequel to this wild, "Dionysiac" episode that God makes known both the importance of and the connection between distinguishing the clean from the unclean and distinguishing the holy (*qodesh*, "apart as sacred or holy," possessing an original idea of *separation*) from the profane (*chol*, "common"; from a root meaning "to bore, to wound, to dissolve, to break"—in short, "to destroy wholeness and form").

God's first speech after this episode of the strange fire gives something of a dietary law to Aaron and the priests—no wine or strong drink before entering the sanctuary—and introduces us for the first time to the all-important and related distinctions, holy and common, unclean and clean, using the same verb, *lehavdil* (the root is *badal*), "to separate or distinguish," that was so prominent in the first chapter of Genesis and *which has not been used in this way since*: "And that ye may make distinction between the holy and the common and between the unclean and the clean, and that ye may teach the children of Israel all the statutes which the Lord has spoken unto them by the hand of Moses" (Leviticus 10:10–11). This is the context for the laws of purity which follow.

Chapter 11 is, in fact, only the first of several chapters that articulate the distinction between the clean and the unclean, the holy and the common. Each deals with what might be described as "transgressions" of the natural boundaries between the human being and his surroundings: Chapter 11, food—that is, that which crosses the boundary coming from the outside in; Chapter 12, childbirth, and Chapter 15, bodily issues, things that cross the boundary going from the inside out, and, in the first and very special case, with the bodily separation of one life coming out from within another; in between, Chapters 13 and 14 deal with a disease that translators have called leprosy (but that experts now believe to be a different disease, as yet unidentified); as described in the text, it is a disease of the living boundary itself, one that effaces the surfaces separating the inside from the outside and that erodes and alters the human form. The laws that especially separate the Israelites from other nations, and that legislate the separation of clean and unclean, concern themselves with regulating "threats" to the embodiments of the principle of separation. The principle for separating clean and unclean is none other than separation itself. We cannot but think of the Creation.

The principles important to Genesis 1—place, form or kind, motion, and life—are all at work in Leviticus 11.* The animals discussed are presented according to their place: first the land animals (vv. 2–8; also vv. 41–45), then those of the waters (vv. 9–12), finally the fliers, birds and insects (vv. 13–23). To be clean, land animals must have completely cloven hoofs and must chew the cud; animals that go upon the belly or upon all fours, that have many feet, that swarm upon the earth, or that do not chew the cud are unclean. To be clean, water animals need fins and scales. Among the fliers, we are given only a list of named unclean birds; but among the winged swarmers—that is, insects—those that leap on jointed legs are clean; those that, though winged, walk on all fours are unclean. Though I cannot account for all the details, I observe that the criteria used to identify the clean and the unclean refer to their *form*, their *means of motion*, and how they *sustain* life—that is, what they eat to live—specifically, whether they eat other animals or not. Ruled out are creatures that violate any of the principles of Creation: place, form, motion, and especially the original dietary code, the one that would least disturb the created order. Ruled out are:

1. Creatures that have no proper or unambiguous *place*; for example the amphibians.

2. Creatures that have no proper *form*, especially the watery ones,
   (a) by having *indefinite* form, with fluid shapes, lacking a firm boundary defined, say, by scales—that is, jellyfish or oysters;
   (b) by having *deceptive* form, like eels (fish that do not look like fish); or
   (c) by having *incomplete* form—like the incompletely cloven-footed animals.

---

*The observations that follow agree largely with those of Mary Douglas[10] and Jean Soler[11] though they were arrived at independently and are made in a completely different spirit. These scholars are content to discover the patterns and logic of what Soler calls "the Hebrew mind." They do not consider the possibility that those patterns and that logic might reflect truly the intelligible patterns of the world, or that the insights of and about this people might have universal anthropological meaning.

3. Creatures that violate proper *locomotion*, such as those animals that live in the water but walk as on land (lobsters); those that live on land but swarm as in water ("all the swarmers that swarm on the earth"; in Genesis 1, the swarmers belonged in the waters); those insects that have wings for flying but that nevertheless go on all fours—that is, walk (the insect leapers, though they have legs, are treated as more akin to the true fliers, and are clean); also, those with too many legs (centipedes) or no legs at all (that go on their belly, for example, snakes, worms); and those that go on all fours—that is, on their paws (and thus use their hands as feet).

4. Creatures that violate the *original dietary code*, showing no respect for life—that is, the carnivorous ones; this consideration is especially evident (a) in the unclean birds, those we can identify being mainly birds of prey; and (b) in the requirement of chewing the cud, the mark of the ruminant animals that eat what God originally gave all animals to eat, the green herb of the earth.

Let us consider more closely a few of the particular requirements. The clean and unclean land animals are distinguished according to their feet (parting the hoof) and according to their diet (chewing the cud)—that is, according to motion and eating. The fish are distinguished by their form (fins and scales) and their mode of locomotion (fins);* the birds presumably by what they eat; the winged hoppers by how they move. *How* an animal *moves* reveals its relation to its *place* in the whole. *What* an animal *eats* reveals its relation to other parts of the whole. If they have fitting relations, they are clean.

Hoofed animals are grazing animals: Their feet are fit only for walking and moving, not for grabbing and clawing; they are footed to stand in the world (and generally poised well above the ground,

---

*The omission of a dietary criterion for the water creatures may be related to a fact perhaps embarrassing to my suggestion that carnivorous animals are, ipso facto, not to be eaten: Fish eat other fish. Yet this may really pose no great difficulty. Many cultures do not regard fish as animals—some peoples of the Far East call fish "the *vegetable* of the sea"—and this judgment is somehow also reflected in the fact that some vegetarians will eat fish. In the creation of fish in Genesis 1, God bade the waters "to swarm swarms," as if fish were a certain exuberant manifestation of the being of the seas themselves. Fish are certainly less separable from and independent of the waters than are the land animals regarding earth. The easier procedures of Koshering fish are another sign that they are not regarded as full-blooded animals.

more erect than the carnivores), not to tear at it. Cud chewers are so far from eating other animals that they finally chew and swallow only the homogenized stuff they have already once swallowed and raised: When the pig, a notorious omnivore, is declared unclean, the Torah says it is because "he does not chew the chew," using the cognate accusative construction (*vehu gerah lo yiggar*; 11:7), presenting by implication, as it were, the ideal of the perfect fit of activity and object. The pig is a would-be ruminant gone bad: One should chew not life but chew—that is, that which is fit for chewing. The chew chewers are poles apart from that first accursed and most unclean animal, the belly-crawling serpent, which is in fact a moving digestive tract and which "voraciously" swallows its prey whole and live.

By attending to these natural differences of animal form, the dietary laws of Leviticus refine and improve on Noachic law. At first, in the covenant with Noah, all animals were given to all men as food, as a concession, save only not the blood. Avoiding the eating of blood does indeed show some respect for the life that one is nevertheless violating. But the common principle of vitality—blood—itself ignores and homogenizes the distinctions among the *kinds* of animals. It shows respect for life but not for separate living form. Focusing only on blood ignores especially the distinction between those animals that do and those that do not honor in their eating the original separations of the world. The Levitical laws of purity reintroduce those early distinctions: The Children of Israel are not to incorporate animals that kill and incorporate other animals.* The restrict-

---

*The reader might wonder why, if my explanation is correct, the Israelites are not enjoined to eat only the defilers rather than the animals that are clean. After all, why should man's hunger be set against those creatures whose ways are least offensive, while the guilty are allowed to cavort, humanly unmolested? The following rejoinders can be offered. First, eating and being eaten are not punishment; therefore the clean animals are not being dealt with unjustly, nor are the carnivores getting away with murder. Second, and more important, eating is incorporation; one eats only those whose qualities one wants to share, but one rigorously abstains from those whose qualities one finds abominable. To incorporate a defiler is to defile oneself. This conclusion need not require a belief in the material transfer of psychic properties through ingestion; symbolically, one dirties and pollutes oneself by pursuing, by contact with, and especially by taking in the unclean. It is instructive to compare this logic focused on purity with that of the utilitarian Benjamin Franklin, who asserts that he gave up vegetarianism when he remembered that fish eat other fish: "Then thought I, if you eat one another, I don't see why we mayn't eat you. So I din'd upon Cod very heartily and continu'd to eat with other People, returning only now and then occasionally to a vegetable Diet. So convenient a thing it is to be a *reasonable Creature*, since it enables one to find or make a Reason for every thing one has a mind to do."[12]

ed carnivorousness of Israel tacitly acknowledges the problem of carnivorousness. The Children of Israel are also not to incorporate or have contact with beings that do not honor in their motion the original separations of the world. These restrictions on their free-dom, which rule out animals that take "illegitimate"—that is, order-destroying—liberties, tacitly acknowledge the problem of freedom. In all these ways the dietary laws build into daily life constant con-crete and incarnate reminders of the created order and its principles and of the dangers that life—and especially man—pose to its preser-vation. In these restrictions on deformation and destruction, there is celebration of Creation—and of its mysterious source.

In a certain sense the dietary laws push the Children of Israel back in the direction of the "original" "vegetarianism" of the pristine and innocent Garden of Eden. Although not all flesh is forbidden, everything that is forbidden is flesh. Thus any strict vegetarian, one could say, never violates the Jewish dietary laws. Yet though he does not violate them, he could not be said to follow them. For only un-knowingly does he not violate them, and, more to the point, he re-frains *indiscriminately*, that is, without regard to the distinctions among the kinds of living things that might and might not be edible. In this sense the strict vegetarian, though he rejects the Noachic per-mission to eat meat, shares exactly the indiscriminate Noachic grouping-together of all the animals and its concentration only on the blood, which is the life.

But why, one might still ask, does not the Torah institute other dietary laws that push back all the way to vegetarianism, reversing altogether the Noachic permission to eat meat? Is not vegetarian-ism the biblical ideal, if the restricted meat diet of Leviticus is really nothing more than a compromise, a recognition that it is too much to expect these stiff-necked human beings to go back to nuts and berries? Perhaps we were wrong to see the Noachic dispen-sation as merely concessive, a yielding to Noah's (and mankind's) prideful bloody-mindedness. Perhaps, looked at again, we can see here also something elevating. Noah, the incipiently civilized man, having spent time in close quarters with the animals, figured out as a result his human difference; he learned that he was more than just king of the animals. He learned that he was the ambig-uous-because-godlike animal, both capable of and in need of self-restraint through the rule of law, and also open to the intelligible order of the multiform world. The result is the new world order after the flood: To mark his self-conscious separation from the animals, man undertakes to eat them; to acknowledge his own godlikeness, man accepts the prohibition of homicide (Genesis 9:3–4, 9:6). Eating meat may indeed be part and parcel—albeit a worrisome one—of our humanization. The recognized humanization of the human animal, it seems, can only be achieved at some cost to the harmony of the whole. This price is noted with regret, but it also must be paid. And it may be worth paying in order to keep the human being ever-mindful of the forms and distinctions that are the foundation of the world. It may be superhuman, and (as some will argue) more godlike, but it may also be less than human—and it surely is paradoxical—for human beings to renounce on the basis of reason their rational difference from the animals, (to renounce also their participation in the transcendent yearnings of Dionysus), and to affirm by an act of choice the pre-human, instinctive diet of fruit and seeds. The Levitical dietary laws fit the human animal in his distinctive uprightness: Celebrating the principle of rational separation, they celebrate not only man's share in rationality but also his openness to the mystery of intelligible yet embodied form.

But there is more to the dietary laws than the celebration of rational order. There is motion also toward the source of that order, toward that which is highest over all. The Noachic covenant with all flesh had denied in a way the dignity of flesh as variously formed and active, reserving it only for blood. Whether as a concession to unavoidable necessity or as a mark of human superiority, the lower, flesh, was permitted, but the higher, life, was not. "Do not eat the high," says the Noachic law on meat. The Levitical permissions and prohibitions say the reverse: "Do not eat the detestable." Only the clean is to be incorporated. The legal distinction between clean and unclean is higher than the natural principle of living and nonliving, even as it incorporates and modifies it. There is elevation in these restrictions. The clean and the holy, once far removed, are incorporated into daily life: Eating the clean, under laws given by the Holy One, symbolizes the sanctification of eating. We conclude with a brief look at sanctification.

Separation and Holiness

At the end of Leviticus 20, in an exhortation that concludes a long ten-chapter section on personal, ritual, and moral purity, God speaks together of separation and holiness. He first calls on the Children of Israel to keep and do the laws, in order to avoid becoming abominations to the land and abhorrent to God, like the Canaanites whom He is casting out before them.* He concludes as follows:

> I am the Lord your God, who have *separated* (*hivdalti*) you from the peoples. You shall therefore *separate* (*vehivdaltem*) between the clean beasts and the unclean and between the unclean fowl and the clean; and you shall not make your souls detestable by beast or by fowl or by anything wherewith the ground teemeth, which I *separated* (*hivdalti*) for you to hold unclean. And you shall be *holy* (*qadoshim*) unto Me; for I the Lord am *holy* (*qadosh*), and have *separated* (*va'avdil*) you from the peoples, that you should be Mine. (vv. 24–26; italics added; the verb *badal*, "to separate," the verb of the Creation, occurs four times)

How does making and observing separations between the clean and the unclean conduce to holiness? What does it mean, "Be ye holy, for I am holy"? I do not know. But I offer one observation and two suggestions.

The dietary laws should remind us not only of the created *order* but of the order as *created*, not only of the intelligible separations

---

*"Ye shall therefore keep all My statutes, and all Mine ordinances, and do them, that the land, whither I bring you therein, vomit you not out. And ye shall not walk in the customs of the nation, which I am casting out before you; for they did all these things, and therefore I abhorred them. But I have said unto you: 'Ye shall inherit their land, and I will give it to you to possess it, a land flowing with milk and honey'" (20:22–24). Among the abominable practices that defile the land, emphasis is placed especially on those surrounding sexuality and generation—failure to observe the crucial distinctions between those with whom one may and those with whom one may not have sexual relations ("uncover nakedness"); failure to honor father and mother; giving one's seed to Molech. These practices especially make a people nauseating, even to the earth which "vomits" them out. To dwell in the land of milk and honey, both sexual and dietary uprightness are required. Leviticus 20 thus revisits and addresses the pre-Abrahamic (that is, uninstructed) excesses of the polymorphously perverse animal—regarding food, drink, and sex—that were presented in the story of Noah: Noah's unwelcome sacrifice of animals, his drunkenness, his son Ham's trafficking in the uncovered nakedness of his father, and Noah's curse on his son ("giving his seed to Molech"). See my essay "Seeing the Nakedness of His Father."⁹

and forms but of the mysterious source of form, separation, and intelligibility. The practice of the dietary laws reflects and achieves the separation of the people, around the rule of separation, to celebrate through obedience the holiness and separateness of the holy *source* of separation itself—and, by the way, also of the bounty of food.

And how might one become holier through observing these separations? Two suggestions. On the one hand, through obedience: One reduces the distance between the holy and the profane by sanctifying the latter through obedience to the former. The low is made high—or at least higher—through acknowledgment of its dependence on the high; the high is "brought down," "democratized," and given concrete expression in the forms that govern ordinary daily life. The humdrum of existence and the passage of time are sanctified when the hallowed separateness of the Seventh Day is brought into human life when it is commemorated as the Sabbath. Likewise the commonness of eating is sanctified through observance of divine commandments, whose main principles remind the mindful eaters of the supreme rule of the Holy One.

On the other hand, through imitation: God seems to say to the creature made in His image, "You should make distinctions because I make distinctions. Because I made the separations that created the world, because I also separated you from the peoples that know Me not that you should be Mine in holiness, so you must make and honor these separations in pursuit of holiness, of more perfect God-like-ness." This suggests that it is also in the fullest rational activity that man imitates and comes closer to God—but with these most important qualifications:

We can discern the distinctions in things, but *we* have not made them separate.

Neither have we made that power of mind that registers the articulations of the world and permits us to recognize distinctions.

The rational man is therefore only an image—and knows it. Brought by his mindful appreciation of forms before the mystery of form and mind, he must bow his head—as he alone can—to powers greater than human reason. The upright animal, his gaze uplifted and his heart filled with wonder and awe, in fact stands tallest when he freely bows his head.

In order that we not forget these qualifications, the dietary laws, like the Creation they memorialize and the world we inhabit, will never be wholly transparent to reason.

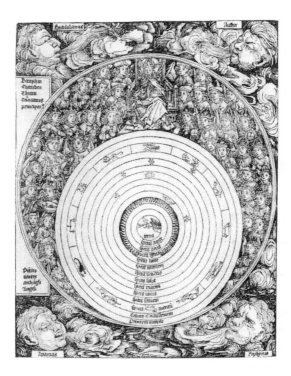

Conclusion

The Hungry Soul and the Perfecting of Our Nature

Without ever leaving the table, we have conducted a full-course inquiry, from metabolism to morality, from digestion to divinity, into how we differ from other animals. Beginning with the universal and urgent need for food, we noted how each living animal, to preserve its lively existence and its formed identity, is appetitively driven outward in space and forward in time, in quest of appropriate material for nourishment. The lack of material, felt as need, opens a gap between self and world; at the same time, need experienced as appetite coordinates the vital activities of awareness and action that bridge this gap, sometimes less, sometimes more, successfully. In the higher animals, the soul energized by hunger gains hunger's satisfaction only through intermediate activities—such as smelling, hearing, seeing, chasing, attacking, capturing, biting, tasting, chewing, and swallowing—activities which themselves become new objects of desire for the hungry soul. Increasingly capable of genuine encounters with the world, with other living forms, and (especially in birds and mammals) with kith and

227

kin, the souls of the hungry acquire new hungers of their own, and for more than nourishment. With the rise of intelligence and especially with its extraordinary development in the upright animal, the hungry soul seeks satisfaction in activities animated also by wonder, ambition, affection, curiosity, and awe. We human beings delight in beauty and order, art and action, sociability and friendship, insight and understanding, song and worship. And, as self-conscious beings, we especially crave self-understanding and knowledge of our place in the larger whole.

All these appetites of the hungry soul can in fact be partly satisfied at the table, provided that we approach it in the proper spirit. The meal taken at table is the cultural form that enables us to respond simultaneously to all the dominant features of our world: inner need, natural plenitude, freedom and reason, human community, and the mysterious source of it all. In humanized eating, we can nourish our souls even while we feed our bodies.

Life, as has been observed, is not just a bowl of cherries; it is also necessarily filled with disappointment, pain, and suffering. The chase is not always successful and, when it is, another animal pays with its life. Human intelligence and reason only compound the paradoxes and dangers of life; greed, vanity, and the will to dominate, no less than awe and wonder, are also passions native to the human soul. Only the rational animal can be perverse, only the rational animal can play the tyrant, only the rational animal destroys the conditions for his own flourishing and that of his fellow creatures. The highly omnivorous rational animal thus stands in need of perfection through the guiding institutions of law, morality, and custom. We have explored here the direction such guidance should take if we are to realize the higher pointings and deeper yearnings of our peculiarly upright nature: pointings toward community and friendship (encouraged by hospitality and shared meals); pointings toward beauty and nobility (encouraged by gracious manners and the adornments of the table); pointings toward discernment and understanding (encouraged by tasteful dining and lively conversation); and yearnings for a relation to the divine (encouraged by a ritual sanctification of the meal).

Though our inquiry has soared high, it has not forgotten its lowly beginnings. On the contrary, we have from the start been singing the virtues of necessity. Necessity—our bodily neediness—can not only be humanized; meeting it knowingly and deliberately can also be humanizing. For those who understand both the meaning of eating and their own hungry soul, necessity becomes the mother of the specifically human virtues: freedom, sympathy, moderation, beautification, taste, liberality, tact, grace, wit, gratitude, and, finally, reverence.

The perfections of our nature are multiple. Accordingly, one should not expect that a single form of humanized eating will embody and nourish them all. Indeed, we have in this book visited a variety of dining forms that manifest in different ways the elevated faces of our humanity: feeding the stranger at our hearth; the well-mannered family supper; the convivial and witty dinner party; the inspiriting feast of the genius Babette; the wisdom-seeking symposium of Plato; the reverent ritual meal. Some forms of dining accentuate the just, others the noble, still others the playful, the artistic, the philosophic, or the pious. Yet each one reveals a common dignified humanity, differently accented and highlighted. Each displays what it means to be the truly upright and thoughtful animal.

It remains only to draw out some implications of this account of nature, human nature, and its ethical pointings. First, regarding our practices, we see clearly what is culturally and spiritually at stake in certain current habits of eating. We face serious dangers from our increasingly utilitarian, functional, or "economic" attitudes toward food. True, fast food, TV dinners, and eating on the run save time, meet our need for "fuel," and provide close to instant gratification. But for these very reasons, they diminish opportunities for conversation, communion, and aesthetic discernment; they thus shortchange the other hungers of the soul. Disposable utensils and paper plates save labor at the price of refinement, and also symbolically deny memory and permanence their rightful places at the table. Meals eaten before the television set turn eating into feeding. Wolfing down food dishonors both the human effort to prepare it and the lives of those plants and animals sacrificed on our behalf. Not surprisingly, incivility, insensitivity, and ingratitude learned at the family table can infect all other aspects of one's life.

Conversely, good habits and thoughtful attitudes regarding food and eating will have far-reaching benefits. Self-restraint and self-command, consideration for others, politeness, fairness, generosity, tact, discernment, good taste, and the art of friendly conversation—all learnable and practiced at the table—enrich and ennoble all of human life. Especially because modern times hold us hostage to the artificial and the "unreal," we do well to remember that the hearth still makes the home, prepared and shared meals still make for genuine family life, and entertaining guests at dinner still nurtures the growth of friendship. A blessing offered over the meal still fosters a fitting attitude toward the world, whose gracious bounty is available to us and not because we merit it.

Beyond these benefits of more refined and upright practices, knowledge of the hungry soul offers us a richer and more truthful self-understanding than is currently available in our dominant modes of thought. For we can now correct the shrunken and misleading opinions about ourselves and our world that are the legacy of our reductive science. We are now in a position to see that hunger hungers for more than fuel, just as eros longs for more than "having sex." The materialistic view of life, though it may help put bread on the table, cannot help us understand what it means to eat. Despite our science's ability to predict and control some natural phenomena, it proves less true to life than an account that takes seriously the soul's natural inclinations and aspirations. Recognizing the soul's roots in our needy animal nature, we can now also free ourselves from the equally shrunken and misleading self-understanding of our existentialist philosophies, which think of human life only in terms of pure mind or consciousness, severed from all meaningful ties to the rest of nature and even to our own bodies. The more natural science and anthropology outlined in this book provide the ground of a human self-understanding that would leave us no longer self-divided, self-denying, self-deceived, and alienated from the world—in short, a self-understanding capable of supporting a dignified and noble view of human life.

In an effort to increase power and efficiency and in the name of so-called liberation and sophistication, we have accepted and even encouraged the demystification of life and the world. Nature we mentally homogenize in preparation for working her over according to our whims. Increasingly blind to the wonderful forms of nature and increasingly deaf to the ennobling forms of civility and ritual, we cultivate a cultural outlook of cynicism, crudeness, and despair. The beauty and bounty of the given world we either ignore or take for granted. Strangely, our telescopes and microscopes (and the technologies that accompany them) have destroyed our perspective on the naturally visible world of ordinary experience. Like the one-eyed Cyclops, we too still eat when hungry but no longer know what it means.

Recovering the deeper meaning of eating could help cure our spiritual anorexia. From it we can learn the essential unity of body and soul, and we can relearn the true relations to the formed world that the hungering soul makes possible. We can see again that living in a needy body is no disgrace and that our particular upright embodiment orients us toward the beautiful, the good, the true, and the holy. We can see which humanly instituted customs, rightly grounded in knowledge of our nature, would help us toward these psychic goals. Understanding more clearly what it means to nourish the hungry soul, we might be better able to satisfy it. Appreciating fully the first necessity of everyday life, we might even be able to begin restoring our ailing cultural spirit. It seems there was wisdom in the apple after all.

Next time you sit down to eat you might wish to keep these thoughts in mind. The truth is right before you—at the table.

Notes

Introduction. *"Good for Food . . . to Make One Wise"*

1. See, for example, my essay "Evolution and the Bible: Genesis I Revisited," *Commentary*, November 1988, pp. 29–39.
2. Some of these are presented in my earlier book, *Toward a More Natural Science: Biology and Human Affairs* (New York: Free Press, 1985; reprint, 1988); see especially chaps. 10–13. See also my essay "The Permanent Limitations of Biology," in *The Ambiguous Legacy of the Enlightenment*, William A. Rusher, ed. (Lanham, MD: University Press of America, 1995).

Chapter 1. *Food and Nourishing: The Primacy of Form*

1. Walter B. Cannon, *The Wisdom of the Body* (New York: W. W. Norton, 1967).
2. See Adolf Portmann, *Animal Forms and Patterns*, trans. by Hella Czech (New York: Schocken Books, 1967). This beautiful book by the late Swiss zoologist gives the best account I know of the meaning of animal form.
3. Kass, *Toward a More Natural Science*, p. 173.
4. Hans Jonas, *The Phenomenon of Life: Toward a Philosophical Biology* (New York: Harper & Row, 1966; Chicago: University of Chicago Press, 1982).
5. Adam Schulman, "Wholes and Parts: Quantum Physics, Aristotelian Physics, and Environmentalism" (lecture delivered at a symposium on "The Green Revolution: The Philosophical and Scientific Basis of Environmentalism," Michigan State University, May, 1992).
6. Jonas, "Is God a Mathematician?," *op. cit.* p. 86; italics added.
7. Ibid., pp. 85–86.
8. See Portmann, *Animal Forms and Patterns*.
9. Jonas, *The Phenomenon of Life*, pp. 106–107.

233

Chapter 2. The Human Form: Omnivorosus Erectus

1. See *De Anima*, Book II, chaps. 1–3.
2. Jonas, *The Phenomenon of Life*, p. 57.
3. Charles Darwin, *The Expression of the Emotions in Man and Animals* (Chicago: University of Chicago Press, 1965), p. 309.
4. For an excellent general treatment of this subject, see Mary Midgley's *Beast and Man: The Roots of Human Nature* (Ithaca, N.Y.: Cornell University Press, 1978).
5. Erwin Straus, "The Upright Posture," in his *Phenomenological Psychology* (New York: Basic Books, 1966), pp. 137–165.
6. Ibid., p. 138.
7. Ibid., p. 139; italics added.
8. Ibid., p. 141.
9. Ibid., p. 142.
10. Ibid., p. 143.
11. Ibid., pp. 150–151.
12. Ibid., p. 156.
13. Ibid., pp. 154–155.
14. C. S. Lewis, *The Four Loves* (New York: Harcourt Brace Jovanovich, 1960), p. 97; italics in original.
15. Straus, "The Upright Posture," p. 162. See also Jonas, "The Nobility of Sight," in *The Phenomenon of Life*, pp. 135–156.
16. Ibid., p. 162.
17. Ibid., p. 162.
18. Readers who wish to pursue these matters should see Hans Jonas's "Image-making and the Freedom of Man," in his *The Phenomenon of Life*, pp. 157–182, on which this and the next paragraph are largely based; Jacob Klein's profound discussion of memory, recollection, imagination, and thought—which includes a remarkable explication of Plato's famous image of the divided line—in his illuminating and beautiful book, *A Commentary on Plato's Meno* (Chicago: University of Chicago Press, 1989), pp. 108–172; and Eva T. H. Brann's magisterial study, *The World of the Imagination: Sum and Substance* (Savage, Md.: Rowman & Littlefield, 1991).
19. See Curtis A. Wilson, "*Homo Loquens* from a Biological Standpoint," *St. John's Review*, Summer 1983, pp. 3–17. See also E. H. Lennenberg, *The Biological Foundations for Language* (New York: John Wiley & Sons, 1967).
20. See Portmann, *Animal Forms and Patterns*.
21. Wolfgang Schad, *Man and Mammals: Toward a Biology of Form*, trans. Carroll Scherer (New York: Waldorf Press, 1977), p. 33.
22. Libbie Henrietta Hyman, *Comparative Vertebrate Anatomy* (Chicago: University of Chicago Press, 1942), p. 256; italics in original.
23. Jean-Jacques Rousseau, "Discourse on the Origin and Foundations of Inequality Among Men," trans. Roger D. Masters and Judith R. Masters, in

The First and Second Discourses, ed. Roger D. Masters (New York: St. Martin's Press, 1964), pp. 105–106.

24. Ibid., pp. 113–114.
25. For a rich discussion of these and related matters, see Schad, *Man and Mammals*.
26. Ibid., p. 266.
27. G. H. Schubert, quoted in Schad, *Man and Mammals*, p. 34.
28. Jean Anthelme Brillat-Savarin, *The Physiology of Taste, or Meditations on Transcendental Gastronomy*, trans. Arthur Machen (New York: Dover, 1960), p. 15. This classic and delightful exploration of eating, from the sense of taste to the philosophical history of cooking, was first published in France in 1825.
29. Ibid., p. 22.
30. Ibid., p. 30; italics in original.
31. Ibid., p. 30; italics added.
32. The phrase is from C. H. Waddington, *The Ethical Animal* (Chicago: University of Chicago Press, 1967). This is perhaps the finest recent attempt to explore the biological basis of man's ethical nature.
33. Aristotle, *Politics*, 1253a31–37.

Chapter 3. Host and Cannibal: From Fressen to Essen

1. Homer, *The Odyssey*, trans. Richmond Lattimore (New York: Harper & Row, 1965), 3:67–74.
2. Aristotle, *Nicomachean Ethics*, 1156a31.
3. Genesis 18:1–8.
4. *Odyssey*, 9:252–255.
5. Ibid., 9:268–271.
6. Ibid., 9:273–279.
7. Ibid., 9:369–370.
8. Ibid., 9:83–97.
9. Herodotus, *Histories*, trans. George Rawlinson (New York: Modern Library/Random House, 1942), 3:99–100.
10. Plato, *The Republic*, trans. Allan Bloom (New York: Basic Books, 1968), 372b.
11. Rousseau, "Discourse on Inequality," op cit. , pp. 141–142.
12. For a marvelous discussion of men's devotion to rice and its sociopolitical meaning, see the chapter "Rice: The Tyrant with a Soul," in Margaret Visser's wonderful book *Much Depends on Dinner* (New York: Collier Books, Macmillan, 1986), pp. 155–191.
13. Margaret Visser, "Salt: The Edible Rock," ibid., p. 65. My discussion of salt relies heavily on this essay.
14. Ibid., pp. 76–77.
15. Ibid., p. 67. "Bread (grown, harvested, ground, leavened, and baked) and

salt (found, won, collected and efficiently transported) together cover the field: they represent man as Farmer, patiently and wisely nurturing his crops, but also as Hunter, Scientist, Adventurer, and Organizer."
16. *The Bacchae* of Euripides is the classic treatment of this problem.

Chapter 4. Enhancing Uprightness: Civilized Eating

1. Margaret Visser, *The Rituals of Dinner: The Origins, Evolution, Eccentricities, and Meaning of Table Manners* (New York: Grove Weidenfeld, 1991).
2. Brillat-Savarin, *The Physiology of Taste*, p. 132.
3. Ibid., pp. 132–133.
4. Aristotle, *Nicomachean Ethics*, 1106b1–5.
5. For a superb exploration of the history of this process, rich in concrete detail, see Norbert Elias, *The Civilizing Process*, especially vol. 1, *The History of Manners*, trans. Edmund Jephcott (New York: Pantheon, 1978).
6. It is dedicated to an eleven-year-old boy of high birth, "The Most Noble Henry of Burgundy, Youth of Outstanding Promise and Son of Adolph, Prince of Veere."
7. The book was an instant success, with at least twelve editions in 1530 alone. English, German, French, and Czech translations appeared within the decade. As early as 1534, it was being introduced in England as a schoolbook for the education of boys. At least until the nineteenth century, it was the most widely read of Erasmus's works; more than 130 editions are known. A modern English translation by Brian McGregor is in *Collected Works of Erasmus*, vol. 25 (Toronto: University of Toronto Press, 1985).
8. This passage is quoted from the 16th-century Whittington English translation, in order to give the more graphic flavor of the original. Hereafter I will quote mainly from the McGregor translation, except in a few places where the more archaic usage captures the point better (marked [W]).
9. See the discussions in Elias, *The History of Manners* and Visser, *The Rituals of Dinner*, to which my own presentation is indebted.
10. From Antoine de Courtin, *Nouveau traité de civilité* (1672), quoted in Elias, *The History of Manners*, p. 92; italics added.
11. Visser, *The Rituals of Dinner*, p. 189.
12. Ibid., p. 187.
13. Elias, *The History of Manners*, p. 123.
14. Visser, *The Rituals of Dinner*, p. 186.
15. Elias, *The History of Manners*, p. 118.
16. Ibid., p. 120.
17. Erwin Straus, "Shame as a Historiological Problem," in *Phenomenological Psychology*, pp. 217–223; quotation at 219. This profound little paper makes clear how shame is natural to man, central to human existence, and indispensable for happiness.
18. Ibid., pp. 222–223.

19. Ibid., p. 220.
20. Brillat-Savarin, *The Physiology of Taste*, aphorism 4, p. 1.
21. *The Autobiography of Benjamin Franklin*, introduction and notes by R. Jackson Wilson (New York: Modern Library, 1981), p. 106.
22. Aristotle, *Nicomachean Ethics*, 1118a23–b5.
23. Ibid., 1119a11–21; italics added.
24. Ibid., 1119b15–18; italics added.
25. Ibid., 1119b6–11.
26. Ibid., 1119b11–15.

Chapter 5. Freedom, Friendship, and Philosophy: From Eating to Dining

1. Tolstoy, *War and Peace*, trans. Louise and Aylmer Maude (New York: W. W. Norton, 1966), p. 102.
2. Judith Martin, *Miss Manners' Guide to Excruciatingly Correct Behavior* (New York: Warner, 1983), p. 492.
3. See, for example, Mary Douglas, "Deciphering a Meal," *Daedalus* 101:61–81, 1972. See also such works of Claude Lévi-Strauss as *The Raw and the Cooked* and *The Origin of Table Manners*.
4. Martin, *Miss Manners' Guide*, p. 481.
5. Ibid., pp. 165–166. Miss Manners clearly disapproves of such practices.
6. *The Autobiography of Benjamin Franklin*, pp. 10–11. As Franklin makes clear in many other passages in *The Autobiography*, he was in fact hardly indifferent to what he ate. See, for example, the famous story about how he abandoned vegetarianism, pp. 41–42.
7. Aristides, "Merely Anecdotal," *American Scholar*, Spring 1992, pp. 167–176, at p. 170. This essay—written by a master story-teller and conversationalist—is altogether a marvelous appreciation of the nature and worth of anecdotes.
8. Isak Dinesen, *Babette's Feast and Other Anecdotes of Destiny* (New York: Vintage books, 1988), p. 16.
9. Ibid., p. 23.
10. Ibid., p. 25.
11. Ibid., pp. 26–27.
12. Ibid., p. 6.
13. Ibid., p. 33.
14. Ibid., pp. 30–31.
15. Ibid., p. 35.
16. Ibid., p. 36.
17. Ibid.
18. Ibid., p. 38.
19. Ibid., p. 39.
20. Ibid., pp. 40–41.
21. Ibid., p. 41.

22. Ibid., pp. 46–47.
23. Ibid., p. 48.

Chapter 6. Sanctified Eating: A Memorial of Creation

1. See, for example, Matthew 15:11: "Not that which goeth into the mouth defileth a man; but that which cometh out of the mouth, this defileth a man." See also Mark 7:18–20.
2. U. Cassuto, *A Commentary on the Book of Genesis* (Jerusalem: Magnes Press/Hebrew University), 1961.
3. Leo Strauss, "On The Interpretation of Genesis," *L'homme* 31, no. 1 (1981), pp. 5–20.
4. Ibid., pp. 12–13.
5. Ibid., p. 13.
6. Robert Sacks, *A Commentary on the Book of Genesis* (Lewiston, N.Y.: Edwin Mellen Press, 1991). This book was first published in serialized form in *Interpretation: A Journal of Political Philosophy*, beginning in May 1980 (vol. 8, nos. 2/3) and ending in May–September 1984 (vol. 12, nos. 2/3).
7. Immanuel Kant, "Conjectural Beginning of Human History," trans. Emil Fackenheim, in *Kant On History*, ed. Lewis White Beck (Indianapolis: Bobbs-Merrill, 1963), pp. 55–56.
8. Rousseau, "Discourse on the Origin and Foundations of Inequality Among Men," p. 102.
9. Leon R. Kass, "Seeing the Nakedness of His Father," *Commentary*, June 1992, pp. 41–47.
10. Mary Douglas, "The Abominations of Leviticus," in *Purity and Danger* (London: Routledge & Kegan Paul), 1966.
11. Jean Soler, "The Dietary Prohibitions of the Hebrews," *New York Review of Books*, June 14, 1979.
12. Franklin, *The Autobiography of Benjamin Franklin*, pp. 41–42. See also R. Jackson Wilson's discussion of this episode, and of other passages about eating, in his Introduction, pp. xix–xxvii.

Index

Aaron, 217
Abraham, 106*n*, 216*n*
  hospitality shown by, 103–5
Absorption, 26
Action
  appetite as guide to, 48
  discriminate, 45
  human openness in, 97
  power of, 44, 45–51, 59, 227
    in higher animals, 53–54
  voluntary, 52, 53
Action space (lived space), 48–49, 67
Aggressiveness, meat eating and, 84, 85
Agriculture, 121–23
Agroikos (humorless oaf), 180
Akolasia (unrestrainedness), 155
Alienation, causes of, xv
Ambiguity, moral. *See* Moral ambiguity
Amoeba, eating mechanism of, 22
Ancient Greeks
  network of relations based on offer-
    ing hospitality, 102–3
  wine making and, 124–27
Anima. See Soul
Animality of human beings, 59–62
  nobility and transformation of, 159
  wine in excess and, 126–27
Animal rights, 118
Animals
  clean versus unclean, laws concern-
    ing, 218–20
  man's dominion over, 60n, 205, 206
  relations between man and, 60–61

Anthropophagy. *See* Cannibalism
Appetite(s), 3, 51–52
  correlation of human freedom and
    human, 83
  as deepest principle of life, 48
  dietary laws as restraints on, 208
  as forward looking and purposive, 49
  of hungry soul, 227–28
  beyond nutrition, in higher animals, 53
  power of, 44, 47–51, 59
  revealing man as ethical animal,
    91–92
  table manners to control internal,
    140–41
  taste and, 87–92
Argument, 171
Aristophanes, 82*n*
Aristotelian view, 3
Aristotle, 25n, 36, 63
  on friendship, 102
  on hand as tool, 67*n*
  on liberality, 174, 175
  on man as best and worst of animals,
    92, 93, 112
  on moderation, 155, 156, 157, 208
  on soul, 60
Arm, human, 67–70
Artist, culinary, 183–92
ATP, 28
Autonomy, human omnivorousness and,
    208–10
Awareness
  human openness in, 97

Awareness (*continued*)
omnivorousness and growing, 56
power of, 44, 45–51, 59, 227
appetite as guide to, 48
discriminate, 45–46
in higher animals, 53–54
use of term, 45n
of wholes, human sight and, 71
Aztecs, ritual cannibalism practiced by,
113–14

Babel, city and tower of, 213
"Babette's Feast" (Dinesen), 183–92
Bacchus (Dionysus), 126–27
Bacon, Francis, 4
Bacteria, 22
Bible, the
biblical anthropology of eating,
208–15
dietary laws in. *See* Sanctified eating
hospitality taught in, 103–6
human food in, 118–19
relations between man and animals
in, 60
Biosynthesis, 26, 31
Birds, uprightness of, 67n
Blood, prohibition against eating, 119,
211, 212n, 220, 222
Blushing, 61n
Body and soul, essential unity of, 231
Body language, 66
Bomolochos, 179–80
Bread as human food, 120–25
salt as relish for, 124
shift from fruit to, 211
Brillat–Savarin, 88, 133, 134, 152, 161,
167, 177
Buddhist teaching of nirvana, 4
Buffoon, 179–80

Cain, 211, 216n
Callatians, 114n
Cannibalism, 99–100, 107–14, 131
natural grounding of taboo against,
109–10
types of, 108, 113–14
Cannon, Walter B., 29n
Cardinal virtues, 174n

Carnivorousness, 21. *See also* Meat eating, human
animals unclean due to, 219
extreme, 116–17
human, 84–85
covenant with Noah and concession to, 212
extreme carnivores, 116–17
Cassuto, U., 199n
Cause of nourishing, 31–34
Chinese, utensils (chopsticks) used by,
145
Civility. *See also* Civilized eating
criticisms of, 132
defining, 131–32
ethics and, 132
Civilization
hospitality and, 107
humanization through, 211
salt usage and rise of, 123
Civilized eating, 129–60
mood and its display, 150–51
regulating hands, mouth, and eyes,
141–50
table as place of meal, 133–38, 228
table manners, 13–14, 131, 181
basic, 138–41
reasons for, 151–54
virtue of eating, 154–60
Clean and unclean, distinction between,
217–20, 222
holiness and, 223–25
Cleanliness at table, 139
Commitment, meal at table as, 134–35
Communication, 170–71
Communion, human openness to, 70
Community, table manners to promote,
152
Companionship, 70n
Complexity, specialization and, 23–24
Composition, concretion versus,
30–31
Conduct. *See* Table manners
"Conjectural Beginning of Human His-
tory" (Kant), 210n
Consideration, table manners to show,
152
Conventions, 99. *See also* Customs

Conversation, 170–74
  meaning of, 172–74
  root of word, 172
  wittiness and, 178–81
Cook, the, 183–92
Corporealism, 5, 7, 8, 9, 34, 59, 114
Covenant between Noah and God,
    211–12, 220
Crafts, accessibility to lateral space and
    exercise of human, 68–69
Creation, the, 60n, 199–207
  dietary laws and celebration of, 221
  main principles at work in, 201–5
  order of, 200–201
Culinary artist, 183–92
Culture, modification by, 13
Customs, 98–127. *See also* Civilized eating
  cannibalism, taboo against, 99–100,
    107–14, 131
  hospitality toward strangers,
    100–107, 131
  of human food, 117–27
  need for, 98
  potential savagery versus excellence
    and, 93
  relation between our nature and, 12
  subhuman eating, 116–17
  vitalism, 114–15
Cyclopes, Odysseus in land of, 110–13

Dairy and meat products, prohibition
    against mixing, 215*n*
Darwin, Charles, 61–62
Darwinism, 5, 61
*De civilitate morum puerilium (On Good
    Manners for Boys)* (Erasmus),
    139–41
Definitive tongue, 81*n*
Demystification of life and world,
    230–31
Dentition, 3
  human, 86–87
  mammalian, 85–86
Dependence, hospitality and recogni-
    tion of mutual, 106
Descartes, René, 4, 34
Descent of Man, The (Darwin), 61
Deuteronomy 4:6, 198

Diaresis (division by two), 204
Diet
  dentition and, 85–87
  freedom (and human difference)
    demonstrable in, 83–84
  unspecialized character of natural
    human, 85, 86–87
Dietary laws, Jewish, 193–225
  biblical anthropology, in Genesis,
    208–15
  dietary laws of Leviticus, 14, 215–22
  Genesis 1 and, 199–207, 218
  holiness as true concern of, 216–17
  original dietary laws, 211–12, 219–20
  reasons for, 208
    questioning, 197–98
  separation through, 212–13
    holiness and, 223–25
Digesting, 26
Digestive tract, 22–23
Digestive waste, 26–27
Dinesen, Isak, 183–92
Dining, 14, 161–92
  culinary artist and the moment of
    truth, 183–92
  at dinner party, 164–70
  table talk, 170–74
  virtues of, 174–83
Dionysus (Bacchus), 126–27
Distance
  implicit in upright posture, 66
  inner "experienced," 68
  mediated first by imagination and
    then thought, 73–74
  powers to overcome, 53–54, 66
  between self and world, 66
  between taster and tasted, 89
Divinity, relation to. *See* Sanctified
    eating
DNA, information carried by material
    in, 43
Dominion over animals, man's, 60*n*,
    205, 206
Douglas, Mary, 218n

Eating, 2–3, 24–27
  civilized. *See* Civilized eating
  defined, 25

Eating (*continued*)
　important socioeconomic aspect of, 2
　paradox of, 13, 97
　in public, 148–50
　reasons for studying, 11–12
　sanctified. *See* Sanctified eating
　scientist's view of, 9–11
　subhuman, 116–17
　table manners to facilitate, 152–53
　transformation involved in, 26
　　composition versus concretion,
　　　30–31
　　as form preserving and form de-
　　　forming, 13, 54–56
　　metabolic, 28–29
　　as transitive and intransitive verb, 25
　virtue of, 154–60
Eidos, 36–37
Eleutheriotes (liberality), 174–78
Elias, Norbert, 144
Emergent form, 39n
Empedocles, 40
Endocannibalism, 108
Energy, food for, 27–28
Environmentalist movement, 4
Epicureanism, 3
Epstein, Joseph, 178, 179
Erasmus of Rotterdam, 139–41, 145,
　147, 150, 151
Ethics
　civility and, 132
　human appetite revealing man as eth-
　　ical animal, 91–92
　nature and, 3–8
　rationality and, 76–79
Evolution, theory of, 59, 61
Exocannibalism, 108
Exodus, 216
"Experienced" distance, inner, 68
*Expression of the Emotions in Man and
　Animals, The* (Darwin), 61
Eyes, human, 70–76
　regulating use at table of, 147–48

Face, human, 70–76
Family, as most fundamental group,
　100–101
Feasting, 14. *See also* Dining

Feed, to
　reflexive sense of, 24–25
　transitive sense of, 24
Fermentation, discovery of, 124
Fish, omission of dietary criterion for,
　219n
Fishbane, Michael, 106n, 210n
Flood, the, 211
Food
　defining, 21–24
　God's instruction to man about,
　　206–7
　human, 117–27
　microscopic view of, 22
　need for, 19–20
　origins of word, 24
　as relational term, 22
　relative to mouth versus to gut,
　　23–24
　uses of, 27–31
　utilitarian attitude toward, dangers of
　　increasing, 229
Fork, use of, 142, 143
Form. *See also* Human form
　clean versus unclean animals based
　　on, 218, 219
　defined, 35
　emergent, 39n
　idea of, 14–15
　independence of, from its own mate-
　　rials, 41
　intangibility of, 42n
　looks and, 36–37
　material and, 34, 35–39
　organic, powers of, 44, 45–51, 59, 227
　persistence of, 41
　potential, 39n
　primacy of, 40–44, 55
　unifying and specifying properties of,
　　36–37
　as unimportant to eater, 21
Form-at-work, 38–39
Franklin, Benjamin, 154–55, 157, 172,
　220n
Freedom, human, 83–84
Friendship, 70n
　at the dinner table, 182
　guest-friendship, 102

Frugivores, 21
Fuel, food as, 27–28
Functioning form or organization, 38–39

Galileo, 4
Garden of Eden, story of, 1, 77, 89n, 208–11
Gastronomic cannibalism, 108
Gender-alternate seating, 169–70
Generosity, 175–77
Genesis, 199–215, 218
  biblical anthropology in, 208–15
  the Creation in, 60n, 199–207
  human food in, 118–19
  relations between man and animals in, 60
Gestalt, 36
Gland field, 81n
Glycolytic cycle, 23
"Gnostic touching," hand as organ of, 67–68
God, man in image of, 205
Gods, hospitality demanded by, 102–3
Good, use of term in Genesis 1, 207n
Gossip, 171
Gourmandism, 90–91
Grace, 177–78, 182, 191, 192
Gratitude, 178
Grosse Fresser, der (great devourer and glutton), 98
Groups
  organization of humans into, 100–101
  table and formation of, 136
Growth, food for true, 29–31
Guest-friendship, 102
Guests. *See also* Hospitality
  handicapped, special needs of, 169
  relations between hosts and, 100–107
  selection for dinner party, 165

Habituation, learning manners through, 159–60
Ham (Noah's son), 213, 223n
Handicapped guest, special needs of, 169
Hands, human, 67–70
  regulating use of, at table, 140, 141–43

Head, human, 70–76
Herbivores, 21, 116, 117
Herodotus, 116
Hesiod, 95
Hierarchy of living forms, 51–56, 59
Hobbes, Thomas, 3
Holiness
  separation and, 223–25
  as true concern of dietary laws, 216–17
Holy and common, distinction between, 217–20
Home, hospitality and recognition of meaning of, 106
Homeostasis, 29
Homer, 102, 110, 137n
Horace, 151
Hors d'oeuvres, 166
Hospitality
  cannibalism as inverted, 107–14
  meals and, 133
  Odysseus' adventure with the Cyclopes and, 110–13
  refined, in dinner party, 174–83
  toward strangers, 100–107, 131
  vitalism as parodied, 114–15
  wine and, 126
  of the world, animal need met by, 46–47, 55
Hosts, hostess
  at dinner party, 169
  guests and, relations between, 100–107
  root of English word *host*, 101
Human food, 117–27
  bread, 120–25, 211
  meat, shift to, 119–25
  rice, 122–23
  salt, 123–24
  wine, 124–27
Human form, 57–93
  animality of, 59–62
  arm and hand, 67–70
  as the best and the worst, 92–93
  denial of dignity of, 112, 113, 114, 117, 118
  distinctiveness of, 62–63
  ethical aspect of, 76–79
  head and face, eyes and mouth, 70–76
  as omnivorous animal, 79–85

Human form (*continued*)
    taste and appetite of, 87–92
    teeth and jaws, 86–87
    upright posture of, 63–66
Humanism, 9
Humanities, retreat from pursuit of wis-
        dom of, 6–7
Humanization
    through civilization, 211
    meat eating and, 119–25
Hunger, origin of appetites in, 27
Hungry soul, 27, 227–31
    knowledge of, 230
Hunting, humanization and shift to,
        119

Image, recognizing distinction between
        original and, 72–73
Image of God, man in, 205
Imagination, human, 73–74
Imitation, sanctification of eating
        through, 224
Independence of form, 41
Indeterminate openness, 78
Information, 35
    true growth as, 29
Inge, William Ralph, 17
Injustice, Sodomite, 106*n*
"Inner" experience, 39
Instincts, 82–84
Inviting guests to dinner party, 165
Isaac, 216*n*

Jacob wrestling with mysterious being,
        213–14
Japan
    festive meal in, 167–68
    utensils used in, 145
Jaw movements, human, 87
Jewish dietary laws. *See* Dietary laws,
        Jewish
Jonas, Hans, 40n, 49, 54*n*
Judgmental self-consciousness, emer-
        gence of, 77–78
Justice
    in distribution of food at table, 137
    need for, 98
    potential savagery versus excellence
        and, 93

Kant, Immanuel, 210*n*
Kaplan, Simon, 150*n*
Kin selection, theory of, 109
Klein, Jacob, 36, 82*n*
Knife, use of, 142, 143–45
Krebs cycle, 23

Languages, meals and birth of, 133
Lateral space, accessibility to, 68–69
Law. *See also* Dietary laws, Jewish
    natural, 3, 4
    need for, 93, 98
    Noachic, 211–12, 221, 222
Leviticus, Book of, 196
    dietary laws of, 14, 215–22
Lewis, C. S., 70*n*
Liberalism, 110
Liberality, virtue of, 174–78
Life
    paradox of, 13, 54–56
    as principle at work in the Creation,
        201, 203, 204
Lived space, 48–49, 67
Living forms
    biblical account of, 204–5
    hierarchy of, 51–56, 59
Locke, John, 3
Locomotion, clean versus unclean ani-
        mals based on, 219–20
Looks, form and, 36–37
Lot, treatment of strangers by, 105
Lotus-Eaters, Odysseus in land of,
        114–15, 120

Machines, differences between organ-
        ism and, 37–38
Maimonides, 215
Mammalian dentition, 85–86
Manners. *See* Table manners
Material(s)
    continuous exchange of, 41
    defined, 35
    form and, 34, 35–39
Materialism, 33–34, 40
Mathematization of nature, 4
Matter
    classical argument for primacy of, 40
    as ultimate "material," 36
Maturation, process of, 29

Meals at table, eating, 133–38, 228
Meat eating, human. *See also* Omnivorousness, human
   first instance of law permitting, 211*n*
   humanization and shift to, 119–25
   meat as relish, 120, 123
   origins of, 84–85
   prohibition against mixing dairy prod-
      ucts and, 215*n*
   serving of meat, 144–45
Mechanism, as ethically subversive, 5
Menu at dinner party, 166–67
Metabolic combustion, 28
Metabolism, 44
   continuous exchange of materials
      through, 41
   as forward-looking and purposive, 50
   in higher animals, 52
   responsibility for, 31–34
   transformations in, 28–29
   vital powers implicit in, 44, 45–51
   wasteful character of, impact of,
      26–27
Metallurgy, salt usage and rise of, 123
Mind, ancient view of, 25*n*
Miss Manners (Judith Martin), 166–67
Moderation, 154–57, 181, 208
Mood at table, display of, 150–51
Moral ambiguity, 208*n*
   human foods and, 127
   of sacrifices, 216*n*
Motion
   laws of, 33
   as principle at work in the Creation,
      201, 203, 204
Mouth, human, 75
   food relative to, 23–24
   multiple functions of, 75, 80–82
   rules concerning, 145–46
   specializations in, 79–80
Murder, prohibition of, 212

Nadab and Abihu, sacrifice of, 217
Naturalism, 8–9
Natural law, 3, 4
Natural rights, 3–4
Nature
   agriculture and new human relation-
      ship to, 122–23

   beneficence of, hospitality as recogni-
      tion of, 106
   ethics and, relation between, 3–8
   man's upright posture and natural
      opposition to, 65–66
   mathematization of, 4
   in modern natural science, 4–8
   objectified view of, 4, 9
   property in, 122
   relation between culture and our, 12
   as suggestive teacher, 12
Neatness at table, 139
Necessity
   Cyclopes' denial of natural, 112, 113
   eating with others while meeting,
      147–48
   of food, 19–20
   God's instruction to man about,
      206–7
   hospitality and perception of, 106–7
   manners to dignify and grace, 154
   virtues of, 229
   wine and elevated life beyond, 126
Nicomachean Ethics (Aristotle), 155, 174
Nirvana, 4
Noachic law, 211–12, 221, 222
Noah, 211–12, 213, 216n, 221–22
   covenant with, 211–12, 220
   sacrifice offered by, 212, 217, 223n
Nobility, 157–60
   sacrifice and, 176n
Noble virtues, 174n
Nourishing, nourishment
   cause of, 31–34
   as continuous necessity, 44
   food for, 28–31
      for growth, 29–31
      for organic self-maintenance, 28–29
   mediated, among higher animals, 52–54
Nucleotides of DNA, 43
Nutrition, taste and needs of, 88–89

Obedience, sanctification of eating
   through, 224
Objectivity, doctrine of, 4, 9
Odysseus
   in land of Cyclopes, 110–13
   in land of Lotus-Eaters, 114–15, 120
Odyssey (Homer), 102

Omnivorousness, human, 3, 13, 21, 97–98
  growing awareness and, 56
  human autonomy and, 208–10
  rationality and, 79–85
  taste and appetite and, 87–92
  as ultimate in homogenization, 92
Openness, 55–56, 68, 69
  to communion, 70
  experience of taste manifesting,
    89–90, 91
  indeterminate, 78
  Levitical dietary laws celebrating, 222
  receptive, 68, 69n, 78
  unique preparation of humans for, 97
  unspecified possibility, 69
Opposites, capacity to discern and
    desire, 92–93
Organic form, powers of, 44, 45–51, 59,
    227
Organic self-maintenance, food for,
    28–29
Organization, 37–38
  animal, meaning of, 48
  functioning, 38–39
  joinings and motions of material parts
    caused and governed by, 42–43
  persistence of, 41
Organs, 37
Organ transplantation, 108n
Ovid, 57, 63
Ownership, 122
Oxidative phosphorylation, 23

Padaeans, 116–17
Paradox
  of eating, 13, 97
  of life, 13, 54–56
Parts and wholes, relation of, 30
Persistence of form, 41
Physical appearance at table, 139
Pig, dietary laws against eating, 220
Pirke Aboth, 193
Place
  clean versus unclean animals based
    on, 218, 219
  as principle at work in the Creation,
    201, 203, 204
Plato, 36, 82n, 120, 125, 202, 204, 211n
Pointing, 69–70

Politics, emergence of, 212–13, 214
Polyphemos, 110–12
Posture at table, 139–40
Potential form, 39n
Powers of organic form, 44, 45–51, 59,
    227
Preparations for dinner party, 165–66
Productive mental capacities of human
    beings, 73–74
Property in nature, 122
Protective shame, 147, 151
Psyche in all living things, 48, 60
Psychic power, 44, 45–51, 59
Public, eating in, 148–50
Purity, Levitical laws of, 217–22
Purposiveness, 49–50

Questionable animal, man as, 76–79

Rationalism, 7, 9
Rationality, 75–85
  autonomy and, 208–10
  ethics and, 76–79
  human form and, 75–76
  Levitical dietary laws celebrating, 222
  omnivorousness and, 79–85
  potential savagery versus excellence
    and, 92–93
  relations between nonrational and ra-
    tional in man, 12
  table as embodiment of human,
    136–37
  upright posture and, 63–66
  wine and elevated life beyond, 126
"Real life," craving for, xiv–xv
Receptive openness, 68, 69n, 78
Recitals, 171
Reflection, 74
Reportage, 171
Reproduction, as forward-looking and
    purposive, 50–51
Republic (Plato), 120, 211n
Respiratory patterns during speech,
    human, 76n
Responsibility for metabolism, 31–34
Restriction, primary need for, 98
Ribaldry, 181
Rice as human food, 122–23
Rights

animal, 118
natural, 3–4
Ritual cannibalism, 108, 113–14
Rousseau, Jean–Jacques, 82, 83, 84,
    119, 122n, 123, 180*n*, 211
Rustic, the, 180

Sacks, Robert, 207*n*, 212*n*
Sacrifice
    laws regarding, 216–17
    Noah's, 212, 217, 223*n*
    nobility and, 176*n*
Salt, use of, 123–24
Sanctified eating, 193–225
    biblical anthropology, in Genesis,
        208–15
    dietary laws of Leviticus, 14, 215–22
    Genesis 1 and, 199–207
    separation and holiness, 223–25
Schad, Wolfgang, 80n
Schulman, Adam, 40
Science
    disjunction between world-as-experi-
        enced and world-as-known-by, 6
    notion of causation in modern, 33
    view of nature associated with mod-
        ern natural, 4–8
Seating at dinner party, arranged,
    168–70
Second Discourse (Rousseau), 119
Self
    distance between world and, 66
    emergence of life and emergence of
        genuine, 44
Self-consciousness, human, 77–78, 93,
    97, 98–99, 210
Self-forgetting, table manners to allow,
    153
Self-indulgence, 156
Self-maintenance, food for organic, 28–29
Separation
    of clean and unclean, Levitical princi-
        ple for, 218
    dietary laws to distinguish between
        peoples, 212–13
    holiness and, 223–25
    as principle at work in the Creation,
        201–4
Serpent in Garden of Eden, 209

Sexual nature, shame and, 77
Shame, 117, 236*n*17
    blushing and, 61*n*
    protective, 147, 151
    sexual nature and, 77
Sight, human, 70–76
Sitting at table, 135–36
Smell, taste and, 88
Sociality
    germ of animal, 50*n*
    mediated nourishing among higher
        animals and, 52
    shift to meat eating and new modes
        of, 119
    upright posture and, 63–66
Socrates, 125
Sodom, city of, 105, 106*n*
Sodomite injustice, 106*n*
Soler, Jean, 218*n*
Sophrosyne (moderation), 155
Soul
    in all living things, 48, 60
    essential unity of body and, 231
    hungry, 27, 227–31
    three great powers of, 13
Space, action (lived), 48–49, 67
Specialization, complexity and, 23–24
Speciation, 55
Species, recognition of, 37
Speech
    human respiratory patterns during, 76*n*
    human tongue and, 80–82
    rules about eating and speaking, 146
Spenser, Edmund, 17
Spirited element (thymos), meat eating
    and, 120
Spiritual distress, causes of, xv
Staring, rules against, 147–48
Starvation, cannibalism in face of, 108
Stimulus–response theory, 47
Stoic version of natural law, 3
Strangers, hospitality toward, 100–107,
    131
    Odysseus' adventures with the Cy-
        clopes and, 110–13
Straus, Erwin, 63, 66n, 67, 68, 82*n*, 147
Strauss, Leo, 199*n*, 202–4
Subhuman eating, 116–17
Symposium (Plato), 82*n*, 125

Table
    eating meal at, 133–38, 228
    setting, 137–38
    shape of, 136
Table manners, 13–14, 131, 181
    basic, 138–41
    reasons for, 151–54
Table talk, 170–74
Taboo
    against cannibalism, 99–100, 107–14,
        131
    in use of knife, 143–44
Tabula, 136
Tact, 177
Taste, 79, 80
    appetite and, 87–92
    latitude and educability of, 88–89
    needs of nutrition and, 88–89
    psychic experience of, 88
Taste buds, 24, 81
Technology, ethical use of new, 5–6
Teeth and jaws, 3
    human, 86–87
    mammalian, 85–86
Temperance, 154–57
Thomistic version of natural law, 3
Thought, human form and prospects
        for, 75–76
Throwing, 69
Thymos (spirited element), meat eating
        and, 120
Tolstoy, Leo, xiv, 165
Tongue
    comparative anatomy of, 81*n*
    human, 80–82
Torah, dietary regulations in. *See* Sancti-
        fied eating
Touch
    laws regarding touching, 196*n*
    taste and, 88
Toward a Natural Science (Kass), xiii

Transformations through eating, 26
    composition versus concretion, 30–31
    metabolic, 28–29
Twain, Mark, 97

Upright posture, 63–66
    head and face, eyes and mouth in, 70–76
    human arm and hand and, 67–70
    human openness due to, 97
    at table, 135–36
"Upright Posture, The" (Straus), 63
Utensils, use of, 137–38, 142–45, 229

Vanderslice, Steve, 126*n*
Vegetarianism, 84–85, 117–18, 221
    subhuman forms of, 116, 117
Vertebrates, similarities in, 62
Virtue(s)
    of dining, 174–83
    of eating, 154–60
    of necessity, 229
Vision, human, 70–76
    eidetic character of, 71–73
Visser, Margaret, 143, 144
Vitalism, 114–15
Voluntary action, 52
    food-gathering, multiple reasons for,
        52, 53
Voyeur, 148, 149–50
Vulnerability, hospitality and recognition
        of mutual, 106

Waste, digestive, 26–27
Wholes and parts, relation of, 30
Wine as human food, 124–27
Wittiness, 174*n*, 178–81
Wonder, human form and prospects for,
        75–76
World relations
    human form and new, 68–70, 83–84
    of living things, 55, 59